# FRENCH PAINTING
## IN THE
# SIXTEENTH CENTURY

## Louis Dimier

## ARNO PRESS · NEW YORK · 1969
A PUBLISHING AND LIBRARY SERVICE OF THE NEW YORK TIMES

Reprinted from a copy in the library of the
Fogg Museum of Art, Harvard University

Library of Congress Catalog Card No. 74-88821

Manufactured in the United States of America by Arno Press Inc.

# FRENCH PAINTING
## IN THE
## SIXTEENTH CENTURY

FRANCIS I.

BY THE PRESUMED JEAN CLOUET.   LOUVRE

# FRENCH PAINTING
## IN THE
# SIXTEENTH CENTURY
## BY L. DIMIER

LONDON: DUCKWORTH AND CO.
NEW YORK: CHARLES SCRIBNER'S SONS
1904

*This book has been translated from Monsieur Dimier's*
*French MS. by Mr. Harold Child*

À MADAME EUGÉNIE STRONG

RESPECTUEUX HOMMAGE

# CONTENTS

## CHAPTER III

## CHAPTER IV

## CHAPTER V

## CHAPTER VI

## CHAPTER VII

## CHAPTER X

## CHAPTER XI

## CHAPTER XII

## CHAPTER XIII

## CHAPTER XIV

# ILLUSTRATIONS

The greater number of these subjects were photographed specially by A. Giraudon, of Paris.

The reproductions are from blocks made by Messrs. Walker & Cockerell and Messrs. J. J. Waddington, Ltd.

The photographs facing pp. 184 and 186 were taken by kind permission of the Duke of Sutherland and the Earl of Carlisle.

# INTRODUCTION

THE present history embraces the period which extends in France from the accession of Francois I. to the death of Henri IV., with the addition, by way of preface, of the reigns of Charles VIII. and Louis XII.

These reigns saw the commencement of the Renaissance in France; and the author of a history of art in general during that period would have no need to offer his reasons for including them. The new elements of the style inspired by the antique, which the example of Italy was introducing into all the countries of Europe, appear prominently in the sculpture and architecture of the French during those reigns; but in the case of painting there is less reason for including them in the scheme. The same influences, no doubt, were at work there too; but in the first place, the paintings of the day were confined to illuminations, and in the second place, the Gothic principles which, in spite of these developments, continued to prevail in this branch of art more than in the rest, have the effect of making this epoch a matter somewhat out of place in a book that is concerned with painting only. I should have found no lack of reasons, then, for omitting these reigns from the present work. My inducement to retain them in the face of this objection is the necessity of showing what condition French painting was in when François I. undertook to restore, or rather to

A

found it.   Moreover we shall acquire a certain additional information from the inclusion in our history of the faint foreshadowings of the works with which it deals.

It was no part of my purpose to find room here, except when accident and circumstance compelled me, for the history of illumination.   Nor have I attempted to swell my work with anything about tapestry, glass-painting, or enamelling.   These matters are treated of separately in dealing with other centuries, and I was of opinion that they should find no place in the history of the sixteenth.

My object in this book has been to set forth, so far as exact research has enabled me, the first chapter of the history of modern painting in France, a service to which the ablest writers have so far done no more than pave the way.

All that has been published hitherto in the form of connected history amounts to absolutely nothing.   On the other hand, all the special researches, the publication of documents, and the scattered summaries, which we owe chiefly to the scholarly generation of 1850, are worthy of the closest attention, and form the basis of all that follows here.

The Comte de Laborde remains the most illustrious of the men of that generation.   To him are due both the design of bringing together at last all the possible materials for a general history of the French Renaissance, and the greatest number of the discoveries made in that field from the first.   His famous book was never finished, and the first volume (now very rare) appeared crammed with the newest and most various information on all subjects.   The precision of the title is remarkable:  " The Renaissance of the Arts at the French Court."

Two things strike me as noteworthy in these words: the subject is not confined to art in the hands of Frenchmen by birth, and provincial initiative is omitted. In the first point the plan is like that of Walpole in his " Anecdotes of Painting". It has the advantage of making no separation between things that were in reality united—I mean the examples given by foreigners and the native imitation of them; and also, in the case of countries so barren of national painters as France and England then were, of conveniently filling up the spaces, which must otherwise be empty, in a vast scheme of chapters and paragraphs. Many writers, in their anxiety to exclude foreigners, have been conscious of this void, and have tried to fill it by exaggerating the importance of certain mediocre and obscure native artists, till their dearth of interest is only surpassed by their falsification of history.

The second point obviates the necessity of carrying research far and wide into pieces of secondary importance, which lacked the lustre and the influence conferred by the honour of the royal command no less than the excellence which the court alone could pay for, and which owed their occasional reputation to the fact of their being discovered by accident and in some remote corner.

This is the plan maintained for the art of painting throughout the present volume.

Two truths, indeed, become plain to any one who has prosecuted these studies: the excessive preponderance of foreign painters, to the almost total exclusion of natives, in the examples of that art which were produced in France in the sixteenth century; and the determining action in these matters exercised in their own proper person by the kings who succeeded each other during this period.

Everything, or nearly everything, sprang from the
king and the court, and the artists they engaged came
for the most part from Italy or the Low Countries; so
much so, that no researches into the purely native art
and the provincial schools have done much to advance
this study. That, however, is the direction in which
French students, sharing a tendency common to all
Europe, have now for some time been aiming their
efforts; and that is the reason why this movement,
however brilliantly opened, has not yet reached an end.
Since Laborde, Chennevières, Reiset, and Montaiglon,
there has been no advance, except in the history of the
art of portraiture, which is due to the researches, no less
patient than profound, of M. Bouchot, present keeper of
the Cabinet of Prints in Paris.

These are the masters I have followed in the researches,
the results of which will be found in this volume. As
regards the stylists and Italianising painters, the chief
of them has already been dealt with in my book on the
life and work of Primaticcio.* The story of the disciples
of Flemish painting is now being prepared for publication
in a work on " Portraiture in France in the Sixteenth
Century." These two movements and schools contain
nearly the whole of my subject. This book does not
exhaust them. Many explanations remain to be given,
many discoveries to be made; but at least the following
pages may claim to supply the essential part of the
matter and a systematic and precise statement of all the
points in this history which have been established up to
the present.

* L. Dimier : *Le Primatice, peintre, sculpteur et architecte des rois de
France*, in 8º.  Paris, 1900.

# CHAPTER I

Did the Renaissance injure the development of the School of French painting ?—What that school consisted of in the time of Charles VIII. and Louis XII.—The Moulins pictures—Poyet, Bourdichon, Perréal —The School of Tours—The illusion of the critics adverse to the Renaissance—The impossibility and error of resisting its influence— Examination of contemporary Italian works—Solario in the pay of Cardinal d'Amboise—The imitation of Italy—Too faint to bring the Renaissance into painting—This introduction really due to Janet and the period of the reign of François I.

THE dawn of painting in France at the Renaissance is one of the questions hotly debated by French historians. Some statement on the subject could only be omitted from the pages of this history at the penalty of leaving it incomplete. However anxious we may be to keep to the presentation of the facts we have acquired, however carefully we may aim at avoiding, in a book of this kind, all wearisome polemics, we have no choice but to touch on the question which for twenty years and more has lain at the threshold of our subject, and to which students have continued to give an ever-increasing attention.

Some, indeed, assert confidently that painting flourished in this country long before the first effects of the Renaissance had begun to be felt here. Nay, more ; if we believe these writers, these first effects came in contact in France with schools already established, which the new principles of that epoch could do nothing but cross and pervert. The result was that what is known as the

Renaissance was really, in this respect, but the destruction
—or rather, since it was welcomed by the French, the
heedless and barbarous immolation—of the national
genius on the altar of the foreigner. The Renaissance
meant the disowning of the past, the Renaissance
meant the corruption of the future and the renunciation
for all time of promises, the total repudiation of which
can never be sufficiently regretted. Hence it arises that
the history we are now beginning is generally approached
with all sorts of recrimination, amounting almost to
spite, which casts an unexpected note of passion into
temperate and peaceful matters. A writer of this school
is convinced that his duty is to avenge the spirit of the
Middle Ages, which was formerly sacrificed to that of
the Renaissance and has since been misjudged by
posterity. The result of this attitude is that his story
goes hand in hand with a mournful and uniform preference
for anything that may appear to retain some touch of
the preceding age, above the works that carry the
imprint of the tendencies of their own century. His
book, as a whole, forms an address for the prosecution
and culminates in distressing conclusions. The preconceptions with which the writer started are the main
cause of this collapse; and an impartial examination of
the facts may do something to avert it.

The truth is, more than one proof is lacking to the
oft-repeated assertions that a flourishing school of French
painting was in existence about the year 1500. It is
impossible to set down here all that might refer either
to the famous school of Burgundy or to Fouquet; and
I mean, therefore, to confine myself to less ancient works
and artists, whose names are now beginning to be heard

in all mouths, and who have been serviceably enumerated
in certain recent articles.*

The works I would mention are these: the triptych
of St. Antoine at Loches, dating from 1485, which represents Christ on the Cross, and bears a mysterious
monogram, " F. I. B.," which so far has not revealed the
identity of the painter; next, the excellent portrait of
Charles-Orland, son of Charles VIII., painted at the
age of two years and two months, in 1494; and lastly,
the retable at Brou representing St. Jerome and a
legend of St. Sebastian, in two divisions. All these
pictures, of unequal merit though they are, might nevertheless reasonably constitute, throughout the reign of
Charles VIII., the beginning of a school, if only the
writers who extol them and bring them to the notice
of the public would produce sufficient evidence of their
being the work of French hands.

M. Benoit himself agrees that the " Legend of St.
Gilles," one panel of which is in the National Gallery in
London, and the retable in the Palais de Justice, though
included in his list, are really of Flemish parentage.
I should like to be certain that the case of the others
is not the same. Two portraits, of the Duke of Bourbon
and his wife, the famous Anne, daughter of Louis XI., †
dating from 1488, together with a spurious Jeanne la
Folle, ‡ which he accepts as their daughter, Suzanne de
Bourbon, suffice him for the reconstruction of the work

---

* Lafenestre: *La peinture ancienne à l'exposition universelle ; Gazette
des Beaux-Arts*, 1900, vol. ii. p. 376. Camille Benoit: *La peinture française à la fin du XV^e siècle ; ibid.*, vol. ii. p. 89.

† Nos. 1004 and 1005 in the Louvre.

‡ In the collection of M. Yturbe of Paris.

of a painter whom he names "the Master of the fleur de lis," or "of 1488." But there is nothing to prove that any such master was a Frenchman, and, moreover, it is difficult to follow the author in some of his arguments, when he attributes to the same painter the admirable picture at Glasgow, representing a prince of the House of Cleves, with his patron saint.* For whatever historical importance may be attached to this master of 1488, he can only be admitted to the second rank as artist. The portraits of the Bourbons in the Louvre are crude in colour and trivial in handling. As for the Glasgow Cleves, what justification is there for classing it as French work, and what reason, in the entire absence of any works connected with it, for altering the old attribution of it to Hugo Vander Goes?

It is contended that these works and their like can be neither Flemish nor Italian, since they take after both schools at once. But, as a matter of fact, why should they not be the work of some Italian student of the Flemish manner, or more probably of some Flemish imitator of the Italians? If we have no knowledge of any artist in whom this fusion may be found so clearly determined, is there anything more incredible in the assumption of some such unknown master among the Flemings than among the French? But, it may be objected, why one more than the other? Because a masterpiece in painting is a thing of so much importance that we hold ourselves bound to look for some contemporary manifestation of the same merit. Such

---

* Exhibited several times in London, and more recently at the Exhibition of Primitives at Bruges.

a manifestation may be found in Flanders, while in France nothing of the kind is known.

Two or three works of this quality duly authenticated as French would be enough, I admit, to give this kind of attribution some probability; but that is precisely what is lacking,* at this period in particular. There are people who argue these questions as if it were possible to draw a deduction in the abstract of the character of French painting. But a school can only be known by its works; it can take no definite shape from vague hypotheses, but only from a comprehensive view of its practice, which its authentic productions can alone supply.

Meanwhile, we need not hesitate to acknowledge that the court of Moulins in Bourbonnois, the patrons of which were painted by the mysterious master of 1488, took some interest in painting, for that court was equally the origin of the famous "Virgin in Glory," which is known as the triptych of Moulins.

For my own part, I believe the painter to have been an Italian. By some he has been turned into "the Master of Moulins," the painter, as they would like to believe, of a small "Virgin with Angels," of very inferior quality, which is the property of the Brussels Museum,† and of a Magdalen with the donor, a woman, in the collection of M. de Somzée, which does no more to enhance

---

* I have not forgotten, in the preceding age, Fouquet, Nicolas Froment, and Enguerrand Charonton : on the contrary, the inferiority of the two last is what confirms my opinion; and as to Fouquet, it must be confessed that, though an excellent illuminator, he was very unsuccessful in oils.

† Purchased in 1902 from the Huybrechts collection at Antwerp.

the merits of the master. At the Moulins Museum, again, there is a " Legend of St. Lawrence " and a " Legend of St. Etienne," which have succeeded in winning for this town the credit, not of the career of a native painter, nor even of what is called a school, but of the exercise of a petty patronage of painting, which is certainly a remarkable thing at that period. In this the Duke of Bourbon and his wife were imitating, at the extreme end of the century, what King René had attempted in the preceding age in the shelter of his court of Provence.

The sum total yields not a single work that can be guaranteed to be French, and only two or three of striking merit. I will go so far as to add to this hypothetical list the portraits of Charles VIII. and Anne of Brittany which were discovered by M. Bouchot on a binding panel * in the cabinet of manuscripts in Paris.†  Although they form the cover of a book, they are painted on wood in oils and of a fair size; and these are in every way deserving of mention in this work. Merit they have none; but their manner is interesting in its relation to Fouquet, whose tradition is here continued and markedly corrupted. That may be a good reason for holding them to be French.

We see, then, beyond question, a sad dearth of paintings. And the number of painters' names to be gleaned

---

* That is, a wooden binding into which is slipped a detachable panel.

† Latin, No. 1190. Bouchot : *Les portraits peints de Charles VIII. et d'Anne de Bretagne à la Bibliothèque Nationale : Bibliothèque de l'École des Chartes*, 1887. The author of the critical catalogue of the Exhibition of Primitives at Bruges joins these portraits to the preceding, affirming them all to be the work of Jean Perréal, of whom more later. This simplified opinion has found no disciples.

from the accounts and various documents of the time is no greater. Even in the little which has survived, the text is so doubtful that we cannot always be sure that we are not paying honour to the name of some mere maker of scutcheons and banners or of some painter of buildings. What were the Chiffelin and the Lallement, of whom we read under the reign of Charles VIII.?* A certain Jean de Courmont painted a Virgin for Queen Anne.† Jean Poyet did for her a "Book of Hours"‡ which I only mention here in order to give prominence to the name of an artist to which some celebrity was attached in the course of time. It is not known whether Poyet painted anything beyond illuminations. This too may perhaps be the right place to bring in once more the painter, Jean Hay, mentioned in 1503 by Lemaire de Belges in his *Plainte du Désiré*,§ though no one has succeeded yet in identifying him conclusively.

Bourdichon flourished from 1484 onwards, and Jean Perréal, called de Paris, from 1490. These two, with Poyet, are the most famous names of the reigns of Charles VIII. and Louis XII. But the first, again, has left nothing but illuminations, the great "Book of Hours" of Anne of Brittany, and two other manuscripts of the same kind.‖ Of the second we have not a single authentic work.

* Müntz: *Histoire de la peinture française*, vol. i. pp. 223, 224.

† In 1492. Laborde: *La Renaissance des Arts à la Cour de France*, p. 272.

‡ In 1497. *Ibid.*, p. 274.

§ Printed at the end of the *Légende des Vénétiens* by the same author, in 1509. It has been suggested, without probability, that he is identical with Jean Clouet, called Janet, of whom we shall have more to say later.

‖ Noted by M. Male: *Trois œuvres nouvelles de Jean Bourdichon: Gazette des Beaux-Arts*, 1902, vol. i.

And the truth is that this " Book of Hours " of Anne of Brittany,* which is usually lauded as marvellous work, is in reality exceedingly feeble for all the minuteness of its execution, and inspires no regret at the loss of whatever this painter † might have achieved in oils. It saw the light in 1503.

Perréal's life is more interesting. There is no doubt of his having painted pictures. Besides this, he undertook great architectural designs and public decoration ; and at the same time we find him working for the engravers.‡ He had visited Italy in the train of Louis XII. in his Milanese expedition. In fact, everything points him out to the historian of the arts in France as the most important man of his time. It is true, however, that, as regards painting pure and simple, the part assigned to him by the documents is extremely small. This will be evident from the following summary.

In 1497 he was sent into Germany to paint a celebrated beauty, whose name we do not know.§ In 1500, when he was at Milan in the train of Louis XII., the Marquis of Mantua asked him for a picture, a commission from which he begged to be excused. ‖ In 1507 he painted for the king the portrait of Guillaume de Montmorency and several other members of the court.¶ That is all : the

---

* Cabinet of Manuscripts, Paris. Latin, 9474.

† *Nouvelles Archives de l'art français*, t. viii. p. 3.

‡ Maulde-Laclavière (*Jean Perréal, dit Jean de Paris : Gazette des Beaux-Arts*, 1895, vol. ii. ; 1896, vol. i.) has collected all that is known of this artist.

§ *Heptaméron* of the Queen of Navarre, novel 32, 4th day.

‖ *Notices et documents de la Société de l'histoire de France*, p. 297.

¶ Perhaps only in an illumination. Maulde-Laclavière regards this as certain, and even adds that it was in the margin of a song ; but the document says nothing of the kind. *Revue de l'art français*, 1896, p. 9.

evidence concerning Perréal's practice as a painter amounts to no more. When we consider that, in spite of this, frequent mention of this artist has been discovered, we must be surprised at the very small number of the instances just given.

Critics, therefore, have not refrained from increasing this equipment by the addition of a large number of those attributions which can easily be shifted in passing from one artist to another. Some say that he must certainly have been the painter of the " Charles-Orland"; others like to recognise in him the Master of Moulins.* There is nothing to prevent his having been the master of 1488 as well. But in the absence of all information on the point, the wiser course will be to form no conclusion, and to leave the field clear for subsequent discovery.†

The next question is this : Where, besides at Moulins, lived the handful of painters who worked for the court of France? The first place to be mentioned is Tours, an important art-centre at this period, the native town of Fouquet, where, no doubt, his memory still survived to inspire some emulation. Poyet and Bourdichon worked in this city. Perréal, in spite of his surname, de Paris, passed the greater part of his life at Lyons. We find no mention of any school of painting at Aix or Avignon. As for those of Douai and Valenciennes, so glibly introduced into most histories of the French school, I can only ask how the idea of them could possibly be entertained.

---

* See Note † on p. 10.

† Maulde-Laclavière's attempt to assign the illuminations of the *Gallic Wars* to Perréal is less inoffensive inasmuch as it takes the credit of this work from Janet, who nevertheless has every right to it. See below, p. 32.

Neither Bellegambe in the former place, nor Marmion in the latter,* can be ranked with the painters of Tours; for neither Douai nor Valenciennes, though they were annexed later, were ever considered in those days as dependencies of the court of France. Why not go a step further in the same direction, and since Maubeuge is in France, claim Mabuse for the French school? Martin Schoen, in whose days Alsace was French, might just as well be appropriated; and some day, when we reflect that there is no historical difference between Tournay and the towns of Northern France, there will be nothing to prevent our enriching the same school with the name of Roger van der Weyden.

"Franco-Flemish" is the modest suggestion. Franco-Flemish is admirable; but I would ask where its significa-tion is to stop, if it includes, as I believe it does, with perfect justice, all the valley of the Meuse and all the French-speaking Low Countries.

The foregoing is a precise account of the condition of what people like to call French painting from the begin-ning of the reign of Charles VIII. till about 1515, when François I. ascended the throne. I have taken nothing away from the picture which its admirers offer us: I have even given it a few supplementary touches. They add, it is true, that, if so little exists, the fault lies with time and oblivion. But, at least so far as the names of painters are concerned, there appears to be absolutely no hope of disinterring any of the smallest renown; for every new contemporary mention of them that is dis-covered merely repeats its predecessors till one is sick

---

* The catalogue of the National Gallery of London lends countenance to this mistake, so far as this painter is concerned. It is not certain that the two pictures there, Nos. 1302, 1303, are his work.

of them.  This dearth of names explains the dearth of
paintings better than any gratuitous suppositions of
destruction in the past, and false attribution in the present.  Nowadays it is the custom to repeat persistently
that any number of pictures reputed to be Flemish,
or even German, will soon reveal their French origin.
Now that is the sort of statement that people are readier
to make as a general proposition than they are to support
in detail.  There is no such great room for questioning
the attributions of the pictures of the Flemish school as
we are wished to believe; and whatever the future may
have to teach us, one thing is certain—the best places are
full, and the painters of all the best pictures are named.
What France has lost for ever (and the quantity can
certainly be but small) had no merit to redeem it.  In
a word, I am not arguing solely from the present state
of the science, but from the conclusions which the discoveries actually made now enable us to form.

One thing which I believe to have helped to lead
criticism astray in this question, is the hope of a reconstruction of the history of art, which sprang from the
discovery of Fouquet and his exceptional excellence.
His excellence as an illuminator I do not dispute.  I
grant it to have been very rare in this branch of the
art, and equal to that of the best masters.  But, though
I may credit him with several admirable successors, I
have still to discover his immediate heir; and, what
is more, I cannot help observing that after his death,
which took place before 1481, there is an interval of
at least five-and-thirty years before the period we have
reached.  Can any one point out the French school
during those five-and-thirty years?  Can any one show

painting abundantly and continuously practised at Tours
(which is a favourite instance) in oils or even in distemper, a medium of which Fouquet undoubtedly left
examples? We have nothing approaching to such a
state of things. The names of two or three artists,
some illuminations (and such illuminations!) in a " Book
of Hours "—these are all that can be produced. Well,
I am not writing a history of illumination, and con-
sequently I am bound to observe that this period is
all but barren of the art that forms my subject.

To come back to the original question: What is it
that the Italian influence is accused of having corrupted
in France? To reproach it with sterilising so utterly
sterile a school is to be wilfully blind. If it is a question
of the corruption of taste, on what is the complaint
grounded? Is the taste of the " Hours " of Queen Anne,
or that of those portraits of the Duke of Bourbon and
his wife, or of Charles VIII. and Anne of Brittany,
so exquisite that there need have been any question
of saving its delicacy and purity? But it was French
taste, and therefore preferable? What matter, if it
was bad? What matters French taste, or the taste of
any other country, when the genius of the nations under-
goes such radical changes in the course of the centuries?
It is puerile to attempt to stem those changes, or to
desire to judge them by anything but their results.
But enough of these reflections. What made the Italian
influence necessary was the growth of new needs which
the restricted talents we have just examined could never
have satisfied. There was soon to be a demand for
painters to decorate the castles and places of assembly
of the court. Work of that kind needs other hands

than those of the illuminators, the painters of triptychs and portraits, that we have so far met with.  Could any one pretend to restrain so natural a taste, and, while Italy was producing her Mantegnas and Lionardos, demand that the French of the same period should confine their pleasures to such as their Bourdichons or their Masters of 1488 could provide?

In any case, we have reached the moment at which they asked for something better.

Examples are few at the outset.  The taste for painting was but little developed, and it was not yet applied to the walls of chambers.  At Cardinal Amboise's at Gaillon, as in King René's castles, the walls were hung with leather or cloth ornamented only with a simple pattern.  Nor were pictures collected as yet, as we know from the inventories of this same Cardinal d'Amboise and of Queen Anne of Brittany.  In the colony of artists which Charles VIII. settled in his castle of Amboise on his return from Italy, there is really no painter.*  However, he brought several pictures from Naples;† some of them, doubtless, were kept by the queen.‡  At Gaillon Cardinal d'Amboise had a "Descent from the Cross" by Perugino, and a "Nativity" by Solario.§  Hurault, Bishop of Autun, had brought from the Monastery of St. Mark at Florence a "St. Catherine" by Fra Bartolomeo.||  The total was but small as yet, for the interest was still unborn.

* *Archives de l'art français.*  Documents, vol. i. p. 100.  Guido Mazzoni, called Paganino, who bears this title, was a sculptor only.
† *Ibid.*  Documents, vol. ii. p. 306.
‡ Leroux de Lincy: *Anne de Bretagne*, vol. iv. pp. 153, 155, 157.
§ Deville: *Comptes du Château de Gaillon*, p. 540.
|| Villot: *Catalogue du Louvre*, part ii. p. 38.

There seems to have been more activity in retaining
and commissioning artists.   Benedetto Ghirlandaio, for
instance, spent some time in France, beyond question
at the behest of some prince,* and left a trace of his
visit in an " Adoration of the Magi " in the Church of
Aigueperse in Auvergne.   Seven or eight Transalpine
artists were brought over to decorate the Cathedral of
Albi with frescoes which may still be seen there.   King
Louis XII. himself, both previously to 1507 and during
his stay at Milan, entreated Lionardo da Vinci to work
for him, and with this object wrote a letter, after his
return to France, which has been preserved.†   Finally,
Cardinal d'Amboise, writing with the same intent to
Mantegna, calls him "the greatest painter in the
world." ‡

This famous minister of Louis XII. was the first
amateur of his time, and France had not seen his like
since the Duc de Berri.   His castle at Gaillon was the
wonder of the reign, and, from what we can learn of it,
a wonder in the history of the arts in France.§   Twenty-
five years before Fontainebleau, this prelate conceived
the design of building a house as only the Italians had
built them before, with lodges, terraces, and porticos,
decked with marble ornament and embellished with
fountains and statues.   When it came to the chapel,

---

* Vasari, *Opere*, Milanesi's edition, vol. vi. p. 532.

† *Documents inédits sur l'histoire de France*, "Miscellaneous," vol. i.
p. 679 ; and *Revue de l'art français*, 1886, p. 5.

‡ *Revue Historique*, 1892, Jan., Feb., March, p. 57, n. 3.

§ The remains of this castle, now turned into a house of correction, may
still be seen on the site, between Vernon and Pont-de-l'Arche.   One of
the façades has been reconstructed in the court of the École des Beaux-
Arts at Paris.

the cardinal desired it to be painted in fresco, and it
is evident that not one of the painters that France could
then furnish was considered equal to the task. Solario
was summoned from Milan, and journeyed over in the
year 1507.* He stayed nearly two years at the castle,
and there is every reason to suppose that this long
sojourn was occupied in some considerable work. Yet
another Italian, named Geraulme Tourniol,† had painted
the house at Lidieu, a dependency of this castle.

Solario's commission at Gaillon is the first important
event in the history of Italianism in French painting.
The great fame of the painter, the greatness of the work,
the magnificence of the prelate who employed him and
the high rank he held in the kingdom, all united to
render the event illustrious. This was the first step in
those famous attempts which, as we know, were multiplied
in various ways from François I. onwards, and differs
from them in nothing but the fact that the painter was
only engaged for a time. Man had not yet come to feel
the need of the permanent presence of artists and of
engagements for life.

We know now how and by whom, before the reign of
François I., Italian influence entered France. The history
of that influence must be completed by showing what
manifestations of it there are in the French or so-called
French works enumerated above.

In the first rank stands the Moulins triptych, which
I should not have placed in this category, were it not

* Deville : *op. cit.*, pp. 361, 363.

† *Ibid.*, pp. 69 and 124. The author would like to make this painter out
a Frenchman ; but the form of the Christian name, Geraulme, adapted
from Girolamo, attests his origin.

for the kinship assigned to it with two other paintings, which I admit to be rightly so included. The sole reason alleged for believing this triptych to be French is that the faces of the angels are French in type. But it must be plain to every one that that proves nothing; for it is not disputed that this work, containing, as it does, the portraits of the Bourbon family, was painted in France. What is there surprising in the supposition that French models sat for some of the other figures too?

There is no proof, then, of the French origin of this picture, nor even any palpable reason for presuming it: in proof of its Italian origin, on the other hand, we have the style of the work, the design, the colour, the general appearance. These indications may be deceptive, no doubt; but if it is imprudent to trust to them absolutely, where, I would ask, is the prudence of those who believe in the French origin on still less evidence or even on none at all? Nothing can avail to counterbalance the probability intrinsic in the work itself, but documentary evidence; and no such evidence has been discovered.

The Brussels "Madonna" and the Somzée "Magdalen" also betray the influence of Italians, but in the case of the latter it is a very different influence from that which we see in the Moulins triptych. In the triptych there is more of Ghirlandaio, in the "Magdalen" more of Mantegna. The name of this latter painter thus meets us in this history from several quarters at once. We shall have to mention it again in dealing with Bourdichon, whose "Hours" is another example of the influence of this master, and in general of a decided imitation of Italy. It is a certain fact, then, that from the reign of Louis XII. and in the leading painters of the time this aim

was making itself felt even in illumination, of all branches
of art the least subject to classic influence.

As to Perréal, it is not questioned that he too followed
this bent: all his biographers admit it, his whole life
bears witness to it. The design for the tomb of the
Duke of Brittany, which is his work, shows him, in its
restrained ornament, a direct imitation of the Transalpine masters.

From that date, therefore, it was the fashion, in painting as in other things, to copy Italy; and it is this
characteristic that makes it right, as I have said, to begin
the history of the renaissance of that art, as of all others,
with the reign of Charles VIII. We find, however, a
certain difference which renders the case of painting
peculiar in this matter. That is, that for all its frank
imitation of Italy at this period, it continues to retain
the Gothic laws almost unaltered. This may be due,
perhaps, to the fact that we are compelled to judge the
style of this epoch principally from illuminations, which
for us remain its chief productions. While in architecture
and sculpture alike a very deliberate change of style is
noticeable about the time of the first Italian expedition,
in painting, on the other hand, the works of that date
preserve so close a resemblance to those of the preceding
age, that we are led to throw them together, and defer the
marking of the dawn of the new order until the accession
of François I.

In fact, neither the Italianism of pictures like the
Somzée " Magdalen " nor that of Bourdichon's " Hours " is
complete enough to mark off a new epoch. There is good
reason against regarding them as a revival of what had
already appeared in Fouquet, and has been noted by all

historians.  The fact is, that the schools of Northern France
always imitated Italy to a certain extent, just as the Middle
Ages were always gathering some information or under-
going some influence from classical antiquity.  Those who
desire to mark with absolute exactness the hour of birth
of the Renaissance are not concerned to seek out the first
faintest traces of this influence.  What determines that
hour is the predominance, at last acknowledged and
formulated, of three elements, which sometimes appear
together, sometimes preceding and introducing each other :
Italianism in fashion, Latinism in culture, and classicism
in the investigation and theory of nature.  This triple
change marks the end of the Gothic and the beginning of
the new age.

Now the Gothic continued to live in the painting, as we
know it, of the reigns of Charles VIII. and Louis XII. ;
while it had entirely disappeared from the art of one Jean
Clouet, called Janet, whose earliest attributed works date
from about 1515.

Janet's painting is not like Fouquet's, nor like that of
the master of 1488, nor any of the painters noticed above.
With due allowance for every difference, his art may be
said to spring from Holbein and from Lionardo.  He is
assumed to have been a Fleming, and may fitly be classed
among the Flemish masters with Schoorel, Sotto Cleef,
and the supposed Mostaert of M. Gustave Gluck,*
painters who retained nothing of the immediate or trans-
mitted Italian influence but a correctly classical manner,

---

* This writer attributes to a Flemish painter, Mostaert, a set of portraits,
of which some at least display a strongly characteristic style, which agrees
with what I advance here.  *Jan Mostaert : Zeitschrift für bildende Kunst*,
1896.

largeness of design, an aim at fulness, simple and not excessively broken drapery ; in short, all that is opposed to the complexities and grimaces of the old style.

Janet brought to the court of France neither the Romanism of Van Orley nor the Italian methods of Mabuse; nevertheless he must be acknowledged to have possessed more of the spirit of the Renaissance than those two masters.* Granted that its activity was but small and proportionate to the genius of the artist; in its own sphere it was in complete conformity with the new methods which were coming from Italy and transforming the art of painting throughout all Europe.

To speak precisely, I should define Janet as a Fleming of the Renaissance. The full realisation of the second quality entitles him to the place I assign him here; while thanks to his Flemish character the detractors of the Renaissance forgive him and recognise his connection with the old French masters.

For it is a fact that those old masters belong to the sphere of Flemish influence; those, that is, of the fifteenth century. The painters of Tours, and those of King René, Fouquet, Bourdichon, Charonton, and Froment, all exhibit this character in an equal degree; and not the least surprising fact is that the very historians who are so jealous when there is any question of Italian influence, find it easy enough to bear with the imitation that came from Flanders. In the pictures they ascribe to France we see time after time that this imitation even becomes in their eyes a passport and a patent of originality. No doubt

* It is true that Michiels compares him to Van Eyck. But in that case, how is it that so many experts have confounded, and continue time after time to confound, his works with Holbein's ?

this confusion may partly explain why these writers, accustomed as they are to hail the national school in the methods of the Low Countries, regard as profanation the attempt that was made to replace them at length by the manner and methods of Italy.

Janet lacks these methods; and that characteristic unites with his connection with the Flemings, to win him the favour of this party. For all that, he broke away from the style of the preceding age no less than Rosso and Primaticcio were to do in their own way. Janet was no innovator either in subject or in general arrangement; his pictures are not in themselves the effect of a new demand of the age; the need there was of him had nothing to do with new manners; and yet there is nothing in him of the Primitive. That is obvious to all. It is quite useless to try and make him out the disciple and successor of the old masters for whom so much merit is claimed. Janet owes no more to Fouquet than Schoorel to Gerard of St. John or Holbein to Martin Schoen. True, there is nothing to prevent the discovery of intermediaries between these two kinds of masters, but the only result of such a discovery will be to mark the stages of a revolution, pacific indeed, but profound, and so far without analogy in all the history of the art in Europe.

All these reflections will assist the comprehension of what follows concerning Jean Clouet and his almost unique position in art. It is remarkable, indeed, that a painter of Flemish training and only secondary ability was to be the first to render an account in France of the new style, and to inaugurate in painting the Renaissance in this country.

# CHAPTER II

WHEN I speak of Janet, it must be clearly understood that the work I call his has not been guaranteed to be so by indisputable proofs. The examples which it includes lack neither the abundance nor the unity of style which declare the hand of a single creator, and their character and merit agree with what we have just read of him. But there is no decisive argument to prove that their creator was Janet. And although the work in question may justly be presumed to be his (on what grounds I will explain later), we still have no right, strictly speaking, to call the master who executed them anything more than the supposed or the *presumed* Janet. I shall not fail to avail myself of that title whenever, in passing from documents which reveal the authentic Janet to some specimen of what I take to be his work, I find it necessary to make these reservations concerning both the painter and the paintings.

Let us acknowledge without hesitation that there is
no work in existence which has been proved to be Janet's.
All the statements that have been made at various times
on the point are nothing but hypotheses. The foregoing
reflections should be applied, not exactly to Janet, but
to the presumed Janet, until some happy find reduces the
two names to one and the same.

The authentic presence of Janet at the French court
is first found in the year 1516,[*] which was the second
of the reign of François I. He was then using his own
name of Jean Clouet. The name under which he
is known is found written indifferently as "Janet,"
"Jeannet" or "Jehannet," and "Jamet" or "Jehamet."
This last form remains unexplained, and has thrown
some doubt on the origin of a word that might otherwise have been easily regarded as a diminutive of Jean.
From an indisputably genuine document [†] we learn that
he was not a Frenchman, and even that, in spite of the
favour he enjoyed, he never was naturalised. He was
born, no doubt, in the Low Countries, and we may suppose that his name was Clouwet. M. de Laborde has
given currency to a putative genealogy of this artist,
and makes him out to be the son of a Jean Clouet of
Brussels, who was painting in 1475.[‡] There is no proof
of this descent, which, indeed, would appear probable

---

* Bouchot : *Les Clouets et Corneille de Lyon*, p. 60.

† The deed of gift made by the King to the artist's own son of his
father's estate, which had escheated to the crown. Laborde : *La Renaissance des Arts à la Cour de France*, p. 578.

‡ Laborde : *Renaissance*, p. 11. For this reason this author and several
others always refer to Jean Clouet as the second of the name, and his son
François as the third. The reader should be warned of the mistakes this
leads to.

only if the name of Clouet were, as a matter of fact, much rarer than it is: in the course of the sixteenth century we find many families bearing this name. The high reputation which Jean Clouet enjoyed is attested by plenty of documentary evidence, and although the great lustre surrounding the name of Janet in this and the succeeding centuries was chiefly due to the fame which his son acquired later, it is recognised that he himself was equally popular in his own time.*

He bore the title of Groom of the Chamber to the King, and received a salary which at first only amounted to 180 livres,† but was soon raised to 240.‡ These sums seem extremely small by comparison with those paid later to the painters enticed from Italy; but it must be observed that the latter, whose hands were full of great works and the control of the workmen who executed them under their supervision, were entitled, according to the ideas of that age, to more pay than an artist occupied in painting small portraits. For that, in fact, was the only branch of painting which Janet practised, and the examples of it filled all this epoch.

In the eyes of the historian of art, the great abundance of portraits is the original and interesting feature of this period of the accession of François I. Nothing like it had been known before, and we must wait till the year 1515 to see the very extraordinary development

---

* See the praise accorded him in the document cited above, and the importance of several of the royal commands. Laborde: *Renaissance*, p. 15. *Comptes des Bâtiments du Roi*, vol. ii. p. 257.

† Laborde: *Renaissance*, p. 571. A clerical error, no doubt, is responsible for the number appearing as 1800 livres in the Louvre catalogue, compiled by Villot.

‡ Laborde: *Renaissance*, pp. 15 *et seq.*

of this branch of the art. Paintings innumerable and
drawings by the thousand have survived from that age,
to hand on to the remotest posterity the features and
the form of all the noteworthy people of the time, in
the state as well as at court. In spite of widespread
destruction, still further increased by the revolution of
1789, the quantity that remains is surprising. The
modern collections of the Château d'Eu,* of Azay-le-
Rideau,† Chantilly and Versailles are famous testimonies
to this fact. Of drawings, which count for much in
this domain, no less striking an exhibition is offered
by the collections of Castle Howard and Stafford House,
since transferred to Chantilly, and those of the Cabinet
of Prints in Paris, and of St. Petersburg. In the seventeenth century the collection of Gaignières,‡ in the eighteenth those of Fevret de Fontette,§ as well as those
of the Castles of Ancy-le-Franc, Ussé, St. Ange, and
many other places,‖ without including even the specially-
formed galleries of copies like that which may still be
seen at the Castle of Beauregard, bear witness to this
extreme fertility. The estate of Catherine de Medici
included more than a hundred such portraits;¶ that of

* Dispersed since the death of Louis Philippe, except the gallery called
the Guise Gallery, which was saved, I believe, in the recent fire.

† Sold in 1901.

‡ See the inventory, published by M. Grandmaison, *Bibliothèque de
l'École des Chartes*, 1892, p. 12.

§ Manuscript inventory, Cabinet of Prints, Paris, Ye 68. The rest
scattered through the alphabetical dictionary of portraiture added by
Fontette himself to the *Bibliothèque Historique* of P. Lelong, vol. iv.

‖ Enumerated and described in Clairambault's notes, Cabinet of Manuscripts, Paris. Clairambault, 1321. The gallery of St. Ange is mentioned
in Dargenville, *Voyage des environs de Paris*, p. 298.

¶ Bonaffé: *Inventaire de Catherine de Médicis*, pp. 77, 150, 155.

Marie of Luxembourg at La Fère shows a list of fifty; *
at Saumur, Duplessis-Mornay had arranged a series
which ran to not less than 125 examples.† Not all
these specimens dated back to the time of François I.;
but this vast number was a result of the fashion which
came then into vogue and was destined to last throughout the whole century.

The result of this rage for portraits was that people
were not content with the necessarily limited number of
originals. The works of the masters of the time were
copied and recopied a hundred times, often by unskilful
and sometimes by absolutely clumsy hands. This was
the case not only with the portraits of kings and queens,
which have been multiplied thus in all ages, but with
those of any one at court—a feature which is peculiar to
the period under consideration. Not even the number of
painted portraits and painted copies was enough: there
was a demand for quicker and cheaper satisfaction. The
original chalk-drawings were copied, in the same medium,
an infinite number of times, far oftener, indeed, than the
paintings; and these drawings were commonly bound into
albums and preserved as family treasures. ‡

A vast number of these albums must have perished,
but a vast number still exist. We need only mention
that of the King's Cabinet, the two in the Louvre,
the Brisacier album and that of the Sorbonne in the
Cabinet of Prints in Paris, that of the Arts-et-Métiers
in Paris, the late M. Courajod's (now the property of M.
Anatole France), the Bethune and Destailleur albums at

* *Revue de l'art français*, 1895, p. 81.
† *Gazette des Beaux-Arts*, 1879, Aug., Sept.
‡ Bouchot : *Les portraits au crayon de la Bibliothèque Nationale*, p. 1.

Chantilly, the Valori at Lille, and the Méjanès at Aix in Provence.*

There were other albums, now scattered and lost to sight, like the Fontette and the Mariette (the latter passed later into the possession of Walpole), which are among the most worthy of mention. To judge from what remains of these albums of copies, it must be confessed that they retained scarcely anything of the merit of the originals. The execution is so poor that they could never have found a place in any history of art for their own sakes, but solely on account of their relation to what preceded them. They form a unique and striking testimony to the strength of a taste by which French society was then possessed.

And yet, execrable indeed though they are, they are none the less of value as aids to the study of the questions before us, and of the art of figure-drawing. They prove the existence of portraits now lost; the multiplication of them is a guide to the popularity attached to certain types, on account either of the workmanship or the subject. Finally, it is clear that anything which is not found among such a vast number of instances can never have existed at all; and therefore, in assigning dates to the originals, we can tell from these albums the exact moment when portraits in the style of Janet began to be common.

I have given that moment as the year 1515. It would be better to say "about 1515," if it is true that some, at least, of the Preux de Marignan had been executed earlier.

---

* I hope to give a complete and analysed list of these albums, with a concordance of the portraits.

The following is a list of these Preux de Marignan, so
named because they fought side by side with King
François I. in that famous battle: Gouffier de Boisy,
Grand Master of France; Admiral Bonnivet, his brother;
Lautrec; La Palisse; Anne de Montmorency; the Sire
de Fleuranges of the house of Lamarck-Bouillon, and the
Sire de Tournon. The combination of these seven great
men is put on record by the famous manuscript of the
Gallic War,* the border of which has the complete set of
their portraits in miniature. The date of the manuscript
is 1519; but if we may trust in certain notes which contain the ages of these men, the original drawings must
have been made at an earlier date, and even before the
battle. Most of the ages agree in putting the drawings
back to 1514.† For these drawings do really exist; we
know them both in the originals ‡ and as reproduced in
several albums of first copies.§ One other portrait in
these albums goes back to the same date, that of Mary
of England, wife of Louis XII.: ‖ this could only have been
painted during the single year she spent in France, which
was before the accession of François I.

Such were the beginnings of this school, and the first
works that heralded it. No one can doubt that Jean
Clouet was the chief master of it, and the most eagerly

* Cabinet of Manuscripts, Paris. French, 13,429.

† Fleuranges, born in 1490, is said to be 24; Montmorency, born in
1492, to be 22; Boisy, born about 1473, to be 41; Bonnivet, born about
1480, to be 34. La Palisse alone, who was 57, and could not have been
born before 1462, could not have been painted before 1519.

‡ Boisy, Bonnivet, Lautrec, La Palisse, and Tournon at Chantilly;
Cases VII., Nos. 14, 9, 55, 21, and VIII., 5.

§ Fleuranges in the Bethune album and elsewhere; Montmorency, an
odd copy at Chantilly, Case V., No. 4.

‖ In the Aix and Lille albums and an album in the Louvre.

sought after of its artists. The drawings of the Preux de Marignan are rightly included among those ascribed to his name; so that the earliest of the works that must be attributed to him, and the mention of his name in the documentary archives, appeared almost at the same moment.

And now we come to the reasons which justify this attribution.

The invaluable Castle Howard collection of drawings, which passed, as I have said, to Chantilly, reveals on examination a number of different hands, two or three of which stand out from the rest by their clearness of character and their superior order of workmanship. One hand in particular may be recognised by several marks, to which we shall return later, and which are decided enough to enable us to base upon them a list of the works of the same artist.* Now, what connects these works is not only the style of the drawing, but also the date attested by the age of the sitters and by the costume they are wearing; and the result is to settle, within two or three years, the limits of the life or the career of the anonymous artist who made them. They were beginning, as I have said, in 1514: they go on without a break until about 1540.† In 1540, or at the latest 1541, Jean Clouet died. That is one of the strongest presumptions in favour of seeing in this painter the artist of the drawings, especially when we consider that Janet's importance, in the quantity as well as the merit and repute of his works,

---

* Bouchot: *Les Clouets*, p. 16, and the manuscript catalogue of the Chantilly drawings.

† This statement is sufficient to refute the opinion of Maulde-Laclavière, who ascribes the Preux de Marignan to Perréal, who died before 1528.

is borne out closely both by the number and excellence of these portraits, and the eminence of the sitters. They included people no less than the king and his family, the Bourbons, the Guises, the Montmorencys, and all the greatest ladies of the court, all drawn direct from nature, and all, therefore, personal clients of the master. By this means we may determine the work of the presumed Janet, which it will be profitable to make known to the world and to present under this name. A few painted pieces may be added to the number, according as pictures in oils are discovered painted after the original drawings. Only a few of these paintings can be allowed to be genuine works of the master, as showing an execution precisely like that of the drawings. An exact list of them will be found below. The remainder are certainly copies after pictures of the same kind, which are unknown or lost.

The presumed Janet was not the only painter of the Gallic War. Illuminations painted by another hand, and signed, may be seen side by side with his. They represent various historical scenes in a style that resembles Lucas van Leyden. The artist writes his name "Godofredus Batavus." I am led to mention him here as presumably a friend of Janet's, partly by his association in a work in which Janet seems to have had a hand, and partly by the authenticated fact that Janet was in close relations with a painter named Guillaume Geoffroy,* who was possibly the same as this Godofredus, and came from the Low Countries of the North.

Possibly that was Janet's native country. We do not know in what year he had left it for France; but it

---

* He stood godfather to one of his children. Herluison, *Recueil des Actes concernant les artistes français*, p. 82.

appears certain that Paris was not the place where he came to settle, and that he went first to Tours. The painters, since Fouquet, who had made this town illustrious, have been named above. The importance of Tours in those days as an art-centre is attested also by the existence of a kind of official studio, which we find in full activity in 1520 under the control of Babou de la Bourdaisière, with sculptors, tapestry-makers, engravers of choice stones, jewellers and painters all subsisting on the king's bounty.* We cannot say for certain that Janet had been of this body; but at any rate he lived side by side with them and must have passed several years in this town. He had financial interests there, and we know that there he met his wife, who was the daughter of a jeweller.† We find him there in 1522. In the following year his wife was living there alone,‡ and it is certain that from 1529 he was settled with her in Paris,§ already perhaps in the neighbourhood of the parish of St. Innocent, in the cemetery of which they were buried.‖

Of Janet's manner of life, either at Tours or in Paris,

---

* Grandmaison : *La tapisserie à Tours en 1502.*—Société des Beaux-Arts des Départements, 1888, p. 235.

† She was called Jeanne Boucault. These two points are certified by an ancient document.—Laborde, *Renaissance*, p. 567.

‡ The same document.

§ This fact is misunderstood by M. Bouchot (*Les Clouets*, p. 11), who quotes there certain documents which really bear out my statements. In 1529 (O.S. 1528), the court being at Blois, a messenger of the king ourneyed to Paris in quest of works from Janet.—Laborde, *Renaissance*, p. 15. In 1537, the king being at Fontainebleau, Janet's wife brought to the castle from Paris more works of her husband's.—Laborde : *Comptes des Bâtiments*, vol. ii. p. 237.

‖ The fact is mentioned in the will of the younger Janet.—*Revue de l'art français*, vol. i. p. 117.

THE DAUPHIN FRANCIS, SON OF FRANCIS I
BY THE PRESUMED JEAN CLOUET.   ANTWERP

*From a Carbon-print by Braun, Clément & Co., Dornach, Alsace*

of the connections he formed and the pupils he taught, all details are lost to us. Deprived as we are of any biography of this artist, and forced to recover his chief characteristics from the barren documents in the archives, matters of this kind must always remain hidden. The documents preserve nothing but the knowledge of his relations with the court; and any further light can only be sought from what we may be permitted to consider as his work.

The manuscript of the Gallic War which we have mentioned above contains, besides the portraits of the Preux de Marignan, a portrait of François I. himself,* a drawing of which was certainly the original of a portrait in oils, of which a bad copy may be seen at Chantilly.† I ascribe this to 1519, because it is incredible that the painter could have chosen, for a picture dedicated to the king, an old drawing as his model. About the same time there appeared the same artist's excellent little Dauphin François in the Antwerp Museum; ‡ and five or six years later a second portrait of the king, now in the Louvre.§

---

* In a separate volume of the same manuscript.—British Museum, Harl. 6205.

† Catalogue, No. 241. M. Gruyer wrongly took it to have been painted before the king's accession, at the time when he was only Count of Angoulême.

‡ Born in 1517, and aged about two in this portrait. No. 33 in the catalogue, which perpetuates the false identification with the young king, François II., and the impossible attribution to Janet the younger. The original drawing is at Chantilly, Case II., No. 33.

§ Aged about thirty : he was born in 1496. The date of this piece is settled as follows. There is a copy of it in Méjanès album at Aix in Provence ; and it can be proved that this collection was made anterior to 1525. See p. 37, note. Catalogue, No. 127. The original drawing at Chantilly is Case I., No. 52.

This was all before the battle of Pavia and belongs to the old court, the court of the king's youth and of a world that was soon to disappear. That was the time at which these albums of copies carried from fête to fête and from castle to castle the lofty mien of the king's companions and the simple beauty of the ladies of Queen Claude, reflections of the beginning of a reign and of a France the like of which had never been seen before.

Chief of this triumphant band is François I. His own portrait stands at the head of the album, and he likes to turn over the leaves for the pleasure of adding to them the merry reflexions, often licentious and always biting, which the thought of the sitters suggests. Ancient testimony shows him visiting Mme. de Boisy and suggesting epigrams and mottoes to be written under each of the portraits. The album of which this story is told has been preserved, and we may read in it to-day the mottoes, presumably of the royal invention.* The book I mean is the Méjanès album at Aix in Provence, † and has more than one title to be mentioned here, being the

---

\* Charles Sorel in 1647 in his *Solitude*, p. 327, whence Father St. Romuald took the anecdote for his *Trésor Chronologique*, vol. iii. p. 203. All modern commentators have understood that Mme. de Boisy herself made these drawings, but the text says nothing of the kind.

† Described, with several engravings, in Rouart : *François I. chez Mme. de Boisy ; notice d'un recueil de crayons enrichi par le roi François I. de vers et de devises inédites*. M. Bouchot in his *Portraits au crayon* refuses to recognise this album, because the anecdote comes in 1519 and the album is not so old. But it must be remarked that the anecdote seems only to be dated by the fact that Mme. de Boisy is then called the *wife* of Arthur de Boisy, who died in 1519. But, in ordinary language, the word does not necessarily imply that her husband was still alive.

oldest of all the known collections, and formed, as we can prove, between 1521 and 1525.*

What better means could there be of bringing back the society of the time and forming an idea of the faces which sat for Jean Janet's drawings? First we have the king; then Madame la Duchesse, his sister, so called before her second marriage made her Queen of Navarre; then the infant sons and daughters of the king, Monsieur le Dauphin, Monsieur d'Orléans, afterwards Henri II., Monsieur d'Angoulême, Mesdames Charlotte and Madeleine, the former of whom became Queen of Scotland and the latter Duchess of Savoy. And then, under the fire of the royal jests, the whole court begins to file by: ladies old and young, honest women and coquettes, widows and maids, fat and thin, sometimes honoured with a compliment, saluted with a bow or caressed with a free jest, sometimes lashed with a stinging taunt; seigneurs, men of battle or courtiers, treated as friends, cordially praised or wittily blamed; we see them all, men and women, taking up again under our eyes their familiar path and showing us the very faces that they wore.

Here are the Preux de Marignan, Boisy, La Palisse, Tournon, Lautrec, nearly the whole of them, and living still; here is M. de Vaudemont of the house of Lorraine, who was to die at the siege of Naples; M. d'Albany of the house of Stuart, in all the fire of his gay youth; Chabot, not yet an admiral, " more lies than love," says the king;

---

* After 1520, because Captain Tavannes, who is there said to be "regretted by his friends," was still alive; before 1525, when Brion, whose name appears there unqualified, was made admiral, and Mdlle. d'Assigny, there called by her maiden name, became Mme. de Canaples by marriage.

M. de Bourbon, the Constable, who was soon to turn
traitor to his king, bearing in his appearance the youth
that was never to come back to him. Under him the
king writes, " grey but not old." Brosse, who turned
traitor with him, and his sister of Avaugour, "more
foolish than loyal "; under the portrait of Chandiou we
find, " too small for the cart and too big for the horse ";
under that of Captain Tavannes, " deservedly regretted
by his friends." And now for the ladies : the king's
young aunt, Mme. de Nemours, is greeted with the
gallant phrase, " what she conceals would be the glory of
others ; " the aged Mme. de Bourbon, a survival from the
Moulins triptych, the daughter of Louis XI. and step-
mother of the Constable ; Mme. de Larochefoucauld, who
took the Comte de Sancerre for her second husband ;
Diane de Poitiers goes by in all the splendour of her
youth, under her old name of *Grand Sénéchale*, and
honoured with the courteous madrigal: " fair to see and
virtuous to know "; Beauvais; Tényé; Mme. du Vigent,
and the ladies of the " little circle," or particular friends
of the king; and above them all the entitled favourite,
Mme. de Chateaubriand, trailing in the wake of her
fortunes the whole house of Foix represented by her
three brothers, Lescun, Lesparre and the unhappy
Lautrec, whose military incapacity was to let loose the
coming disasters; " better figured than painted," adds the
king.* At Casaulde, a lady of Queen Claude's, he shoots
this compliment: " honest, fat, and pleasant in season ";
at Mary of England, whom he courted, this insult: " more
dirty than queenly "; at the fair Assigny, who comes

---

* I take this to mean, " her figure is better than her complexion."

modestly among the last pages of the collection, this simple praise: "the best made of all."

And here, unexpectedly and strangely, we find, joined to all these faces and surviving fifty years of history, the mistress of Charles VII., Agnes Sorel. She figures here as the illustrious woman to whom (and not to Jeanne d'Arc) belongs the credit of the deliverance of the kingdom at the time of the war with the English. Her appearance in this book is no exception; scarcely one of these albums but contains her portrait, copied again and again in an infinite number of examples. Under her portrait François I. has written a well-known quatrain, in honour of the lady's political action.

Such are the famous names of the time, and the fashionable portraits that appeared in the ubiquitous albums, and may now be seen in the Castle Howard designs drawn by the pencil of the presumed Janet.

After Pavia all was changed. That unparalleled disaster, preceded by treason and defeat and followed by the captivity of the king of France at Madrid, transformed the reign completely. Two or three years later, the very family of the king is changed. We can scarcely recognise the ancient court of France. Look· at the album of the King's Cabinet,* compiled about 1535, only ten years after the Méjanès. The difference is amazing. We find here a new queen, Eléonore, sister of the Emperor Charles V., with her Spaniards, Manrique and Béatrix, in her train, taking precedence of the ladies of the late Queen Claude. We see new dresses on altered

---

* So called here because it was in the King's Cabinet before those at present in the National Library. Numbered A by M. Bouchot in his *Portraits au crayon.* On the date, see his work, p. 22.

figures. The young courtiers have grown old; the beauties of yesterday are faded; the fair Assigny is married: here she is under the guise of stout Mme. de Canaples; the old "little circle" have lost their figures and their spirits. A newer youth has ousted them, the ladies de Gié, and Mdlle. Bry, unknown to the old album. Mme. la Duchesse is Queen of Navarre. Mme. la Régente Louise of Savoy is dead, Mme. de Chateaubriand disgraced: one after the other, included henceforth as historical curiosities, they pass across this new society in a melancholy procession of the faces of yesterday, the Preux de Marignan who fell before Pavia, Brosse, Vaudemont; whose names, forgotten now, banished by recent ills to the farthest background, seem to forgather in the far distance with the fabulous memory of Agnes Sorel.

Throughout this great change Janet remains, to copy the faded beauties and bearded captains, to paint the king at forty, as he had painted him at twenty-five. Far from deteriorating, his art seems to develop with the years. The portrait of Duke Claude of Guise in the Uffizi Gallery at Florence, which ought to be presumed his work, painted in 1530, may serve as an instance.*

Would that we possessed, and were able to add to this list, the only picture which is known for certain to have been the work of Jean Clouet, the portrait of the mathematician Oronce Finé, which was painted in this

---

* Aged about thirty-five years in this portrait; he was born in 1496. Catalogue, No. 252. The copy of the original crayon at Chantilly, Case IV., No. 71.

*Spooner*

MAN UNKNOWN, HOLDING PETRARCH'S WORKS
BY THE PRESUMED JEAN CLOUET. HAMPTON COURT

same year, but is now known only by a print! * A little later we have the excellent portrait at Hampton Court of a man unknown, holding a volume of Petrarch,† the fourth and last of the oil paintings which we may look upon as his—a fitting work to crown a catalogue all too short, but a source of promise and encouragement.

I have still to note, in this new period, the portrait of Mme. de Vendôme, which we know from the copy at Versailles,‡ and which is executed on a scale singularly large by comparison with that which the presumed Janet commonly used. Possibly, as years went on, he was emboldened to undertake the covering of more space, and to seek by this means to resemble the contemporary Flemish portrait - painters — but before this isolated example the more becoming course will be to abstain from comment.

It cannot be determined exactly when Jean Clouet, called Janet, died. But we know that he was no longer living in December 1541,§ and we find him still alive and standing godfather at a christening on the 8th of July 1540.‖ His death, then, must have taken place between these two dates.

---

* Engraved in *Hommes Illustres* by Thevet, who vouches in his life of Finé both for the authorship of the work and the age of the sitter. He was then thirty-six, and was born in 1494.

† Dated by the costume. Catalogue, No. 192. I have discovered the chalk original of this picture at Chantilly, Case VIII., No. 131.

‡ Dated by the age of the princess, who was born shortly after 1488. Catalogue, No. 4039. The original drawing by the presumed Janet, Chantilly, Case III., No. 174.

§ See the document cited above, p. 26, note †.

‖ *Revue de l'art français*, vol. ii. p. 20. M. Bouchot is wrong in placing his death in the preceding year. It is true that he disappears from

Such, within the narrow limits imposed by rigorous criticism, were the principal features in the career of this celebrated painter. It would be tedious to add a list, were it only of the best of the drawings at Chantilly,* which must be ascribed to the presumed Janet. Besides the originals of several works contained in the Aix or the King's Cabinet albums, there are many excellent portraits at Chantilly of which no copy exists elsewhere. The ladies of the "little circle," some of the Preux de Marignan, members of the families of Foix, Gié, Nevers, Tavannes and many other famous houses, Queen Eléonore's ladies of honour, prelates, and numbers of unknown subjects are crowded into this choice collection, the most striking gems of which are the Sire de Canaples, the Maréchal de Montejean and a woman unknown of exceptional vigour and charm.† It is in this collection that the period may be seen in its entirety, in all the delightful medley of a powerful and brilliant court. We have here the days before and the days after Pavia, the two courts and the two reigns. Princes of the blood, women, warriors, cardinals, great officers of state, doctors, the king's household, the government, the provinces— all are united in an unequalled whole. We pass from dauphins in bibs to the duennas of the court in their old-fashioned garments, from the iron glance of captains to the sprightly youth of courtiers, from the ample majesty of court prelates to the roguish freshness of

the king's household after 1539; but the case is just the same with all the rest, the household meaning absolutely nothing. *Les Clouets*, p. 61.

* All this collection was engraved while it belonged to Lord Carlisle. Ronald Gower : *Three hundred French portraits representing personages of the court of François I.*

† Cases VIII., Nos. 106 and 176, and XIX., 246.

PORTRAIT OF A LADY
BY THE PRESUMED JEAN CLOUET.   CHÂTEAU DE CHANTILLY

beauties in favour, from the careworn brows of ministers of state to the tender charms of young girls. Nowhere, and in the art of no country, can a similar sequence be found, to present in so light and easy a form and adorned with the charm of a wise and simple art, the summary of a whole epoch.

The manner in which this kind of work was carried on is now proved.* Janet used to visit all these sitters in their own houses and draw portraits of this nature with the greatest care in coloured chalks. That finished, the model had sat for the last time. The oil-portrait was executed in the studio, working from the drawing only; manuscript notes used sometimes to direct the choice of colours. During this part of the work new accessories were added at need,† and this fact prevents our regarding these drawings as portraits commissioned for their own sake or as anything more than preparatory studies. In addition to these changes the painter would add, in the studio, the hands, a book, or some drapery.

There was nothing in this, however, even when the pictures were finished, to prevent the drawings being valued. I do not know that we need look for any reason other than that of profit. It is certain that the people of those days did not care to sit often. In the large number of these portraits which have survived it is remarkable how few different types we meet with. Those few were copied and recopied without limit. Was a certain portrait

* Thanks to the research and the ingenious commentary of M. Bouchot: *Les Clouets*, p. 13.

† An example to remember is the Dauphin François's plumed hat, substituted in the Antwerp painting for the indoor cap which he wears in the Chantilly drawing. He was drawn, then, from nature and dressed up in the studio.

wanted suddenly to complete a new illumination or other
work, there was the drawing already made and kept in
the studio, to be used again. And since others besides the
artist who had made the drawing often found that they
wanted the likeness, copies were taken from this original
and no doubt carried off to other studios to begin the
same services there. Many of these copies, which, as it
evidently appears, never belong to any album, and by no
means badly done, owe their existence, no doubt, to this
practice, and were meant for the use of artists. Copies of
copies were for the public only. But artists or public, and
good copies or bad, I imagine that leave to make them was
not to be obtained without payment; so that the trouble of
preserving the original drawing helped to pay the painter·

After all, these drawings, the originals, that is, rank as
the most important works of the epoch. That is a fact
that is beginning to be recognised; they are becoming so
popular that amateurs of art go so far as to value them
almost as highly as Holbein's. But certain limits must be
kept, and to compare Janet with so great a master is more
likely to lower than to exalt him. To judge him by the
works we have mentioned, it must be admitted that his
knowledge is limited and his means restricted. I am not
speaking of the composition, which is just as cramped and
as archaic in Holbein and the contemporary Flemings, but
solely of the drawing, in which Holbein triumphs. The
presumed Janet has a stiffness and dryness which are very
far from the flowing and supple handling of the Basle
master. The principal features of the face are put in
their place with no refinement, and the rest is added
without precision and with only a moderate feeling for
nature. The nose, the eyes, and the curve of the lips are

given with a light and sure touch; but the beard and hair, like the plume on the hat, are either composed of equal and tedious little strokes or simply scribbled in. The point we are glad to make is, that never have modest resources been carried into expression with greater care or truer intelligence and dexterity. His narrow science knows its own limits, and by gauging itself correctly obtains an opportune sureness which more able artists often lack. Above all, chalk was a medium that suited him. He used it with a perfect ease that was a source of ever-recurring charms. In his simple and lively fashion he addresses himself to all tasks, and only handles each in its proper degree; rounding the forehead, hollowing the fold of the eyelid, softly arching the nostril, setting at the corners of the mouth those pleasant curves which cause the large planes of the face to move and settle, delicately balancing the points of symmetry, and in the non-symmetry of three-quarter faces recalling in the modelling of one cheek what he notes in the contour of the other with perfect elegance. Black chalk and pale sanguine are both used: the former caressing the cheeks with fine close strokes, touching in imperceptible reflected lights in the hollow of the nostrils or the insertion of the eyelashes, winding along the delicate contours of the ears, enveloping the chin with a large and subtle line which holds the whole structure together; the latter moving across the face in firm and careful steps, relieving projections, suggesting the bony structure, marking sharply the strong shadows, giving a spiritual emphasis to the complicated modelling of the forms, sometimes giving the eye its colour or applying those flashing touches by which the eyeball sparkles and lights up, then playing freely on

the accessories, subtly pleating the delicate linen, relieving
the cloak with a few touches, strengthening and bringing
out the slanting cap, sweeping in the hair and beard with
heavy strokes, replacing, whenever the painter's knowledge
failed him, exact imitation by pleasing audacity, and
merit by a cunning that is both witty and modest. These
works of themselves prove the painter a colourist; he
mingles the two tones that his chalk afforded him with
perfect taste; in his hands the combination gives a
thousand ingenious effects, a thousand new colours, in
which the tones of the flesh are varied at will.

The colour of the oil-paintings adds little to this
pleasure beyond the natural delight of contemplating
finished works. The texture is pure, as usual with the
painters of the Low Countries; the execution is delicate
and smooth, the outlines are harder than in the chalk.
The total effect is equally pleasing in its suggestion of
ingenuity and the adroit management of resources.

Exception, however, must be made from these strictures
in the case of the anonymous portrait at Hampton Court,
in which all the charm of the chalks is revived in the
enchantment of rich and limpid colour. Those who used
formerly to ascribe this portrait to Holbein, though still
far enough out, were not this time so grossly mistaken in
their respective merits. The excellence of certain details
is indeed surprising. The gloved hand has much that is
masterly in it.

And now we have come to the end of all that can or
ought to be said of Janet. For twenty-five years he
practised his art at the court of France; and the length
of this period combines with his success to make him one
of the painters inseparable from the memory of François I.

We should like to know how the king came to be acquainted with him, and how first he took him into favour.  It would be instructive to know the king's share in the introduction of this kind of portrait, and how the painter's talent and the taste of the monarch combined to establish it.  We cannot doubt that each had a share, and that the art, like others in those days, was partly due to the royal initiative.

Franços I. has sometimes been represented as enamoured of Italy alone, and interested only in the talents of that country.  It is doing him an injustice to take no account of the value he attached, in his truly universal taste, to the art of the Low Countries.  In 1529 we see him acquiring from Flanders *genre* paintings, peasant scenes and humours in the style of Bosch, and later of old Brueghel.*  Shortly before, with the idea, as it seems, of giving Janet a rival, he had entreated Schoorel to enter his service.†  This painter was working successfully at Utrecht.  He refused the king's offer.  Perhaps, too, it was about the same time that Joost van Cleef of Antwerp, also a portrait-painter, who is known in England under the name of Sotto Cleef, was sent for to paint the king himself, the queen and the other royal

---

* Laborde : *Renaissance*, p. 24, note.  They were the work, perhaps, of Jean Maudyn of Antwerp, who painted this class of picture at that time.  For another purchase of Flemish pictures see Laborde : *Comptes des Bâtiments du Roi*, vol. ii. p. 207.

† Van Mander : *Livre des peintres*, Hymans' edition, vol. i. p. 315. The date is fixed as follows.  According to this author it happened soon after Schoorel's return from Italy.  Now an autograph letter of his proves that he was still there on the 26th May 1524.  The battle of Pavia was fought on the 24th February following, and compels us to place the invitation after the captivity of Madrid,

persons of the kingdom.* This commission was only momentary, and there was nothing in the episode to prevent Janet's pursuing his career without a rival.

It is true, however, that during his last ten years we can point to his companions; but they were his own brother and son. The former, who has been discovered by a lucky chance,† is known nowadays under the name of Clouet de Navarre, because it is in the service of that king and queen, she being a sister of François I., that he has been found to be living in the year 1529. As to Janet's son, François, it is difficult to divine the date of his earliest works; but since we see him in honourable renown in 1541,‡ the starting-point of his career as artist may perhaps go back so far as 1530.

Moreover, the list of drawings, which I range under the name of Janet the younger, begins about 1534, a date which corresponds in all points with this supposition.

When Janet's son was born is another point we cannot determine. He had a sister named Catherine§ of no concern to this history except for her relationship.

---

* Guichardin: *Description de tout le Pays-Bas*, p. 132. This must have happened some time before 1540, since Sotto Cleef died in that year, and the madness from which he suffered put his last years out of the calculation.

† A letter of Marguerite d'Angoulême, believed to be of 1529, who calls him "the painter brother of Janet, painter to the king." Génin's edition, p. 242. The reference to the archives have been found to be incorrect, so that it has been impossible so far to hit upon the letter. M. de Laborde has wrongly taken the Janet mentioned for François, son of Jean, and jumbled the relationship. M. Horsin-Déon (*Essai sur les portraitistes français de la Renaissance*, p. 46) informs us that a document in the archives of Vienne, in Viennois, calls this new-comer Claude.

‡ Document cited above, p. 26, note †.

§ See p. 207.

François Janet no doubt was his father's pupil. The earlier of the drawings I referred to are stamped with his influence; and beneath it we may perceive a perfection of drawing which was to carry him much higher in his art. We may suppose that owing to his talent he was allowed to participate in the elder Janet's works; and, since the method of producing these paintings was as I described it above, that he played the part of copyist in oils of the drawings made by his father; but there is nothing to prove that this was so.

# CHAPTER III

The designs of François I. in regard to Italian art—His taste for paint-
ing—Lionardo da Vinci in France—His death—Andrea del Sarto
—His works for the king and for Semblançay—His departure
—Squazella—Death of Bourdichon and Perréal—The second-rate
Italians—Guetty, Belin, called Modena, Pellegrino—The works,
hitherto wrongly attributed, which may be assigned to them—The
king's dealings in Italy — His agents — Raphael, Giulio Romano
—State of the schools in Italy—Mantua and the Palace of Te—
Relations of François I. with Florence—Rosso engaged, then Primaticcio.—Fontainebleau—The school so named—Our task to define
it clearly.

Every one has heard tell of the great efforts made by
François I. to naturalise Italian art in France : I shall use
the word art, without qualification, to express the art of
painting, the only branch with which we are concerned here.

We have seen above what France's contribution was
in this branch, and that it amounted to nothing at all.
Neither Bourdichon, nor, doubtless, Perréal, who both
were still flourishing at the beginning of his reign, were
the kind of artist that was wanted to fulfil the vast designs
which the king was meditating, and the effect of which
will be seen shortly. The former painted a portrait of
the king in 1506 * ; that is all that we know of his
work about that time. So far as Flanders was concerned,
the court of Mechlin was offering under Marguerite of
Austria an example of brilliant patronage, but we do not

* *Archives de l'art français :* Documents, vol. iv. p. 22.

see what the king could have looked for there beyond
portraits and *genre*-pictures. Neither Van Orley nor
Mabuse, this princess's favourite painters, had anything
to offer, either of their own or their pupils' work, which
François I. could not have found in a far superior degree
of excellence in Italy. Besides, no one would have thought,
at that time, of going anywhere else, when it was a
question of procuring work of a certain order, for Italy
alone was able to furnish it.

The king's ambition in this direction knew no bounds.
He had visited the country, and seen with his own eyes
examples of the greatest achievements of the art. He
was the first King of France to show this taste for painting. It seems that his predecessors, and even Cardinal
d'Amboise himself, had valued it below the other arts, and
only as their handmaid. The new king proclaimed himself the champion of painting, and of the loftiest that the
art was then producing. What he longed to possess and
to carry into France was the great frescoes of the Milanese,
and the wonders of Florence, which had been described
to him ; the unheard-of display of arrangement, of pose,
of noble drapery and sublime expression, the ostentatious exhibition of all the resources, the frenzy of all the
spells of the art, well fitted, indeed, to enchant the
imagination of one who is commonly shown to us as
supported till then on the triptychs of Loches and the
masters of 1488.

We must not forget that François I. was really an
amateur of the art, not merely a patron, like Louis XIV.
for example. He had the taste for artistic things which
comes of the pleasure they give and the power to appre-
ciate it. In this his character is more like that of Charles I.

of England. Cellini, who may be trusted on this point, in the course of his famous Memoirs, puts into his mouth words like these: "I am an amateur and judge of art. I well remember to have inspected all the best works and by the greatest masters of all Italy." * He went there after Marignan, and visited Milan, Pavia, and Bologna. The journey could not but have given an impulse to his natural disposition, and stamped him, among potentates as among artists, an amateur of the first rank.

In fact, after his return to France, we find pictures becoming in his hands an instrument in diplomatic relations. The "St. Michael" and the "Madonna," now in the Louvre,† were commissioned for him from Raphael by Pope Leo X., who was in treaty with the court of France. Cardinal Bibiena, the legate of the Holy See, presented, for his part, the portrait of the vice-queen of Naples in the same gallery.‡ Charles VIII. had only brought back from Italy the "makers of ceilings and turners of alabaster." § What Francois I. saw first and

* *Life*, Bianchi's edition, 12mo, pp. 359, 301; Symonds' translation, 8vo, vol. ii. pp. 160, 90. A striking proof of this prince's initiative in these matters is the story of the life-sized silver Hercules, which Cellini (*ibid.*, vol. ii. p. 154) says that he had commissioned as a present to Charles V. on the occasion of his journey into France. Rosso made the design, and the work was executed by a certain Chevrier (Félibien, *Histoire de la ville de Paris*, vol. i. p. 354), whose real name was Brimbal (*Archives de l'art français*, Documents, vol. ii. p. 133, and vol. iii. p. 365). Chevrier set about it in such a way that the king vowed he had never seen anything so bad. However, he held to his idea, and to satisfy himself he ordered of Cellini twelve statues of celebrated gods, of which none but the Jupiter was ever seen. A similar tenacity of purpose is to be observed throughout the reign.

† Nos. 1498 and 1504.                    ‡ No. 1507.

§ This expression comes from the above-quoted document, p. 17, note *.

chiefly in that country was the painters. He wanted to take the " Last Supper " from the very walls of Santa Maria delle Grazie, and carry it off to France, and only necessity induced him to resign this impossible project.\* Lionardo da Vinci followed him on his return, and this historical episode is known to every one.

Legend has popularised it, and the invention of men of letters has amplified it; painting itself has multiplied his pictures, till after four centuries have passed Lionardo holds in the public imagination an unique and unparalleled rank in the Renaissance and in French painting. Well, there is no doubt that this great artist did play a part in these events; the difficulty is to decide how large a part.

He arrived in the year 1516,† and died three years later. They gave him a lodging near Amboise, on an estate called le Clos or le Cloux, with a pension of 500 crowns. ‡ This retired dwelling points at least to the fact that they did not expect of him any great works of decoration, the execution of which would have kept him tied to the royal residences. But we have very little information, beyond that, of what easel pictures he painted for the king.

An eye-witness of a visit paid to his studio by Cardinal Louis de Bourbon in 1516,§ reports that he saw there three pictures from his brush : the portrait of a Florentine lady, a young St. John the Baptist, and the famous

* Vasari : *Opere*, Milanesi's edition, vol. vi. pp. 31, 32.

† *Ibid.*, vol. iv. p. 47.

‡ Seven hundred, according to Cellini (*op. cit.*, p. 306; Symonds, vol. ii. p. 95) ; but Vasari is more trustworthy.

§ On the 10th October. The eye-witness was the cardinal's own secretary. Uzielli, *Ricerche*, vol. ii. p. 460.

picture of St. Anne.   He had brought from Italy the
cartoon of this last work,* drawn in 1501, fifteen years
before; † and its great celebrity had apparently enflamed
the king with the desire to have the painting from it.
The portrait of a lady, in which we dare not recognise
La Gioconda,‡ he had brought with him finished.   It
is certain that the "St. John" passed into the collection
of François I., an exact list of which, about 1545, I
have succeeded in compiling.§   On the other hand, the
"St. Anne" never went there, and has come at last to the
Louvre‖ by a totally different road.   The total works
of Lionardo which the royal collection included at that
time were five at least, which were, beside the "St. John,"
the "Virgin of the Rocks," the "Belle Ferronnière," the
"Rape of Proserpine," and perhaps also the "Leda."¶   But
how can we be certain that, during an interval of thirty
years, none of these pictures were bought in Italy?
We must resign the attempt, then, to settle which they
were that saw the light in the studio at Cloux.

The witness quoted above adds that Lionardo was then
paralysed in the right hand, and could only continue to
paint with difficulty, though still capable of "drawing

---

* Vasari, *ut sup.*

† H. Cook, *Trésors de l'art italien en Angleterre ; Gazette des Beaux-
Arts,* 1897, vol. ii. p. 370.   The cartoon is now lost.   The one preserved
at the Academy in London is only a first sketch.

‡ Müntz, *Les tableaux de Léonard de Vinci en France.   Chronique des
Arts,* 1898, p. 266.

§ *Le Primatice,* p. 281.

‖ No. 1598.

¶ It is possible that the picture of this name which we find mentioned
was Michael Angelo's.   The four first mentioned are Nos. 1601, 1599, 1600,
and 1597 in the catalogue of the Louvre.

and teaching." Perhaps we had best be content with this reason for the small quantity of work which he seems to have executed for the king during the three years he lived in France. He had with him three pupils : Melzi, Andrea Salaino, and Battista de Villanis,\* enough to compose a little guild, from which some profit could be drawn. It is true beyond question that François I. drew another kind of profit from this rare retainer, through the lessons he must have learnt, lessons which the difference between their ages rendered natural from the one to the other. Lionardo had played this *rôle* on the other side of the Alps in 1515, when we find him acting as sponsor for the prince, introducing him into that glorious atmosphere in which Milan, Florence, and Rome were ablaze with the three great lights of the Italy of that day, Raphael, Michael Angelo, and Lionardo himself. Something of the same sort must have continued after the return to France. François I. passed much of his time at Amboise in the three years that followed. We find him spending more than two months there at the end of 1516, and nearly six at the beginning of 1518.† We cannot doubt that in those months he saw his painter again, and discoursed with him of the things which he was so eager to learn.

Lionardo died at Cloux on the 2nd May 1519, during the time which the court spent at St. Germain. The king, then, did not see him in his last moments, as Vasari relates, a statement which has been copied from him by

---

\* Mentioned in Lionardo's will. *Société des Beaux-Arts des Départements*, 1873, p. 792.

† These facts are taken from the *Catalogue des Actes de François I.*, the dates in which provide a precise journal of the king's doings.

so many others since. François I. was then in the twenty-fifth year of his life and the fourth of his reign.

Whatever the causes which keep us in the dark about Lionardo's activity during the three years he spent in France, one thing is certain—that he did nothing, by any direct intervention, to advance the artistic renovation of the kingdom which the king incessantly desired. Another Italian painter of great ability, and one of the glories of the Florentine school, Andrea del Sarto, appeared in France a year before Lionardo's death.

We cannot say how François I. induced him to enter his service, and all that we know on the subject has only Vasari's authority.* He arrived, then, in 1518, and painted for the king the famous "Charity" which is admired to-day at the Louvre,† and which figures under the date given above in the collection of Fontainebleau. The same collection contained also a "Holy Family," then known under the name of "St. Elizabeth," also preserved at the Louvre.‡ These two works have all the merit of the others which have carried the name of their painter so high. Andrea was then little more than thirty, and much was to be hoped from the engagement of such a man in the service of France.

Certain people had already begun to reap the fruits of his coming. According to Florent Lecomte, who saw the pictures themselves on the spot,§ Semblançay, the famous Superintendent of Finance, took into his house at Tours

---

* *Op. cit.*, vol. v. p. 29.

† Catalogue, No. 1514.

‡ No. 1515. Vasari adds a portrait of the Dauphin François and a St. John the Baptist for Louise of Savoy.

§ *Cabinet des singularités*, vol. iii. p. 269.

HOLY FAMILY
ANDREA DEL SARTO.   LOUVRE

three pictures by Andrea del Sarto: the "Meeting of Esau and Jacob," the "Manna," and the "Striking of the Rock"; all three painted for the chapel. We know the tragic fate of the Superintendent, who seven years later was hanged at Montfaucon by order of the king. He was then at the height of his fortunes. Andrea had brought with him a pupil, whose name Vasari gives as Szuazzella, a Florentine like his master. If we may believe M. de Laborde,* Semblançay employed Szuazzella also. In the case of the latter, several of his pictures were seen at Semblançay, on the Superintendent's estate near Troyes.

It is equally possible that Andrea del Sarto painted the ceiling of the chapel in the castle of Marmontier near Tours. At any rate there was a painting there in his name, which was noted in the following century by the famous traveller Monconis.†

Matters were progressing thus when Vasari says that Andrea's wife called him home. Apparently this agreed with the king's secret plans. It may be said that by means of Andrea del Sarto we see the first attempt made since the beginning of the reign to set on foot the enterprises which only succeeded later. Although he was esteemed as a painter, he had not been drawn into France merely to paint; and the king, taking advantage of his departure, commissioned him to go at the same time to Rome to look for antiquities. Andrea left at the end of a year's sojourn, promising to return. But his

---

* *Renaissance*, p. 35. He sometimes got his notes confused and quoted from memory: hence it is not altogether impossible that this unsupported assertion is a maimed recollection of the evidence cited in the preceding note.

† In 1665, in his *Journal des Voyages*, vol. ii. p. 59.

morals were light and his honesty but indifferent: he
squandered the money that had been entrusted to him,
and dared never again set foot in France.  And so, once
more, by the unkindness of circumstance, the king's
projects were postponed.  This was in 1519.

His pupil, Szuazzella, remained, and even settled in
France; for Cellini,* in the first journey he made in this
country in 1537, states that he met him there, and even
lodged in his house.  That was nineteen years later.
It is remarkable that throughout so long a time these
two instances remain the sole sources of the biography
of this painter, and that scarcely any other evidence of
him has been preserved in France.  It must not be
doubted, however, that during all these years of residence
the Florentine had multiplied his productions.  Vasari
says that he painted a castle in the provinces: is it
that of Semblançay that he refers to?

Be that as it may, we cannot quit this subject without
mentioning an allegorical painting in the Lille Museum,†
which is believed to represent Justice, and shows the
most evident signs of the influence of Andrea del Sarto
on a pupil of moderate ability.  It has been ascribed
to the school of Fontainebleau; but picture galleries are
wont to use that attribution so generally and so hastily
that it cannot be held to prove much.  But, after all,
I only mention this as a probable effect, in addition to
what has been said above, of the visit of Andrea del
Sarto to France.

The King of France, then, spared neither money nor
favour to retain the Italians; but all his efforts did

* *Op. cit.*, p. 213; Symonds, vol. i. p. 266.
† Catalogue, No. 1011.

not enable him to count on the services of any famous
man from that country. All his schemes failed at once;
and his political disasters soon succeeded in ruining his
designs. The defeat of la Bicocque, the treason of the
Constable of Bourbon, finally the *coup de grâce* of Pavia,
mark a period of catastrophes in the history of the
arts in France.

Up till that date, painting, with the exception of
portraiture, in which Janet was winning fame, went in
jeopardy in this country. In that respect, nothing could
equal the distress of the first years that followed the
captivity of Madrid. Before 1521 Bourdichon was dead,[*]
and before 1529 Perréal. These feeble lights were
extinguished. What some are anxious to call by the
name of the French school had completely abdicated,
and the trouble of giving an account of it is spared
us for this part of our history. It would be difficult
to maintain that Italianism had killed it, seeing how
little that influence had so far amounted to. And
in any case we look in vain for anything left of the
school to spoil and disorder when, in 1531, the famous
Rosso set out from Florence to decorate the castle of
Fontainebleau.

It is a completely paradoxical but yet a genuine
fact that only after this epoch, and under the impulse
brought from abroad, do several names of French
painters reappear, and not without honour; some following the Clouets in portraiture, others the painters of
Fontainebleau in allegory and history.

[*] Grandmaison : *Documents pour servir à l'histoire de l'art en
Touraine*, p. 56.

[†] Charvet : *Jean Perréal*, p. 231.

In the meantime, a few indifferent Italians, in feeble concurrence with the national genius, continued to fill the void which even the persevering efforts made to win over the best of their compatriots had not succeeded in removing.

Bartolomeo Guetty, a Florentine, is the oldest of the names we know. This painter had been in the king's service before his accession to the throne,* and was living then at Amboise. Later we find him at Tours,† where, no doubt, he had settled, with so many others of his profession. After the commencement of the reign we find him a member of the king's household.‡ His death did not take place till after 1532.§ He painted history and illuminations. Another came from Modena, whence he took his surname, his own name being Nicolas Belin. He appears after 1516,‖ and died after 1533.¶ Much later, about 1528, we find Francesco Pellegrino,** a Florentine, whose name is mentioned by Vasari. He enjoyed a place in the royal favour, for when the sculptor Rustici left Florence for the service of the King of France, we see Pellegrino taking part in his introduction.

Pellegrino and Modena were later to have a share in the decoration of Fontainebleau. Guetty designed the histories for the Tennis-court at the Louvre, temporary decorations, no doubt, which contained satyrs and nymphs. The

---

* *Nouvelles Archives de l'art français*, vol. vii. p. 9.

† Laborde: *Comptes des Bâtiments du roi*, vol. ii. p. 367.

‡ Bouchot: *Les Clouets*, p. 60.

§ Laborde: *ut. sup.*          ‖ Bouchot: *op. cit., ut sup.*

¶ Bouchot: *Comptes*, vol. i. p. 94.

** I have collected the information about this painter in *François Pellegrin: Annales de la Société Archéologique du Gatinais*, 1901.

FRANCISCO PELLEGRINO. ALLEGORY
FROM A PRINT

supposition that all this was not of a very high order
is rendered all the more probable by a composition of
Pellegrino's, printed as the frontispiece to a book of
patterns of lace he published in 1530, which comes aptly
to give the measure of a talent no doubt much on a
level with the rest. This work, unique in this respect,
represents an allegory which I cannot resolve, with the
Latin motto: *Exitus acta probat.* The style is poor
but precise, and provisionally instructive in the epoch.

Now I cannot refrain from believing that these second-
rate Italians will some day play a part in unexpected
discoveries. We are so firmly accustomed to recognising
in all the portraits of the time no manner but the
"Clouetic" and the Flemish, and the men I have just
named are so forgotten, that we never think of looking
among them for the Italian painters of certain of these
portraits. But any one who will take an unprejudiced
look at the great portrait of François I. at the Louvre *
will find there nothing but what is pronouncedly Italian.
The choice of the colours, the drawing of the doublet,
the very touch, all are calculated to turn our suppositions that way. The drawing of the face, it is true,
makes in the opposite direction ; but that I can explain :
a chalk-drawing by the presumed Janet, which that
master used elsewhere,† or some copy of this drawing,
served as a model for the face. That is the explanation
of the disparity of style and the confusion of criticism.
But there is no doubt about the rest, and even the hands
are Florentine.

I know of no similar drawing having been used either

* Catalogue, No. 126.        † See p. 35, note §.

for the portrait of Queen Eléonore at Hampton Court *
or for that of Marguerite of Angoulême in the Walker
Gallery at Liverpool; † but it is certain that both of
them show no less marked a difference from the general
run of the works produced under the influence of Janet.

I notice, as no negligible piece of testimony, that
Roscoe attributed the first to Lionardo da Vinci, and
that a "Henry VIII." at Hampton Court, incontestably
from the same hand as the second, has been considered
by many to be an Italian work. Denon attributed the
"François I." of the Louvre to Mabuse, and M. Hymans
proposes Sotto Cleef, both Flemings, but both full of
the Italian influence. But, if I join these three portraits
together here, it is not because I believe them all to be the
work of the same painter, but because I observe in them
all, in different degrees, an air of Italy, which only those,
perhaps, can fail to perceive who have neglected to combine to their mutual intensification these exceptions to
the Flemish manner, which was the common fare of
painting in the France of that time.

We must not forget that the Guettys, the Pellegrinos,
and the Modenas—feeble artists, hack-workers—who
were then serving the King of France, were just the men
to apply themselves in this way to the work of semi-
copyists and passable arrangers.‡

While talents of this sort were providing as best they

* Catalogue, No. 561.     † Roscoe Collection, No. 54.

‡ The portrait of Eléonore is unquestionably not original. Gaignières
had a full-length (Cabinet of Prints, Paris, Oa. 16, p. 13) from which this
bust is slavishly copied. I do not take into consideration the one at
Chantilly, which is inferior. For the rest, neither this portrait nor that of
Marguerite nor the François I. deserve the praise that has been accorded
them.

could for the needs that grew afresh as the court by degrees recovered, the thwarted designs of the king were being renewed more strongly than ever; a fine example of perseverance which perhaps has never been equalled.

To understand what follows we must form some idea of the extraordinary activity which François I. never ceased, through all his political troubles, to exercise for the encouragement of the arts.

We must picture to ourselves the intense interest which led him to keep up relations with the most famous artists in every country and with merchants all over Europe. Vasari and Félibien are full of references to works of art, antique statues, bronzes, and pictures, that were constantly being sent over from Italy to the King of France, proving the uninterrupted dealings of the prince with everything that concerned art in this country. Rome, Florence, and Venice contributed to his wants.* The documents in the archives increase the tale still further. They tell, among other things, of the purchase of tapestries in abundance. We know the names of his agents in several of the towns in Europe, at Antwerp, Milan, Brussels, and Florence. In the last-named city, the office took on the importance of a small state appointment, and the name of the man who filled it has passed into the history of the arts—Jean Baptiste de la Palla, who is mentioned, one might say, on every page of Vasari. He would send the king now a picture by Fra Bartolomeo, now a marble by Michael Angelo, now a sculptor to enter his service, collecting with avidity a thousand things for his master, until he roused the in-

* See a summary of these dealings in my *Primatice*, p. 55.

dignation of his countrymen, who dubbed him the valet
of the foreigner and almost a traitor to his country.*

There was no less vigour in the direct relations with
the artists.   It cannot be doubted that, after the journey
which followed Marignan, the king kept them up in great
numbers.   Palpable proofs of his correspondence with
Raphael are the incense-burner, engraved by Marc-
Antonio, which Raphael designed for the device of
François I., and the tapestries of the *scuola nuova* ordered
of the master for Leo X.†   The great number of designs
for tapestries which we afterwards find Giulio Romano
supplying in like manner ‡ prove how far Raphael's chief
pupil had inherited this distinction.   Moreover we find
François I. writing with his own hand direct to Michael
Angelo.§   All this implies a continuous action, the effects
of which were no sooner thwarted than they started
afresh and took shape again, till at length they reached
their end, and, by throwing once more the net of his
promises and his attractive reputation, the King of France
succeeded in drawing from his coveted Italy the men who
were to be responsible for the development of the French
renaissance in historical decoration.

It will be necessary to review, in a few words, the state
of Italy after the dispersion of Raphael's studio, from
which, we might say, as Cicero said of the school of
Isocrates, men of genius spread over the world like the
Greeks from the Trojan horse.   After this event the school
of Rome was first decapitated by the flight of Giulio
Romano, who fled to Gonzaga at Mantua, to escape

---

* Vasari : *op. cit.*, vol. vii. p. 262.
† Laborde : *Renaissance*, p. 971.        ‡ *Le Primatice*, p. 111.
§ *Archives de l'art français :* Documents, vol. v. p. 38.

punishment for the famous obscene prints which he had just designed. Three years later, in 1527, the sack of Rome completed the ruin of this school by the dispersion of all the artists whom Clement VII. had retained there under his protection. The horses of the Constable of Bourbon were stabled in the chambers of Raphael, and we can well believe that art could never recover from such a blow. Florence, on the other hand, continued to prosper under the splendid impulses given to artists by the designs for the "Pisan War" and the "Battle of Anghiari," which had not yet lost their effect. The ever-living style of Michael Angelo was suppressing there by degrees the example of Lionardo, whose last follower in this city was Andrea del Sarto. Close to Andrea came Pontormo; and Piombo, who had long been working in Rome, belonged no less to the school through the instruction of Michael Angelo.

Giulio Romano, however, in his retirement at Mantua, began to fill that city and all Italy with the noise of his amazing works. The Vatican being finished, all eyes were turned towards that astonishing palace of Te, on which Isabella d'Este and Gonzaga were lavishing marvels, rivalling the popes, not so much in splendour and magnificence as in novelty, grace, and learning. Mantua had become the capital of art; she was suddenly peopled with artists of her own nurture, and still drawing them from other cities in haste to form themselves on her vast enterprises and under so excellent an influence. The result was a studio prepared to furnish the subjects of the future, and certainly one of the first on which a prince who was an enthusiast in painting and decoration on a great scale was bound to turn his eyes.

E

At that time the fame of the Florentine school was spreading over Italy in the person of a man whom his great abilities had never succeeded in settling. I mean Rosso, who had formed himself on Michael Angelo and copied in a pleasant manner his spirit and his peculiar features. Having failed to make a living out of some pictures painted for the churches of his native place, he had set out thereupon for Rome, and might perhaps have stayed there but for the tragic event which drove the artists away. He continued to wander, and took refuge at Venice; but we cannot doubt that through all these journeyings he maintained a few friendships in Florence. His work preserved such indelible marks of them that he might be said to have carried his country on the point of his brush.

The relations of François I. with the Florentine painters are established by plenty of evidence. Piombo was painting for him at first. No doubt the commissions came by way of this city. The "Visitation," which was afterwards placed in the chapel at Fontainebleau and is now in the Louvre,* was the work of this artist, and he had begun for the king a "St. Michael," which he never finished.† A portrait of Giulia de Gonzaga, also from his brush, passed from the possession of Cardinal Hippolito de Medici into that of François I.‡ In the same way, several paintings by Pontormo, which were at Fontainebleau in the following century,§ must have come from this

* Catalogue, No. 1352.

† Félibien: *Entretiens sur la vie des plus fameux peintres*, 4to, vol. i. p. 442.

‡ Vasari: *op. cit.* All this was before 1531, when Piombo ceased to paint.

§ *Diarium* of Cassiano del Pozzo, edited by Müntz. *Mémoires de la Société de l'histoire de Paris*, 1886.

monarch. That at least is certain * of the so-called
Gaston de Foix, now in the Louvre.† Later, several pictures by Bronzino and Salviati were to prove that these
relations were continued. There is nothing surprising,
then, in the fact that such persistent dealings should have
ended in satisfying the great projects which the King of
France was forming, by the engagement of a Florentine
painter.

Rosso, till then a wanderer, was found in the nick of
time for the post. It is probable that La Palla had a
hand in the introduction, as he had three years before in
that of the sculptor Rustici : the reputation of the man
did the rest.

Finally, in the following year, François I., attracted
by the glamour which the school of Mantua was throwing
round Giulio Romano, turned towards it, and drew from
it, to reinforce Rosso, the best of its pupils, Primaticcio
of Bologna. Rosso arrived in 1531, Primaticcio in
1532.‡

In this second half of the reign everything seemed
ready prepared to make use of such services. Formerly,
from Lionardo and Andrea del Sarto nothing more seems
to have been asked than scattered works and easel pictures.
Had the king's ideas further developed in the interval,
and are we to believe that this time he knew more precisely what he wanted ? Or had circumstances prevented
him before from preparing to realise them ? In any case,
this time all was ready ; nothing was wanted but the
painters ; and their place is so clearly marked that it is

* See p. 54, note §.                    † Catalogue, No. 395.
‡ Vasari states that there was a year between the two arrivals. I have
calculated the second most exactly in my *Primatice*, p. 12.

hard to imagine what would have happened if they had
failed to flock to it.

The matter in hand was the decoration of the Castle of
Fontainebleau, the famous residence of the ancient French
monarchy. It was François I. who had made it famous,
for in the days of St. Louis and Charles V. it had been
but an obscure house. Suddenly its name blazed forth at
this epoch, and its reputation passed the frontiers.

The king loved the place for its situation, which he
called a "delicious desert." Up till 1528, for thirteen years
of his reign, he appears nevertheless to have been content
with his palaces of Amboise and St. Germain en Laye.
He had added to Blois; he had built Chambord. But
neither of them seems to have retained his affections.
The second, especially, on which vast sums had been spent
and which tradition has made his favourite residence, was
extraordinarily neglected. In thirty-two years of his
reign and in several journeys, he spent there no more than
thirty-six days altogether.* Extreme distaste must have
succeeded the choice he had made of this spot for the
squandering of such enormous sums. Nothing of the kind
occurred in the case of Fontainebleau. The workmen were
hurried, the land was bought in hot haste; every one was
pressed into the work at once and on all sides. Chambers,
galleries, vestibules, and gardens were ordered in the mass
and pushed forward concurrently. The estimates for re-
building were made in 1528 : three years later the painters
began their work; in ten years the castle was built, and
the king's and queen's apartments, the places of assembly
of the court, and the embellishment of the gardens finished.

* I have published this calculation as relating to the king's various
residences in the *Bulletin de l'art ancien et moderne*, 1902, p. 303.

When we reflect how slowly all such great works usually
went forward at that time, we are astonished at this swift-
ness, and impressed with an extraordinary idea of the
ardour with which the king encouraged it.

And so there was never again any place which he liked
better. "When he went there," says Ducerceau, "he used
to say that he was going home"; and the most exact calculations bear witness to the many long periods he spent
there. St. Germain kept some place in the order of the
royal predilections, but Amboise was abandoned; the
borders of the Loire scarcely ever saw him again.*

This preference has made Fontainebleau a kind of
summary of the reign. François I. found a place there
for everything he liked in the world. He installed
his library there; his bronze foundry was set up there,
his tapestry manufactories opened; all the precious
things that had been collected for him from all parts of
Europe came at last to Fontainebleau. The style of
ornament which his artists spread over it was called the
Fontainebleau style; Fontainebleau gave its name to
the school of painters which grew up from the imitation
of these artists. Hence this name is found in every history of art, in every manual, in every dictionary of art
that is printed, by the same right as Antwerp, Venice,
and Florence.

In that name is involved the signification of French
painting in the sixteenth century, the sum and total of
the idea formed, in the world of criticism, of the renaissance of this art under the Valois. All finer shades
are lost, all differences ignored in the hasty use of so
general a term. The following chapter aims at fixing

* *Ibid.*

its meaning and defining its scope, so far as painting is concerned. Such definition, perhaps, has never been so necessary as to-day. The name is extremely common; but I question whether there is aught so misunderstood as the thing. We shall see why as we proceed. The history which is now about to begin will give a true idea of its meaning by deduction from its origins and analysis of its results.

# CHAPTER IV

History of Rosso in France—His first picture—Primaticcio—The decoration of Fontainebleau—The credit of it due to Rosso—The gallery of François I.—Its ornament—Its suite of paintings—Now only to be judged from the drawings and the prints—The *padiglione* of Vasari—Other works by the same artist—Works by Primaticcio—The King's and the Queen's Chambers—Assistants of Rosso and Primaticcio—Rivalry between the two masters—The legend examined —The works they did in common : the "Pavilion of Pomona," the "Galerie-Basse"—Favour enjoyed by Rosso—His picture at Ecouen —His death—Idea of his style and his merit—Primaticcio's journey to Rome—Appraisement of the beginnings of the school of Fontainebleau.

V ASARI * and a few monuments and the "Comptes des Bâtiments du Roi" are the only sources from which the present chapter is taken. The last is often incomplete, and the first, so far as concerns Rosso, is nearly always vague and inexact. The result is that after many efforts we must despair of bringing to light all the details of this part of the history.

We know for certain, from documentary evidence,† that Rosso did not come into France on his own initiative, but was summoned by François I. We know neither the day nor the month: the year, as I have said, was 1531.‡

---

* *Opere*, Milanesi's edition, vol. v. pp. 167 *et seq.*
† The text of his naturalisation. Laborde : *Renaissance*, p. 754.
‡ See p. 67, note ‡.

At the end of 1533, we find the work on the great gallery of Fontainebleau,* of which Rosso is known to have been in charge, was already far advanced. Vasari relates that he had begun with some pictures, which the king approved of. If that is true, there is no objection to believing that a " Judith holding the head of Holophernes," which ten years later formed part of the collection of François I., was among the number of these first pictures, perhaps also a " Queen of Naples," " Mars and Venus," and the " Contest of the Muses and the Pierides," the last now in the Louvre,† which Commander del Pozzo ‡ reports that he saw in the following century in the King's collection at Fontainebleau. The same author adds a " Leda " painted after the design of Michael Angelo's. This last picture probably did not come into the king's hands till 1532,§ and four years later Rosso was charged to bring it to the castle.‖ I will not attempt to say when, between these dates, the copy mentioned was made.

The artist was very well received. He had a house in Paris, which can have been but little use to him, since all his occupation was at Fontainebleau ; a pension, which the Accounts show to have been 1400 livres,¶ though Vasari says 100 crowns ; and, if the latter is to be believed,

* Laborde : *Comptes des Bâtiments du Roi*, vol. i. p. 89.

† Catalogue, No. 1486.

‡ *Diarium*, edited by Müntz. *Mémoires de la Société de l'histoire de Paris*, 1886.

§ Herbet : *Dominique Florentin et les burinistes de l'École de Fontainebleau, Annales de la Société Archéologique du Gatinais*, 1899.

‖ Laborde : *Comptes*, vol. i. p. 104.

¶ *Ibid.*, vol. ii. p. 305. *Id.: Renaissance*, p. 756. *Nouvelles Archives de l'art français*, 1876, p. 90.

a general authority over all the works at Fontainebleau. We must add letters of naturalisation * granted by the king after these beginnings, a great favour by which we may gauge the value he set on this artist.

It must be acknowledged that the authority given him did not extend to the immediate direction of all the decoration that was being carried out at Fontaine-bleau, and that after the start this office was divided.

Primaticcio appeared in France between the 23rd January and the 25th March 1532.† He was, if not a competitor and rival, at least a man of importance, treated as such, and entrusted at once with the manage-ment of a staff of workmen like that which was work-ing under Rosso. After 1533 we find the newcomer at work on the king's chamber.‡ His pension was only 600 livres.§ In the same way the appointments each received as artist-managers of the paintings and decora-tions at Fontainebleau were strikingly different. Prima-ticcio had 25 livres a month, while Rosso had 50.|| There could not indeed have been perfect equality between the two. Rosso was thirty-five years of age, Primaticcio only twenty-seven; and while the Florentine was at the height of his career, already known by the works he had done in Italy, the other was but at the beginning of his. It is true that the difference of pay ought not to be considered here without some reservation; for even after Rosso's death, at a time when unquestion-ably the favour of Primaticcio surpassed anything that the former had ever enjoyed, we find his pension still at

---

* See p. 71, note †.                    † See p. 67, note ‡.
‡ Laborde : *Comptes*, vol. i. p. 94.
§ *Ibid.*, vol. ii. p. 366.                || *Ibid.*, vol. i. p. 98.

the same figure, which proves that the deficit was due
to differences of time * as much as of esteem, since in
proportion as the number of artists increased and, in
general, the expenses of his buildings, the king found
himself forced to reduce their salaries.

However that may be, it will be convenient to
contemplate these early stages of the work as divided
into two distinct studios: one, under Rosso, occupied
on the Great Gallery, the other, under Primaticcio, on
the King's Chamber. These were the first works undertaken at the castle, and the first in which the new style
was revealed.

We will speak first of the arrangement, hitherto
unknown, not only in France, but elsewhere. The
principle was a division of the wall in height; the lower
part was wainscoted, and the upper adorned with large
cartouches in a profusion of ornament, each forming
the border of a subject painted in fresco. Not only had
Italy no model of the kind to show, but Rosso himself,
at thirty-five years of age and the summit of his reputation, had never done anything like it. The combination
of stucco and fresco in one or two schemes of decoration of the time, that of the palace of Te for example,
had been treated on totally different principles, and
closely related to those of the ancient works recently
discovered at the Thermæ of Titus on the Esquiline
hill. The form we are considering was to come to light
in France alone; and although it was invented by an
Italian, a traveller of the same nation † who was privi-

---

* The sculptor Rustici, engaged about 1528, had 1200 livres, which,
with Rosso's, makes the highest salaries paid to any of these artists.

† C. del Pozzo : *op. cit.*

leged to see it later has called it frankly " the French
style." All this inclines me to believe that the King of
France himself, the sole person who shared the affairs
of this decoration with his Italians, was responsible for
the first idea, which the painters were charged to carry
out.

Nothing remains of the King's Chamber, to which
the guides to the castle have restored its more ancient
name of the Chamber of St. Louis; but some old prints
and a drawing by Primaticcio himself* enable us at
least to picture its appearance to ourselves, and to establish the comparison with Rosso's gallery, which has been
preserved.

All visitors to Fontainebleau carry away a recollection
of the extraordinary mixture of painting and sculptured
ornament † displayed in the gallery. The high relief
and the abundance of the stucco, which hems in the
pictures on all sides and in places even overlaps their
edges, make a unique and inspiring effect, in which the
balance of the two arts would have been disturbed if
Rosso had not scattered among the stuccos little cartouches of painting and placed grounds of gold behind
them charged with paintings in varied colours. By this
means the union of the two parts becomes as close as
could be. Frescoes and stuccos seem to be born of a
single stroke, and look as if each had risen out of the
other. The King's Chamber was very far from having

---

\* It seems to me useless to refer on all occasions to the sources drawn
on in my *Primatice*, and better to refer to the work itself. For this drawing see p. 17 of that book.

† Long attributed to Primaticcio. The guides perpetuate the mistake.
It is refuted in *Primatice*, p. 301.

this unity in its magnificence. There was a symmetrical stiffness in its arrangement, which clung perhaps to the taste for the antique brought from Mantua and retained from the lessons of Giulio Romano; and although we find there, following the example of what Rosso was doing, little pictures set below the big ones in the cartouches, the ornament of these fragments has not the variety, nor the novelty, nor the *ronflant* of those in the gallery. The separation remains entire between the stucco and the painting, which is surrounded with a large gilded guilloche to keep the huge ornaments at a distance.

From these signs it is easy to tell, in a perfectly new style of this nature, which of the two artists inspired the other. Of the two ways here revealed of filling in the same general arrangement, the original and autonomous is certainly Rosso's. To him, so far as possible in matters of this kind, belongs the credit of this invention and this use of the cartouche, which, once put at the service of the King of France, was promptly to accomplish the grand tour of Europe and become thenceforth one of the commonest *motifs* of the designers of ornament.

But no one else ever made such brilliant use of it. In this respect the gallery at Fontainebleau, which is called the Gallery of François I., remains a perennial subject of admiration. Thirteen great cartouches out of fifteen * remain of the magnificent spectacle, the richness and variety of which are inexpressible. In fact, what may be seen there is quite unlike any of the attempts

---

* The one in the middle, on the same side as the apartments, is Louis XV., and a copy from that opposite it. Just here was the entrance to a chamber decorated with two large cartouches, which have been destroyed.

that had now and then been made previously. Not only
has the artist used original detail to vary the uniform
arrangement of the whole. With the same space to fill,
around the same picture which has to be framed, in every
one of the thirteen cases he has taken up the arrangement of his ornament on a new principle; sometimes
hollowing out niches in the wall, and sometimes reserv-
ing large spaces to paint on. Here we have scrolls, here
bas-relief, here wreaths, here brackets; elsewhere, tall
figures in simple attitudes which hold the whole scheme
of decoration together. At one spot he places columns,
at another a network of rigid lines enclosing flat stucco
borrowed from the ancients. In several places it seems
as if he could not have enough of figures: here are four
genii, four terminals, two statues; elsewhere, again, a
twin cartouche is supported by little children. All ages
have served as models; boys, children, young men and
old men, philosophers, soldiers, augurs, women, genii,
satyrs, standing, sitting, flying, supporting cornices,
running in *frises* round the edges of the frames or
crouching underneath; all the creations of story, all the
marvels of fancy, all the suggestions of archæology and
of history are showered abroad on these walls. In this
charming and tumultuous surge, new ornaments are multiplied without end about the human figure. Fair fruits
woven into wreaths, scrolls, foliage, lions' heads, tragic
masks, ox-skulls, salamanders, leaning masks, shells,
scabbards, urns, then animals, birds, and dogs, make
up a novel harmony.

The consideration of ornament is outside the scope
of this book, but it was impossible to pass over a matter
of such importance without saying at least these few

words about it.  It was Rosso's mark in the palace, his
mark in the school of Fontainebleau and among all
who imitated him.   It is impossible to do justice to
this master without praising the beauty and fertility of
his invention of ornament.  Vasari informs us that he
designed for the King of France salt-cellars, vases,
shells, a complete service, masquerades, and even horse-
trappings.  He was a great master in this branch, and
his swift and brilliant stay at court was marked by truly
illustrious and imperishable characteristics.

As to the paintings by him which are in the gallery,
we must give up the attempt nowadays to judge them
on the spot, so sadly have restorations injured them, and
indeed destroyed them.*  This is a point to be impressed
on visitors to Fontainebleau: we can no longer know
anything about these works except from old prints and
the original designs.   One of these designs is preserved
at the École des Beaux-Arts in Paris.†   It represents
the education of Achilles, and shows the hero and his
master repeated several times in various episodes, collected into one picture, according to the archaic custom
which these sixteenth-century painters had inherited
from the Middle Ages.  From this fragment we may
easily judge of the style of the whole work, better, indeed, than from the prints of Fantose and Boivin, which
never escape being hard.

Vasari has described two oil-paintings which adorned
the two ends of this gallery, and no doubt faced each
other.  One was "Venus and Bacchus" with a satyr

---

* Couder repainted them entirely under Louis Philippe, and Brisset
later repainted Couder's repaintings.
† Muntz: *Guide de l'École Nationale des Beaux-Arts*, p. 173.

THE EDUCATION OF ACHILLES

ROSSO.  ORIGINAL DESIGN FOR THE GALLERY OF FRANCIS I. AT FONTAINEBLEAU
ÉCOLE DES BEAUX-ARTS, PARIS

lifting the curtain and appearing delighted at the beauty
of the god; a child riding a bear, and various ornamental
vases, no doubt of exquisite design, filled up the composition.  The other picture showed "Venus and Cupid," the
latter remarkable for his well-grown and pleasant limbs,
in the person of a boy of twelve years old.  If Vasari's
account is true, these pictures must have been destroyed
in one of the alterations which the castle underwent
later.*

What remains to-day bears witness only to twelve
paintings in fresco † which I will now describe in detail.
The greater number were mythological, and, to tell the
truth, not of the most common order nor the most easy
to decipher.  The artist seems to have delighted in the
less-known passages of Herodotus, Apuleius, and the
Metamorphoses rather than in the scenes which others
had repeated to satiety.  "Venus bewailing the death of
Adonis" ‡ belongs to this latter class, like the "Combat
of the Centaur and Lapithæ at the wedding of Piri-

---

* It is none the less difficult to see where one of these pictures can have
been placed, for one end of the gallery, that towards the White Horse, was
in those days pierced by a doorway, as we see from the arrangement of the
stucco works that remain.  Possibly the picture hung above, on the spot
where there is now the "Dispute of Minerva and Neptune," copied after
an old print.  The introduction of the subject was a fancy of Couder's,
and there is nothing to prove that there had been a painting of it there
before, although it had been somewhere at Fontainebleau, for Van Thulden
copied it there.  His drawing is in the Albertina collection at Vienna.
Several writers have claimed to recognise the second of the pictures
described by Vasari in the "Venus chastising Cupid," which we shall
speak of below; but that does not agree with the text of Vasari, either in
description or situation.

† Primaticcio painted the thirteenth cartouche.  See below, p. 98.

‡ Engraved by Fantose.

thous " ; * but " Cupid chastised by his mother for having
abandoned Psyche "; " Cleobis and Biton drawing the
chariot of their mother, the priestess of Juno"; "The
Burning of Catania," where Amphinomus and Anapicus
are seen carrying their parents on their shoulders,† have
been less frequently painted. To this must be added the
unusual manner in which the painter has chosen to treat
his subjects, which often makes it difficult to recognise
them ; so that it is not surprising that four others have
never yet been explained at all. These are the supposed
" Fountain of Youth "; " The Tempest," ‡ in which some
see an allegory of the battle of Pavia; " The Preparation
for a Sacrifice "§ and the famous composition known to
print-collectors under the title of " The Royal Elephant." ||
This elephant forms part of a triumph, and carries, in the
midst of fleurs-de-lis, the salamander and the cypher of
François I.; at his feet is a stork, and the figures of a
Roman Emperor and of Cerberus are added without
making the painter's intentions any clearer. Finally, at
the end of the gallery, on the side of the Court of the
White Horse and fitly crowning this monument, were two
pictures face to face, representing the government and the
patronage of François I. In the first ¶ the king, in
Roman armour, and surrounded with senators, great
functionaries and warriors, holds in his hand a pome-
granate, symbolising the union of all parts of the State.

* Engraved by Fantose.
† Engraved by Fantose and by Boivin.
‡ Engraved by Fantose.
§ Engraved by Fantose and by Boivin.
|| Engraved, with some alterations, by Fantose.
¶ Engraved by Fantose.

In the other, which is known as " Ignorance cast forth " *
and is the most celebrated of these pictures, François I.
appears crowned with laurel, a book under his arm and a
sword in his hand, entering the temple of Immortality :
in the foreground are several figures of men and women
blindfolded, some asleep, some leaning on their staves,
who appear to be seeking for the entrance to the temple.

It will be useless to add an enumeration of the many
subjects painted here and there in the little cartouches,
in the method I have described.† The most interesting
of these are the " Apollo " and " Diana " in their chariots,
supplementary paintings to the thirteenth great cartouche
in the middle of the gallery. To judge from a print of
them by Boivin ‡ these two pieces displayed in a smaller
compass as much style and poetry as were ever put into
the large pictures. Though painted in fresco, they
resemble enamel in their delicacy and form, and so
minute is the workmanship that for a long time they were
believed to be so.§

If we may trust Vasari, Rosso's works at Fontainebleau
were not confined to the gallery we have just described.
A celebrated passage in this author, which has often
exercised the wisdom of the learned, attributes to him a

---

* Engraved by Fantose and by Boivin.

† The following are a few, of which the engravings have preserved
a more exact account than the work of the restorers : "The Rape of
Amphitrite," "The Rape of Europa," "The Dance of the Dryads,"
engraved by Boivin ; "Glory," engraved by Domenico Fiorentino. See
note §.

‡ See below, p. 98.

§ Guilbert : *Description de Fontainebleau,* vol. i. p. 87. This writer
adds in a note that the gallery contained other enamels, which Primaticcio
destroyed. An examination of the gallery makes this incredible.

second work, which appears to have been of hardly less
importance than the gallery. In the Italian it is called
*padiglione,* and Vasari asserts that this was the name
given to a room "above the first storey of the upper
rooms, which forms the highest storey above all the rest."
There follows a very engaging picture of the multitude of
sculptures and frescoes and of the richness of invention
of the whole. On the subject of this room we need not
enter into a long discourse, which has already been supplied elsewhere ; * but we cannot omit to warn the reader
of the false situation which M. Palustre has assigned
to it in his "Architecture de la Renaissance," that is,
above the grotto of the Garden of Pine-trees. In order
to gather a few new lights on this subject, we have found
it necessary to enter on a very minute chronology, not
only of the buildings, but of the rooms at Fontainebleau,
and to draw up a complete geography of the interior of
this celebrated residence ; the result of which is, in fine,
that we can only apply Vasari's words to one place, and
that is the room on the second storey of the pavilion
called the Pavilion des Poèles. This pavilion was built
close to the lake at Fontainebleau about 1535.† The
Abbé Guilbert says in his guide to the castle that Charles
V. was lodged here in his passage through the country,
which took place five years later. This statement seems
to be justified by a passage in the "Chronicle of King
François I.,"‡ which so describes the emperor's lodging as

* L. Dimier : *Les Logis royaux au château de Fontainebleau, Annales
de la Société Archéologique du Gatinais,* 1898. *Recherches sur la Grotte
du Jardin des Pins. Ibid.,* 1897.

† *Le Primatice,* p. 253.

‡ Edited by Georges Guiffrey ; p. 290. "A sumptuous lodging of
stone," the passage runs, "in the form of a pavilion, completely open. The

to let us recognise this room ; so that, if my calculations
are accurate, the *padiglione* of Vasari formed part of the
apartments assigned to the illustrious guest.

Rosso's decorations in the lofty chamber of the Pavilion
des Poèles cannot have been executed, then, till after 1535,
and several references in the Accounts imply that they
were not entirely finished at his death.*  And certainly
no such chamber in France had ever been called a pavilion :
the word was only applied to the building, and we may
leave the responsibility of the phrase to the Italian
author.

I shall not here quote the description he gives of it ;
because, amidst much magnificent eulogy, it contains very
little detail.  All that can be gathered from it is that the
*padiglione* offered the spectacle of all the gods and goddesses, those of barbarism no less than of antiquity.  We
may imagine what resources of invention and ingenious
extravagance the painter must have put into the former.

The Pavilion des Poèles exists no longer ; it was pulled
down under Louis XV., but the paintings of the time of
François I. had disappeared long before.  The lofty hall
retained nothing of that date but its wainscoting and
perhaps its stucco : the fresco, which, no doubt, had
been injured, had been restored under Henri IV.†

To avoid any omission, we must add a statement of the
same author concerning some works, of what nature he
does not state, which he says were pulled down later in
order to enlarge the main building.  If this report is true,

rooms, chambers, and galleries were richly hung with tapestry and decorated with rich pictures and statues."

\* *Le Primatice,* p. 390.

† By Dubreuil.  See below, p. 262.

it must be applied to a certain gallery, included in the first estimates, which only stood for twenty years, and then was, in fact, destroyed, in 1552, in order to build the Ball-room.* Moreover, the number of cartouches of ornament engraved in the style of Rosso, and even of drawings by his own hand, which survive, with no corresponding paintings in the stucco of the gallery, are a striking confirmation of these statements concerning lost works.

While the Florentine was busy on these undertakings, Primaticcio was completing the King's Chamber with frescoes, of which a few copies in chalk by Van Thulden or Diepenbeck † preserve a faint memory. These pictures represented some of the adventures of the Greeks in the Trojan War. The arrangement was pleasant; but from what we know of Primaticcio in his early days, we cannot doubt that the execution was inferior to that of his later productions.

This first manner of Primaticcio's is exactly revealed in two drawings executed about 1535 (one of which may be seen in the Albertina collection at Vienna, and the other at the Duke of Devonshire's seat of Chatsworth) for the decoration of the Porte-Dorée, then the principal entrance to the Castle of Fontainebleau.‡ These two compositions may still be seen in their original places, but restored by modern hands. One is "Hercules visiting Omphale and allowing himself to be dressed like a woman," § the other a subject unexplained, in which a torch held by a man is lighting up some recumbent figures.‖

* *Le Primatice*, pp. 255, 288.
† *Ibid.*, p. 474.                    ‡ *Ibid.*, p. 306.
§ Engraved by the master with the monogram L. D. and by Fantose.
‖ Engraved by the master with the monogram L.D.

The next work of the same artist was the Queen's Chamber, finished in 1537 *; of this a chimney-piece remains. This room is called in the guides the Salon of François I. The chimney-piece has two fine stuccos and some restored paintings, among others a medallion of Venus and Adonis which the painter took from a drawing by Giulio Romano, carried out in stucco at the Palace of Te.

To the list of Primaticcio's works of that date we must add the King's Hall, with a certain room said to be over the Porte-Dorée, both of which are so completely forgotten that scarcely any mention of them can be found in contemporary documents.† It is not even known what the latter was used for, and the decoration of either remains a matter of conjecture.

Such were the works with which these two famous artists each enriched his part of the renovated residence of the King of France. A great number of assistants worked under them. Vasari states positively that for the gallery Rosso provided nothing more than the designs in water-colour, and that his assistants worked after these. No doubt Primaticcio, less famous than he and in a slightly inferior situation, was not allowed at first to leave all the execution to lieutenants; and in those early days he probably painted and modelled with those he had under his orders. That does not mean that he had no assistants: the " Comptes des Bâtiments " give him, as well as Rosso, the title of " painter-designer," which means that he had his orders carried out by others.

It is true that we find him with fewer assistants than Rosso. I will take no account of any but the principal,

* *Le Primatice*, p. 265.     † *Ibid.*, pp. 264, 278.

who were distinguished by the salary of 20 livres a
month. To mention the painters only, under Rosso
there was Pellegrino, of whom I have spoken, Giovanni
de Majoricy, called Jean Antoine, Claude Badouin,
Charles Dorigny, Joost Fouquet, and Leonard Thiry.
Primaticcio had only two, Belin, called Modena, and
Bartolommeo di Miniato; and the first of these, again,
was only there at the beginning.

Some writers have been fond of saying that though the
direction of the decorations at Fontainebleau was entirely
Italian, the French element was none the less important,
on account of the large number of workmen of that nation
who helped in their execution. That is a statement
which the examination of the documents proves to be
false. Of the seven names just mentioned, only two,
Badouin and Dorigny, were Frenchmen; two are Flemings, Fouquet and Thiry; four are Italians, Pellegrino,
Jean Antoine, Miniato, and Nicolas de Modena.* Of
the little that we know of these painters, some has been
given above, and the rest will follow in its place.

Every one has a general knowledge of the violent
rivalry which, according to most of the biographies,
set our two artists by the ears. The theme has been
embroidered in countless ways, and the story of these
quarrels has had an extraordinary success with authors.
New details have appeared; accessory occurrences have
been added. Champollion-Figeac† relates how, when
Rosso had painted Diane de Poitiers in the thirteenth
cartouche of the gallery, the Duchess d'Etampes, the

* *Ibid.*, p. 40.
† In his monography of the *Palais de Fontainebleau*, written in collaboration with Pfnor.

king's favourite, had the painting removed through
jealousy and her own portrait painted by Primaticcio
in its place. The whole of one episode in the present
history has been connected with these adventures : Primaticcio's journey to Rome, which occurred in 1540, could
have had no other cause! It was his rival, we are told,
who induced François I. to banish him from court.
The king, it is added, soon repented of doing so. In
Primaticcio's absence he quarrelled with Rosso, and
Rosso, unable to endure that his rival should be preferred to himself, took poison in despair, which permitted
the return of the Bolognese artist.*

The truth is, that we do not know in the least
whether Diane de Poitiers, who certainly was the mistress of Henri II. under his father's reign, and from
the times of which we write, was Rosso's friend or not.
The story of the portraits is a sheer invention, with
no more justification than the fact that, though Boivin
engraved a Diana in a cartouche copied from the gallery,
the actual cartouche has a Danae painted by Primaticcio.
But it cannot be said that this Diana is like Diane de
Poitiers, nor the Danae like the Duchess d'Etampes.
Still less can we be sure that the first of these subjects
was ever painted where we now see the second. Even
supposing that it had been intended to paint it there,
the death of Rosso, which occurred before the gallery
was finished, would be enough to explain why the design
was never carried into execution. The rest of the story
though it is drawn from a more ancient source, is none
the less untrue. It rests only on the authority of Guido
and Albani, who said that they took the above account

* Malvasia : *Felsina Pittrice*, vol. i. p. 162.

of Rosso's death from a letter of a certain painter of
Fontainebleau,* and on some notes half a century later
than Vasari.    Beyond  question,  we  must  prefer  the
evidence of this author, who nowhere says a single
word of the quarrel between Primaticcio and Rosso.
The cause he assigns for the death of the latter is entirely different.    It followed, according to him, from
the grief he felt at having had Pellegrino put to the
torture on suspicion of having robbed him.    Pellegrino
was proved innocent, and revenged himself by so scathing
a lampoon that Rosso, reviving the ancient story of the
victims of Archilochus, killed himself in despair.    Vasari,
moreover, does not rest this account on the evidence
of his own authority alone, but in his first edition he
quotes the text of a Latin epitaph composed by the
Florentines on Rosso, which gives the same explanation
of his death.†

And now that the legend is put right, we shall find
less trouble in understanding how it is that, throughout
the ten years of his life at the court of France, we
find Rosso co-operating with Primaticcio in joint undertakings.

The first was a little pavilion in the gardens of
Fontainebleau, called the Pavilion of Pomona from two
pictures representing the history of that goddess which
were painted there. ‡    Rosso directed the work and
painted one of the pictures, the study for which is now
in the Louvre, in the collection His de la Salle.    The
subject is Vertumnus in the form of an old woman

---

* Caccianemici, called Cachenemis, mentioned below, p. 114.

† Edition of 1550, Florence, p. 815.

‡ *Le Primatice*, p. 312.

THE MUSES

PRIMATICCIO.    CHÂTEAU D'ANCY-LE-FRANC

inspiring Pomona with love.* The other, which represents the Gardens of Vertumnus,† is equally known from the original study by Primaticcio, also in the Louvre.

On a second occasion, several years later, we find the two men joined in painting the Galerie Basse above the lake, on the first floor of the Pavilion des Poèles. ‡ The work was considerable, and in the same style as the rest. Part of it, no doubt, consisted of twelve figures in corner-pieces, representing Juno, Pallas, Venus, and the Muses, § by Primaticcio, the studies for which are nearly all in the Louvre.

Finally, and in the very year which preceded the death of Rosso, the same alliance was renewed for the purpose of the decorations with which the King of France wished to embellish the reception of the emperor Charles V. at Fontainebleau. The emperor was then crossing France to fight the revolted people of Ghent. Rosso and Primaticcio worked together ‖ on the ornaments with which his entry was adorned.

All this period seems to have been spent by Rosso in the shelter of a favour which no unpleasantness came to disturb. Vasari says that his train was that of a nobleman. He had, besides his pension and the payment for his work, the revenue of a canonry in the Ste. Chapelle which the king had given him, it is not known at what date. Private patrons employed him; and we have at least one example of the fact in the

* Engraved by Fantose.
† Engraved by the master with the monogram L.D.
‡ *Le Primatice*, p. 305.
§ Engraved by the master with the monogram L.D.
‖ Vasari: *op. cit.*, vol. v. p. 170. It was on this occasion that Rosso designed the figure of Hercules, of which we spoke on p. 52, note *.

picture of " Our Lady of Sorrows," now in the Louvre,* which he painted for the Castle of Ecouen to the order of the Constable de Montmorency.

His age was only forty-five; and his active and brilliant genius should assuredly have been for many years to come the ornament of the country in which he found himself so advantageously settled. His rank was not contested, and Maître Roux, or Red, as they called him, must have been anxious to pursue a career which had opened so auspiciously, and which he must have known himself capable of pursuing. The protection of France had drawn out and intensified his merits, which in Italy had been so buried as scarcely to be suspected, and given his influence a field, the extent of which must have delighted him. But none of these things could prevail against a sullen temper, and its outbreaks caused his death. I have related the event above. That was in 1541; almost at the same moment, it is worth noting, as the death, at the opposite pole of art, of Jean Clouet.

Such was the miserable end of this man of genius. In some respects he was an exquisite artist; and in these, France, if enlightened and exempt from futile preconceptions, will ever be grateful to him for her first initiation. Rosso was the first to reveal to this country the power of painting in her larger enterprises and her nobler functions: in this sense we might say that he was the first painter France had ever had. To a nation fed so far on illuminators and glass-painters, on timid little sacred pictures and lifeless portraits, he brought learned allegory, genial mythology, the infinite song of

* Catalogue, No. 1485.

OUR LADY OF SORROWS
ROSSO.  LOUVRE

imagination, and the profound taste for antiquity which is the source of perpetual rejuvenation.

Certain less praiseworthy characteristics of his manner ought not to obscure this fact: the genius of Rosso, completely imbued as it was with Michael Angelo, was nevertheless profoundly influenced by the style and spirit of antiquity; and I shall point out further on the effect of this novelty on France.

In Rosso this foundation is mingled with smartest outline, superb originality of posture, and admirable movement of the composition. It is true that there is no beauty either in his expressions or his faces. With force and variety and elegance of a certain sort, he lacked tenderness and grace. His Ecouen picture of " Our Lady of Sorrows," though executed with singular skill, is pitilessly hard. He liked to paint terrible expressions, and those he has given to the faces in his " Tempest " verge on the ridiculous in the print by Fantose. His learned drawing sometimes fell into excess, and too easily allowed itself to run to the neglect of nature. There is mannerism in the action of his figures, and even in their repose; the arms and legs have too much movement, assume too much importance in the composition, and constantly encumber it distastefully. But all these failings are corrected and all these faults atoned for by the life and impetuosity which appear in all his works. In a design like that of the " Education of Achilles," his very joy in wielding his brush has given it a wonderful charm. Here indeed is a fine design, a collector's piece, of the kind that was so admired in the eighteenth century, when it belonged to Mariette. What readiness of touch and hand; what suppleness and ductility; what ease in giving the distances with a stroke of the pen, in throwing in the foreshortenings and sweeping the outlines! And what hurried and lively action, what elasticity, what contrasts! What grace of invention, what poetic bloom, culled from the "Metamorphoses," lavished with a magnificence and lightness of hand which neither Primaticcio nor del Vaga ever surpassed! His genius for decoration pervaded his figure-paintings, and has given them a value which rises superior to anything that well-founded criticism can say of them. It relegates them, indeed, to the second rank, but lit with so many flashes of beauty and composed of such striking parts that we scarcely dare envy their painter the first rank which he held for ten years in France.

His influence on painting, which lasted long and left a sensible effect on many artists, was only to yield at last to that of Primaticcio, who took his place in the royal favour and inherited for thirty years the succession which his death left open.

Primaticcio's journey to Rome, which has been linked to false reports of rivalry between the two men, is not in itself a fable. It arose from the king's desire to possess works of art and antiquities, which could only be found in Italy, and could be better procured by a man of taste trained in his service than by a merchant. In fact the commission given to Andrea del Sarto was repeated after a lapse of twenty years. Primaticcio left on the 13th February 1540,* and we find him in Rome on the 31st October following.† The date of his return is not known,

---

* *Revue de l'art français*, 1888, p. 1.
† *Gazette des Beaux-Arts*, 1860, vol. iii. p. 212.

but it was during his absence that Maître Roux died; and thus we might say that, finding himself unrivalled both in merit and importance, he returned only to reign alone over the undertakings at Fontainebleau.

From that moment the history of the Italian school in France began, and though we are still thirty years from the date at which we may best judge it as a whole, the story of its earliest stages calls at once for a few conclusions. The care I have taken to show in its due proportions what talent France had to offer to the king's encouragement, and, on the other side, to state what his plans were and consider what Rome and Florence could do for him, demonstrates conclusively that the conduct of this prince was the most natural in the world. In these concerns the results were neither more nor less than what they should have been; and in such a chain of causes, resolutions, and effects, I cannot see what room is left for hostile criticism to insinuate its strictures.

It has a right, of course, to complain that the painters brought over into France were not a few degrees better, and that they belonged to what, strictly speaking, we call with justice the decadence. But that was a mischance which it was in nobody's power to avoid. The blame must attach to the epoch, and the King of France could not bring back to life the men of the preceding age. On the contrary, what we have seen of his taste compensates somewhat for this disadvantage, if it is true that the right to please and content us is not confined to things of the supremest excellence. All the strictures that have been accumulated on this point are merely fanciful, because they are objectless, except in

one aspect which the late regretted M. Müntz, with his
learned criticism and sound common sense, has alone
succeeded in stating with moderation. Why, he says,
did it not occur to them to look in Venice for the
man they needed? This regret, which implies a
preference for Tintoretto and Veronese over Rosso and
Primaticcio, no one can call excessive. And, indeed, I
do not know that any general reply could be found,
except that François I. had fewer relations with Venice
than with the other parts of Italy, and that perhaps he
was imperfectly acquainted with its painters. This
observation removes the blame, but not the regret.
Another reflection, no doubt, will do more: which is,
that in spite of the loss as regards the proper perfection
of the art of painting, there was an undeniable gain in
the domains of ornament and decoration in general. In
this respect Florence and Mantua were the most advanced
places in the world, and the Venetian style, which was
composed of flat paintings without relief or repose of
any kind, seemed so behindhand to the Venetians
themselves, that we find them some years later being the
first in all Italy to borrow from Fontainebleau the
motives they lacked.*

The great expansion of style of Fontainebleau, therefore, which was effected through ornament rather than
through the figure, was unquestionably due to nothing
but the exclusion complained of. And, therefore, if any
expression of regret is to be allowed, it must be only
in a book like the present, and solely from the point
of view of painting.

That, moreover, is not the point of view from which

* *Le Primatice*, p. 140.

everything must be judged.  The gifts of painters make
the pleasure of amateurs; they are not always equal to
giving importance and fertility to a school.   England,
certainly, in acquiring Holbein, possessed herself of an
artist whose personal merit surpasses all who are to be
named in this book.

But what sterility was his in regard to art in general !
If he formed a few pupils in his particular branch, that
was all he did.   Decorative painting, sculpture, ornament
—not one of them did he bring to perfection.   For, in
spite of a few architectural designs that he left, the
English Renaissance proceeds, not from Holbein, but from
Pieter Koeck and Vredeman de Vriese.   So true is it
that in the school whose history we are writing, we are
forced to look at other considerations besides the strict
excellence of the painter, and to measure abilities not
only by depth but by extent and wealth, the sources of
influence and of fertility.

# CHAPTER V

THE period we now enter marks, by a curious coincidence,
the simultaneous enfranchisement of the two most famous
painters of the century, as different in genius, in application and in style as could be imagined, coming from the
two extremities of Europe to make France illustrious, and
destined to enjoy together for thirty years, and without
rivals, the constant favour of a court and people whose
rapid initiation into the arts was fixing the attention
of the whole world.

Primaticcio and François Clouet made their first
appearance at the same moment. At the same moment
the former's rival, who shared his reputation and success,
and the latter's father, whose established fame was sub-
merging his dawning abilities, disappeared and left them
the field. Both together won enduring glory, monopolised
the royal favour, imposed the standard of their taste,

their style, their manner, the imitation of their qualities
and their defects; passed, with no surrender of their
marvellous fortune, through revolutions in public taste
and changes of sovereign, and faced the tyranny of new
patrons, the caprice of new manners in the course of the
most troubled century in the history of the world.

Together and each by himself they led this life of
imposing triumph; together they quitted it near that
day of blood which is marked in the politics of the time
by the Massacre of St. Bartholomew; as if these parallel
careers, full of a curious symmetry, had been necessary
for the better comparison of talents so widely different
and the measurement of their importance.

I will take Primaticcio first, since in him the history
begun in the preceding chapter is carried on.

His first care, on his return, was to cast in bronze
several antique statues of which he had taken the moulds
in Rome, with the assistance of Vignola, who followed
him to France on purpose to take charge of the work.*
This famous architect, still young and at the outset of
his career, was occupied in this instance on subjects very
different from those which have made him famous;
nevertheless, with the aid of our artist, he succeeded
perfectly in the work, which was taken to Fontainebleau.
The casts they took, a large portion of which may be
seen at the Louvre, have kept the name of this residence
and are still called the Fontainebleau casts.†

Primaticcio's second object was to finish the gallery

---

\* *Le Primatice*, p. 328.

† They are : "The Ariadne" from the Vatican, "The Hercules Com-
modus," "The Apollo Belvedere," "The Venus of Cnidos," and "The
Laocoon." The rest were turned into rifles at the Revolution.

so magnificently decorated under Rosso. I have said
that the thirteenth cartouche, which formed the centre
piece, remained to be painted, and I added that a print
by Boivin has preserved for us the form of this cartouche,
with a Diana in the place of the painting.* There is
nothing, it is true, to assure us that this Diana was
ever intended to be placed there, and the examples of
free copies taken from these ornaments at Fontainebleau
are numerous enough to justify us in believing this to
be one of them.† It must be admitted, however, that
the engraver from whom it emanates, as well as the
perfect exactitude of the part representing the ornaments, leaves less room for this supposition than in
other cases. Finally, a possibly decisive detail is that
two little accessory cartouches are reproduced in this
print with the paintings which they actually received. ‡
It seems, therefore, wiser to believe that the Diana represented belonged to the plan which Rosso had formed
for this thirteenth cartouche, and which was never
finished. It was the custom of the time for the burin
to begin work at the same time as the brush, and for
the painters' works to appear in engravings while they
were still being carried out. No doubt the death of
the painter interrupted this painting; and it is not to
be supposed that any one else charged with the completion of the gallery would have taken up the design
of Maître Roux.

Primaticcio then painted a "Danae"§ which the

* On this question in general see *Le Primatice*, p. 302.
† See Herbet: *Catalogue de l'œuvre de L.D. Annales de la Société
Archéologique du Gatinais*, 1896, p. 21.
‡ See above, p. 81.
§ Engraved by the master with the monogram L.D.

restorations have ruined like the rest; but the design of it is preserved at Chantilly. At the same time—and this is a proof that Rosso's death had certainly left the gallery unfinished—the same artist must have painted, in a little closet which opened into the middle of the gallery, the subject of Semele burnt in the fire of Jupiter.* This painting was soon removed, and nothing is left of the closet.

Everything points in like manner to the belief that another work of Rosso's—the "Salle Haute" of the Pavilion des Poèles—taken in a former chapter to be the same as the *padiglione* of Vasari—which we know to have been completed about that time, was also finished by Primaticcio.†

It has been said and repeated broadcast that this artist, in his hatred of his defunct rival, set himself to degrade his work, and that the gallery was sacked by Primaticcio. On the other hand, an expression in Vasari has been taken to mean that he must have worked upon the stucco, and that the profusion of ornament in this material was of his making. The result of this notion has been that Primaticcio's intervention has grown beyond all bounds, until at last the guides have adopted the course of leaving Rosso the paintings, but presenting all the stucco in this gallery as the work of Primaticcio. That statement is the exact opposite of what I have said above; and the rest is no whit more true. If Primaticcio joined up the stuccos in his own way, it could only have been in the closet which has been destroyed. The gallery that remains shows no trace of any such thing, and, equally, none of any

* Engraved by the above.  † *Le Primatice*, p. 390.

devastation; and a wise decision would be to confine this painter's part in the work to the two pictures which I have just mentioned.

In conjunction with the figures of the so-called " Muses " painted in the Galerie Basse, the drawings and prints that survive show a notable change in Primaticcio's manner. This change took place about 1540. In the paintings of the Porte-Dorée we find something of stiffness and inexperience, of vulgarity in the expression and heaviness in the treatment, and in the drapery now carelessness and now a slavish attachment to the manner of Giulio Romano. They betray the recollection of Mantua, the traditions of the Roman school, and the imitation of the antique. On the contrary, the dominating note of the epoch we have reached is the style of Michael Angelo polished and sweetened by Correggio; all the grace of Parma refreshing and caressing the grandeur of Florence. This is all the more worth remarking because thenceforth that was the style of the master, and the improvement was final.

This was the style of the drawing and composition of the innumerable paintings of his which appeared after this period and formed the basis of his reputation. This was the style of the Ulysses Gallery, the Ball-room and the many others, which we must now describe in detail.

The first was the Chamber of the Duchess d'Etampes,* which still exists as a whole, but so thoroughly repainted † that nothing beyond the stuccos

---

* *Le Primatice*, p. 269.

† By Abel de Pujol, under Louis Philippe. This painter replaced the subjects at haphazard, and even introduced some of his own designing. From the reign of Louis XV. the chamber was used to contain a staircase, and the chimney-piece had been pulled down.

can be regarded as the master's work. They marked his final style, which was always more symmetrical and less prolific than Rosso's, and lacked the beautiful admixture of gold grounds with the ornament and painted medallions with the sculpture. No praise, however, can be sufficient for the beautiful effect of this work, the delicately varied attitudes of the twenty large female figures, standing erect below the cornice, which accompany these paintings. Originally this room, which was altered lately, contained six large subjects only, two rectangles and four medallions. The children above the medallions have a perfect and charming beauty, and so have the raised garlands that accompany them, conceived in the style of Rosso, and no whit inferior. The goats' heads and little terminals of satyrs, in the same style, are no less excellent.

Of the original paintings the detail was as follows. On one side, one of the large pieces represented Campaspe crowned by Alexander,* and the other, above the chimney-piece, the story of Alexander and Thalestris,† the drawing of which is in the Louvre. In the medallions were Alexander taming Bucephalus, ‡ Apelles painting Campaspe and Alexander,§ the drawing for which is at the Duke of Devonshire's seat of Chatsworth, Timoclea, before Alexander, ‖ and Alexander embracing Campaspe, the drawing of which is

---

* M. Müntz calls her Roxana, and considers the subject to have been borrowed from the Italian way of painting the wedding of that princess with Alexander.

† Engraved by the master with the monogram F.G.

‡ Engraved by the master with the monogram L.D.

§ Engraved by the above.                   ‖ Engraved by the above.

in the Albertina collection at Vienna. For the rest, we
know well enough what Alexander we have to deal with,
and what Campaspe too: Mme. d'Etampes could not
refuse this name which allowed the king to figure in the
*rôle* of so illustrious a character. We know from Cellini
how the favourite had taken Primaticcio under her
protection. The friendship between them is announced
with some emphasis in this chamber. May we believe
that the painter intended to represent himself in the
person of Apelles? In any case, the sequel of the story,
depicted as I believe in small cartouches, and showing
the marriage of Campaspe and Apelles by order of
Alexander, can have no application to Primaticcio. In
this sort of allegory it often happens that the same
pseudonym does not always signify the same person.
The honour of becoming the husband of the royal
mistress was assigned to another. The cynicism of the
allusions is in accordance with the morals of the age,
and I cannot help thinking that this painting celebrated
the union of Jean de Brosse * with the fair de Heilly,
which the king himself brought about, creating him duc
d'Etampes in honour of the occasion.

All these subjects, which bear but slender witness to the
painter's sense of the proprieties, do the greatest honour
to his genius. One cannot imagine a better turned or
more gallant allegorical poem in honour of the impure
and insolent triumph of beauty. Throughout the whole
work the supreme elegance, the dignity of composition,
the grace of detail and the variety of subject, surprise
and captivate us.

* The son of Brosse, the friend of the Constable de Bourbon, who
betrayed the king and fell at Pavia.

Into the midst of this gallantry the picture of the taming of Bucephalus throws an apt note of sports and tourneys; the "Timoclea spared by Alexander" recalls no less happily the humanity and courtesy on which the knightly king prided himself; while two little subjects, I believe, the "Festival at Babylon"* and the "Masquerade at Persepolis," † symbolised to a marvel the ingenious and magnificent displays with which this brilliant court amused itself.

The Chamber of Mme. d'Etampes was scarcely finished when Primaticcio turned his labours to the Grotto of the Garden of Pine-trees.‡ The decoration of the garden was going on side by side with that of the apartments.

The grotto was one in the ancient style, decorated with rustic ornaments, in which bossage, rock-work, and shells, arranged in symmetrical patterns, unite, in an extremely novel fashion, natural substances with architecture of the strictest regularity. It still exists, sadly fallen from its ancient fame, in a little court which is now separated from that ancient Garden of Pine-trees, within a few paces of the spot where stood the Pavilion of Pomona, but hidden behind fragments brought from other parts of the castle, and dishonoured by an incipient restoration of the interior.§ Primaticcio had painted the ceiling with three subjects, two of them round, and the one in the centre oval. The last is almost

---

* Engraved by Domenic Fiorentino. The drawing is in the Louvre.
† Engraved by anonymous artist. The drawing is in the Louvre.
‡ *Le Primatice*, p. 309.
§ I have given an idea of this recent restoration in the *Chronique des Arts*, 1900, p. 330 ; and have described its former appearance in *Recherches sur la grotte du Jardin des Pins, Annales de la Société Archéologique du Gatinais*, 1897.

entirely destroyed, and the subject is not known. The designs for the two others are in the Louvre; one shows Minerva, the other Juno, sitting under trellises in the form of cupolas. Arragonite crystals formed several compartments round them, on which various birds and fishes of painted stucco may still be seen, distributed over a ground moulded in scales. Some of the compartments had foliage, and foliage again covered the wall from the ground. Such a building could serve no purpose but that of gallant recreation. It was not used for bathing, as some have supposed, on the faith of a hundred fictitious adventures.* People came there to take the air, and to enjoy the piquant spectacle of these unusual ornaments and the mythological paintings.

These paintings are the earliest of all the works arranged by Primaticcio for the adornment of a vault, and his first attempt at ceiling figures. It was not long before new decorations were to show what might be expected of him in this branch.

Under the pavilion of the Porte-Dorée, behind the portico which we have seen him painting, stretches a hall or vestibule,† which our artist took up in its turn, and finished in 1544. Here he painted four subjects on the slopes of the vault, and two, octagonal in shape, at the top. The former represented Juno at the House

---

* Put into circulation in the eighteenth century by a novel by Mme. de Villedieu, and scrupulously repeated by the guides. They talk of a hiding-place provided with an arrangement of looking-glasses, which the king had constructed there in order to see the ladies bathing. These stories lack the most rudimentary probability.

† *Le Primatice,* p. 306.

of Sleep,* the design of which is in the Florence Museum; Paris wounded before the walls of Troy,† the design of which is in the Louvre; that of Hercules fighting from the deck of the ship of the Argonauts,‡ unhappily painted over, is in the Albertina collection at Vienna; and a subject supposed to represent Tithonus and Aurora § may still be admired in a drawing in the Louvre. The octagonal subjects represented Aurora chasing the Evil Dreams, the design of which, vilely retouched, is at Chatsworth, and Jupiter slaying the Giants with his thunder-bolt. All these were painted with great taste, and, compared with the paintings in the porch, show the superiority that came of ten years of practice and study. These pieces offered the eye by turns the most martial and the most seductive of mythological scenes. Unhappily, every one of them has been repainted, ‖ and even modified, until some of the compositions have changed their meaning.

Thus, then, was Primaticcio pursuing his career, henceforth master of his powers and ready to employ them on the most various kinds of undertaking. The intention of all these works is different. There were no stucco ornaments in the vestibule of the Porte-Dorée: in the King's Closet ¶ we find a still more original design.

We refer to four large wardrobes, which he decorated

---

* Badly engraved by the master with the monogram J.V.

† Engraved by the master with the monogram F.G.

‡ Engraved by the master with the monogram L.D.

§ Engraved by Fantose.

‖ By Picot, under Louis Philippe, like the gate itself, which was described, p. 84. This artist believed them to be the work of Rosso.

¶ *Le Primatice*, p. 262.

with cameos below, and above with various figures representing the cardinal virtues, which stood in pairs,
face to face, on the doors of each wardrobe.  One of
each pair was purely allegorical, the other represented
some hero of antiquity in whom these virtues had been
most conspicuous.  Thus Cæsar goes with Strength,
Ulysses (the drawing of which is in the collection His
de la Salle in the Louvre) with Prudence, Zaleucus with
Justice (the drawings of both are in the Louvre), and
Scipio, no doubt, with Temperance (the drawing of which
is in the British Museum).  Nothing now is left of this
decoration.  This room, once the King's Closet, is now
what they call at Fontainebleau the Council Chamber.
The virtues may still be seen there, but of another kind,
and by more modern hands.  In the days of François I.
the chimney-piece bore one of the most beautiful compositions ever seen at Fontainebleau—the "Forge of
Vulcan," * as described by Virgil.  The original drawing
of this famous piece is in the Louvre.  Above was
"Joseph visited by his Brethren."  The whole was
finished in 1545.

Such were the works which, up to that year, Primaticcio carried out for the king.  The Bathing-hall,†
which occupied him, perhaps, up till 1547, must end this
enumeration.  This was a work that was remarkable for a
mythological flight of the greatest beauty combined with
an extraordinarily spirited execution.  Although we cannot doubt that all the rooms composing this part of the
building were decorated with paintings, I can furnish no
definite information about anything but the Bathing-room

---

* Engraved by the master with the monogram F.G.
† *Le Primatice*, p. 279.

properly so called. Here was painted the story of
Calisto, in four small hemicycles and one large subject
in the vault. First came Jupiter in the form of Diana
embracing Calisto *; next, Diana discovering the preg-
nancy of the nymph, which was composed in two drawings, one now in the Louvre and the other in the Malcolm
collection in the British Museum; then the nymph
changed into a bear, the drawing of which is in the
Louvre. These three, with their piquancy of invention
and lavish suggestions, provided motives for compositions
of strikingly original effect. The fourth hemicycle showed
Neptune with Triton and other marine deities; and in
the vault was Calisto set among the stars. This body
of paintings must be reckoned among the finest of the
master's works, and the most conspicuous for his facility.
Such pieces proved the complete and perfect mastery of
his genius, and the power of producing, with the greatest
facility, the most difficult marvels of art.

Having spoken of this apartment, I cannot omit to
add a word concerning the use, besides that of the baths,
to which it was put. That use was (it seems almost
incredible!) to contain the pictures which composed the
king's collection. It was made up of six vaulted rooms
arranged *en suite* on the ground floor just below the gallery
of Rosso. The Bathing-room was the principal one.
First came two chambers which served for vapour baths
and other cares of the toilet; and beyond it three others
intended for repose. Nothing could have been better
adapted than this arrangement; for the rooms were easy
to warm during the winter, and cool in summer from the
thickness of the ceilings and the terrace which shaded it

* Partly engraved by Boivin.

in front. The view over the lake and the garden-alleys was the most beautiful in the castle. The king's pictures were hung on the walls of these rooms, which were all decorated with stucco in keeping with the paintings that Primaticcio placed there. There, too, were the pictures the king had from Lionardo and Andrea del Sarto, the Raphaels that had been given him, Michael Angelo's "Leda,"* a "Magdalen" by Titian,† and all the fine works which the Louvre owes to this prince, with several others that unhappily are lost. It will be a matter of surprise, perhaps, that such perfect masterpieces should have been deliberately exposed to the causes of destruction presented by such a place. The choice of it shows that pleasure in the arts was included by the King of France among physical recreations. As if to prove, at least, the sincerity of his taste, painting appeared to have no other office in his eyes than that of ministering to pleasure.

Four of these pictures had come under the care of Primaticcio before his journey to Rome, in a manner which needs mention here. The "St. Michael," the "Madonna," the "Jeanne d'Aragon," and the "St. Margaret"‡ by Raphael had been put into his hands to clean. The task throws light on the work, in those days, of the keeper of the king's pictures, a keeper who was equally ready and able to design a setting worthy of their merits.

---

* This celebrated picture, now lost to France, which disliked the freedom of its subject, is now, it is believed, in the National Gallery in London. Reiset: *Une visite aux musées de Londres; Gazette des Beaux-Arts,* 1877, vol. i. p. 246.

† Now in the Bordeaux Museum; Catalogue, No. 150.

‡ Laborde: *Comptes des Bâtiments du Roi,* vol. i. p. 135.

The whole of this large number of paintings and all sorts of decoration is fully proved to belong to the space of barely six years which elapsed between the return from Rome and the death of François I. This, perhaps, would be the place to pause in admiration of this immense activity, if it were not that we must enrich it still further by the mention of the half of the ceiling of the Ulysses Gallery which was carried on at the same time.

This Ulysses Gallery was not destined to approach completion until the following reign. I shall not speak of it, therefore, as yet, but reserve its description until we reach the date at which the last figures were placed there. For the present it will be sufficient to remember that it formed the greatest work of Primaticcio's career, and one of the most extraordinary that have ever been seen.

What follows will serve to gauge the degree of importance to which, in this new period of his life, Primaticcio was raised, and the favour with which he was honoured by the King of France. The choice that was made of him to undertake the journey to Rome marked the dawn of it. The manner in which he acquitted himself must naturally have added to his credit; and soon we find him passing into the front rank in all the enterprises in which the king was then encouraging all the arts at once. He was entrusted, as we have seen, with the management of the foundry; and a tapestry loom, which François I. set up about that time in his palace, was ordered to weave the designs that he presented.* At the same time he was

* *Le Primatice*, p. 384.

making drawings for the Limoges enamellers.*   In short,
his position at the court of the Valois was thenceforth
more a general supervision and direction of all the bodies
of craftsmen than the simple post of painter to the king,
corresponding, in its own day, to that of Lebrun under
Louis XIV.

He had the title of Groom of the Chamber to the
King, and, from 1544, enjoyed the revenues of the Abbey
of St. Martin in Troyes, from which for the future he
took his name in place of that of Bologna, by which
he had been called hitherto on account of his native
town.†  Vasari says of him, as of Rosso, that he kept
at court the retinue of a nobleman, a testimony to the
brilliant fortune with which the king rewarded his many
services.

That consideration leads us to speak of the famous
quarrel which, in the midst of this high favour, he had
to wage with Benvenuto Cellini; a quarrel which, in
celebrity, outdoes that which is supposed to have existed
between Primaticcio and Rosso.   As to authenticity,
one is nearly as badly off as the other.   The grounds
of it are stated by Cellini himself in his " Memoirs,"
which all the world has read; and for long there was
no other information on the point.   The author has
had to be checked, sometimes by some fragment of the
" Comptes des Bâtiments," sometimes by admissions he

---

* That, for instance, of the famous " Apostles " at Chartres, which M.
de Laborde attempted to restore to the French painter, Rochetel, a course
in which a number of manuals have imitated him.  *Le Primatice*, p. 381.

† He is designated by this name of St. Martin so late as the descriptions of Fontainebleau written in the following century.  Several
authorities on this subject have made mistakes through their ignorance of
this fact.

himself has let slip, sometimes by mere probability, and
sometimes by facts of chronology furnished by contemporary documents.    This assistance, slender as it is,
has nevertheless enabled me to restore something of the
truth of the facts.* An unpublished fragment which
I have since printed has added new and indisputable
knowledge, and a more material means of verification.

Cellini came to France in 1540, when the king, who
had asked him for some goldsmith's work, ordered of
him at once twelve life-size silver chandeliers, representing
the twelve greater gods.    But Cellini, who had been
engaged as a goldsmith, began, without the king's
authority, to devote himself to large works in bronze.

Several indisputable sources of evidence agree in
assigning what follows to the beginning of the year
1543.    Primaticcio, being then at Fontainebleau, finds
Cellini bursting in upon him in a fury and accusing
him of having robbed him of the commissions he held
from the king.    All readers of Cellini know the details
of the fountain which he had designed to erect to the
glory of the king and the adornment of Fontainebleau.
The goldsmith has related how the king had approved
of the model and granted him leave to work upon it.
But what was his surprise when, on arriving at Fontainebleau, whither the king had summoned him, he learned
from a treasurer that Primaticcio too had equally received a commission from the king for the fountain !
Primaticcio did not appear to be frightened by the
violent outburst of his rival.    He received him with
affability and declared that he would keep the commission.    Cellini thereupon threatened to kill him, and

* *Benvenuto Cellini à la cour de France ; Revue Archéologique*, 1898,

he asserts that, in consequence, Primaticcio surrendered the commission a few days later.

This fact, however, is certain: Primaticcio was the real creator of this fountain. Another consideration is that in the story of his interviews with the king, the Florentine never dared to refer to any formal commission from the monarch. I have shown how the close examination of these passages, and of several parallel passages, compels us to believe that the order was, on the contrary, properly Primaticcio's own, and that Cellini had pushed himself into the matter without leave from any one; so that his "Memoirs" have reversed the *rôles*.

The other point in this story concerns the Fontainebleau casts, which, Cellini asserts, had never any other object but to lower his own works, by comparison, in the eyes of the king and all the court. According to him, this was the definite object of Primaticcio's visit to Rome; and all that would naturally be attributed to the king's taste for works of art and fine antiquities must be ascribed solely to the effect of the terror which Cellini inspired, and the nets in which his innocence was entangled.

The thought is extravagant; and, what is more, at variance with chronology; for the arrival of Cellini in France could not have been at the latest after the 27th May, and Primaticcio's journey was undertaken more than three months before. But the consequence Cellini draws from it must be held to be quite as fictitious—that famous and often-repeated episode in which we see the antiques cast under Primaticcio's direction, exhibited before the whole court in the gallery at Fontainebleau at the same time as a silver Jupiter, the first to be completed of the twelve gods which the king had ordered.

It is scarcely necessary to recall the cabal which Cellini
declares was being formed against him, and how Mme.
d'Etampes, the king's favourite and Cellini's enemy,
contrived that the king should not come to see it till
the evening, so that its merits should have less chance
of recognition.  Thereupon the artist had a torch placed
in the hands of his Jupiter; an apprentice lit it suddenly,
and the work appeared in instant splendour, while the
antique bronzes, lit solely by the torches of the servants,
not a soul looked at.  Such is the triumph which he
vaunts; and several features of it seem utterly impro-
bable in themselves.  But we have a more important
piece of evidence than any such consideration, an
account, at present unpublished, of the delivery of this
Jupiter, written by an ambassador of Ferrara.*  This
narrative is very circumstantial, and, what is more, the
letter enclosing it is favourable to Cellini.  Primaticcio
is only casually mentioned, as a person of no importance.
But the picture, which shows us, indeed, the great
personages of the court, and Mme. d'Etampes purposely
flying into a rage with the work and its creator, contains
nothing besides the Jupiter.  Primaticcio's antiques are
not there; and not only is there no question of Primaticcio : of the evening, the lighted torch, and the rest,
there is not the slightest trace; which proves that all
this was an invention, and that this quarrel with
Primaticcio has been gratuitousɪy magnified into an
important event.

It is probable that these rivalries, to which the great
popularity of Cellini's "Memoirs" has given so much im-

* L. Dimier : *Une pièce inédite sur le séjour de Benvenuto Cellini à la
cour de France ; Revue Archéologique,* 1902.

portance, made less noise and held a smaller place in the career of Primaticcio. The favour which I have shown him to have enjoyed at that time was not of the sort that has much to fear from the attacks of a newcomer. Ere long Cellini was to depart, in 1545, under the blow of the royal displeasure, which not all his eloquence can disguise.

I come now to speak of Primaticcio's assistants. From that time onwards he was aided just as Rosso had always been, and his position was like that of Giulio Romano at Mantua. A whole colony of artisans of all kinds, whose names are all noted in the " Comptes des Bâtiments," vied with one another in executing his designs. As before, I propose to mention only those distinguished by higher pay, and only the names of painters, giving with each an account of all that is known of him.*

First came four Bolognese, fellow-citizens of the master, and no doubt engaged on his recommendation. Francisco Caccianemici, called Cachenemis, is the least famous of the four. Nothing is known of him beyond his nationality and the references to him in the Accounts. Virgilio Baron only appears during a period of two years, on the eve of the journey to Rome; he was a pupil of Lorenzo Costa of Ferrara.† Giovanni Battista Bagnacavallo was the son of Bartolommeo Bagnacavallo, a follower of Raphael, ‡ under whom, by a curious coincidence, Primaticcio had studied. A number of works by this painter are noticed by ancient writers in the churches and convents of his native town,§ and we

---

* For all these artists see *Le Primatice*, p. 314.

† Malvasia : *Felsina Pittrice*, 1678 edition, vol. i. p. 60.

‡ Vasari : *Opere*, Milanesi's edition, vol. vii. p. 409.

§ Bumaldi : *Minervalia Bononiensium civium anademata*, p. 252. Malvasia : *op. cit.*, vol. i. p. 141.

know that, soon after 1546, he was helping Vasari with
his paintings in the Sala della Cancellaria for Cardinal
Farnese at Rome, which fixes the date of his leaving
France; but no other work of his is known in this country,
beyond the assistance he gave Primaticcio in the works
mentioned above. To him in particular belongs the
execution of the Ulysses and the Prudence on the
wardrobes in the King's Closet. Fantose, whom the
catalogues of prints wrongly confuse with Antonio da
Trento, a pupil of Parmigiano, I have already noticed
as an engraver; in which capacity he devoted himself
to the reproduction of a great number of Rosso's stuccos,
which proclaim him clever in ornament. Thus we find
him in the same way charged to make the tracings for
the arabesques which Primaticcio combined with his
figures in the ceiling of the Ulysses Gallery. No print
of his is known dated later than 1545.

Bartolommeo di Miniato, a Florentine, is distinguished
from these Bolognese by a longer sojourn in France. It
is evident that the others only came for a time, drawn
thither by the large profit to be made from the innumerable works that were then being carried on;
Miniato, on the other hand, was there before them, and
we know that he died there in the year 1548, by a death
as miserable as Rosso's, for he hanged himself.* His
special work was the painting on the wardrobes in the
King's Closet of the Cæsar and the Strength from
the drawings of Primaticcio.

Luca Penni, called Romano, offers more material for
description, and the French Renaissance owed him some
original works. He was the brother of Giovanni Fran-

* *Nouvelles Archives de l'art français*, 1876, p. 100.

cesco Penni, called Il Fattore, a pupil of Raphael. Although Florentine by birth, he was completely Roman in style. Vasari * says that on leaving France he went to England, whence he used to send drawings for the Flemish engravers. The only verification of the last statement is an engraving printed by Jerome Cock of Antwerp in 1562.† The rest of his drawings were engraved by Giorgio Mantovano, by the master with the monogram L.D., by Boivin and by Etienne Delaune, the last three of whom worked in France. It is certain that a great number of these works date back to his residence in this country. His " Ascent of Calvary," the drawing of which is in the Louvre, is definitely dated 1544. Thus he exercised his own activity independently of Primaticcio, chiefly through the medium of engraving. I am not sure that tapestry-making ought not to be added; the Louvre contains two drawings of the "Story of Orion" by this artist ‡ which have been exactly engraved by Delaune and seem to have been made for this purpose. I do not know when he left France, and possibly the archives of England would be the best sources of information on this point. There has been an attempt to attribute to him the paintings in Wolsey's Closet at Hampton Court; but they are not at all in his style. Walpole, on the other hand, made the mistake of confusing him with Bartholomew Penn, who worked under Henry VIII.₁ It is true that by a similar inadvertence Félibien has brought Henry VIII. into the case of Luca Penni, whom he took to be different from

* *Op. cit.*, vol. iv. p. 647.
† Library of the École des Beaux-Arts ; coll. Lesoufaché, Case II.
‡ Nos. 8741 and 8742.

TROJANS BRINGING THE WOODEN HORSE WITHIN THEIR WALLS

LUCA PENNI. LOUVRE

Luca Romano. Milanesi says that a "Madonna" of his is in the collection of the Duke of Sutherland.

We turn now from the Italians to the only Fleming, who first worked under Rosso and after his death entered the studio of Primaticcio. Leonard Thiry is an artist well known to historians of art, and takes an important place, next to Luca Penni, in the French Renaissance. His style, it is true, was impregnated with Rosso's, and could exercise no distinct influence; but his original compositions, which were equally confined to engravings, secured him none the less a great fortune. The most important consists of a series of twenty-five works representing the story of "Jason and the Golden Fleece." A certain Jean de Mauregard commissioned him for the set, and had it engraved by Boivin. The same engraver executed, again after Leonard Thiry, a series of twenty ornamental panels. From the same artist we have also a series of the "Loves of Pluto and Proserpine," and one of "Calisto," engraved with the monogram L.D.* Finally, twelve views of ancient ruins, the drawings of which he left behind him, were engraved by Ducerceau. He soon left France to return to his own country, and retired to Antwerp.†

To all these foreign painters we must add a list of six Frenchmen. Two of them, Badouin and Dorigny, we have already seen at Fontainebleau during Rosso's lifetime; the other four are new: Michel Rochetel, Charles Carmoy, Michel Rougemont, and Germain Mus-

---

* The fact that the monogram is put close to his name has given the erroneous idea that the numerous prints thus marked were his own work.

† This fact is taken from the preface that Ducerceau issued with the previously mentioned series.

nier. Anything more that can be said about them will
be found in a later chapter; but I cannot omit to mention here the anonymous author of several excellent
drawings of this school.

I only know him by these drawings, three of which
are of the characteristic order : one, in the Albertina
collection at Vienna, represents athletic games; another,
which belongs to M. Masson of Amiens, represents Greek
princes banqueting on the seashore, while beside them
a bard is singing; and the third, a queen receiving a
fugitive prince, is in the Staedel Institute at Frankfort.
I can only give one definite fact about this artist, which
is, that he was working in France before 1562. The
famous series of the "Story of Artemisia," in the Cabinet
of Prints * in Paris, was actually designed in that year,
and the composition of the "Boxers," † which is in the
same collection, was copied from the Vienna drawing.
Elsewhere ‡ I have called this anonymous artist "the
supposed Bagnacavallo"; every detail of his career remains to be discovered.

And now this chapter must be brought to an end
by a brief account of Primaticcio's work outside the court,
and what we might call his provincial activity.

It is not known whether the favour he enjoyed with
Mme. d'Etampes brought him any commissions in the
favourite's private castles, at Meudon, Challuau, or Valen-
çay; but Cardinal Ferrara, the brother of the reigning duke
of that city, and Ferrarese ambassador in France, employed him, and so did Dinteville, Bishop of Auxerre, and
one of the leading patrons of the time. The Comte de

---

* See below, p. 189.                    † Folio 28 of the series.
‡ *Le Primatice*, p. 483.

Clermont-Tonnerre and Jean Duthier, Secretary of State
under Henri II., may also be added to the list.  It is
true that no certainty attaches to the chief name in it,
and that our conviction only rests on cogent reasons.

The patronage of the Bishop of Auxerre has been
proved.  Just at that time he was beautifying Polisy,
near Troyes, a magnificent abode in his time, though
scarcely anything is left of it now.  Primaticcio was
there in 1544 in company with other artists, with whom
no doubt he was working at some specimen of his
own branch of art.*  According to Guilbert, in whose
time these paintings were still to be seen, he had painted
for Cardinal Ferrara, in the style of the ceiling of the
Ulysses Gallery, the bathing-hall in the mansion of this
prelate (who was known as the Grand Ferrara) at Fontainebleau.†  Cardinal Ferrara, again, ordered the painting of the abbot's private chapel ‡ in the Abbey of
Chaalis in the diocese of Senlis, of which he was in
charge.  M. Reiset, who knew these paintings before
their unhappy restoration, attributed them to Primaticcio, and all that remains of them tends to confirm
this idea.  All this took place near the date we have
now reached.  Félibien says that the painting of the
chapel of the Castle of Beauregard, near Blois,§ which
he gave to Primaticcio, was begun under François I.;
it was the property of Jean Duthier, who, according
to his account, carried on the decoration of it under
the reign of Charles IX.

Part of the frescoes, again, in the Castle of Ancy-le-
Franc—the recumbent ovals which decorate the Chamber

---

* *Le Primatice*, p. 382.            † *Ibid.*, p. 388.
‡ *Ibid.*, p. 387.                    § *Ibid.*, p. 389.

of the Arts—are in my opinion his work. The subjects
are as follows: Logic, Rhetoric, Physics, Geometry,
Arithmetic, Grammar, Astronomy, and the Muses. In
view of the destruction that was consummated by the
restoration at Fontainebleau, the importance of these
paintings, which have been preserved with only moderate
restoration, would be very great, if it were proved that
they were executed from the drawings and under the
direction of the master. They might give us some idea
of what all these disfigured works were like. In the
painting of " Geometry," the bowed figure of a man in
full vigour is an episode beautiful enough to deserve
special mention here. The Castle of Ancy-le-Franc was
built after 1546, by the Comte de Clermont-Tonnerre,
and this date is our authority for introducing here the
subject of these paintings.

To all this we must add the commission given to our
artist in 1546 by the Duke of Ferrara for a design for
the battle of Marignan, which he wished to have painted
in his country house at Copparo.* Finally there were
the easel pictures, which no doubt Primaticcio produced
in great numbers. Among them was a " Rape of
Europa," † the drawing and a study of which are in the
Louvre, and do not match any series of his other works.

François I. died at the end of the period we have just
sketched, in the year 1547. The event occurred when
the studio of Fontainebleau was in full work, when all the
arts had already been transformed and were in progress
towards the most brilliant future, and when painting in
particular shone out with a lustre which it had never

---

\* *Archivio Storico dell' arte,* 1889, p. 158.

† Engraved by the artist with the monogram L. D.

GEOMETRY

known in France.  The disappearance of the prince from
the scene did not interrupt its development, thanks to
the new king, who took up his father's patronage with
equal moderation and intelligence, and to the fortunate
preservation of the masters who had made the glory of
the past reign.  Primaticcio had yet more than twenty
years to live, and his presence alone was enough to carry
on the school founded in Fontainebleau and to assure it
plenty of recruits.  The case was just the same with
another domain, that of the younger Clouet, whose history I have now to begin.  Both these masters were to
live on and prosper; to enjoy till nearly the end of the
century the praise they had earned from the king who
had chosen them, and imposed them upon his successors
by the force of his prodigious initiative.

# CHAPTER VI

A DOCUMENT well known to connoisseurs ushers the son of the elder Janet, François Clouet, called Janet like his father, into the light of history. It is a renunciation made by the king, for the artist's benefit, of his father's inheritance, which had escheated to the crown as the estate of a foreigner.* It bears date December 1541; and in it the younger Janet is said to have " followed his father very closely in the science of his art." This is the first evidence we have of this painter.

From that date we find him, like his father, holding the office of groom of the chamber and painter in ordinary to the king, with emoluments of 240 livres.† The sum meant that, so far as salary was concerned, he started

---

* Quoted above, p. 26, note †.  Laborde : *Le Renaissance des Arts à la cour de France*, p. 578.
† Bouchot : *Les Clouets et Corneille de Lyon*, p. 61.

where his father had left off; and we cannot but believe
that thenceforward his services were fully employed, and
that the last years of François I. saw the birth of a great
number of his works.

Nevertheless I can only establish a few, and those as
often drawings as paintings, in the various collections
that are known.

To tell the truth, with François Clouet, as with his
father, we still lack perfect certainty about the works
that should be attributed to him. In his case too we can
only draw up a list of presumed drawings, all of them
beyond question from the same hand, and emanating
from a single artist; but there is nothing to assure us
positively that the artist was the younger Janet. In the
catalogue I have compiled, which starts, as I have said,
in 1534, we may note a succession of developments and
an evolution of style which did not come to perfection
until the reign of Henri II., and which were modified
again later. But these gradual and almost insensible
developments offer no argument against ascribing the
whole body of the work to one man. Now the reasoning
which serves for Jean Clouet is appropriate to his son too.
The list of drawings I spoke of begins in the year mentioned above, and does not extend beyond 1572, when
François Clouet died. That is one reason for believing
the work to be his; and the presumption is confirmed by
two other considerations. The elder Janet's life, so far
as we know it, was passed under a single reign; the
younger lived through four. The long list of sovereigns
who reigned in his lifetime offers a special means of
verifying the work to be attributed to him, through the
regularity with which, one after the other, there occur the

portraits of all these kings, together with the queens and
princesses: we may add that they are the best portraits
of them we know.   This argument appears to me strong
enough to justify my dropping, in the course of my narrative, the title of " the presumed " Janet for the painter
whom I see behind the works to be discussed, especially
since I have stated the exact nature of the question at
the beginning of this chapter; and there is yet another
reason which inclines me to follow this course.   That is,
that in the case of François Janet we have something
more to go upon than we had in the case of his father—I
mean an ancient and unbroken tradition in the attributions of the pictures.   The younger Janet was not forgotten like the elder.   In his lifetime his praises were
sung by the writers of the day, and his name has been
faithfully preserved from reign to reign and from generation to generation.   And although the uncertainty into
which this artist's reputation has been plunged has caused
him to be credited with any number of works with which
he had nothing at all to do, there are nevertheless certain
choice pieces consistently ascribed to him, which can on
no account be considered as debatable ground; par-
ticularly when they agree with all the probabilities that
can be deduced.   It should be understood once and for
all that not one of the works that I ascribe to François
Clouet in this book are guaranteed to be his by any
document in the archives or any original attestation.   I
follow probabilities only; but probabilities so convincing
that I must be permitted to consult the convenience of
diction and suppress these reservations in detail.

To François Clouet, called Janet, then, must belong a
portrait of King François I., the lost original of which is

CATHERINE DE MÉDICIS AS DAUPHINE
FRANÇOIS CLOUET, CHÂTEAU DE VERSAILLES

known from a number of reproductions, two of them in
miniature enjoying some celebrity. One is at the Uffizi
in Florence,* the other at the Louvre in Paris.† Both
represent the king on horseback, with a full face and a
thick neck, already showing signs of age and the approach
of the fifties. For that reason it could not have come
from the elder Janet. The original drawing is missing,
but there are enough copies, drawings as well as prints,
besides the two in miniature, to prove its existence. The
most interesting is a chalk-drawing in the Louvre,‡
arranged lengthways and life-sized, excellently drawn, and
reproducing the original exactly. The existence of such
a copy seems to imply some large piece of decoration
taken from the original chalk-drawing like that at White-
hall, the composition of which is preserved by the Duke
of Devonshire's cartoon. Like Holbein's Henry VIII.,
this portrait of the King of France by Janet was drawn
on a large scale to appear in some royal gallery, no doubt
on horseback as in the miniature-painting mentioned above.

A less problematical work is the charming portrait of
Catherine de Medici in the museum at Versailles.§ This
young princess was then dauphine, through the death of
François, the king's eldest son, which had occurred ten
years before. The execution of the picture is delicate

---

* Catalogue, No. 667. M. de Laborde attributed it to the elder Janet,
and has been followed by many other writers.

† Catalogue of Drawings, No. 683. The only difference between the
composition of the two is in the architecture, and in a purple coat added
to the one in Paris.

‡ No. 33530.

§ No. 4074. The chalk-drawing is at Chantilly, hung in the Psyche
Gallery under the title of "Mme. d'Aluye." M. Bouchot discovered the
mistake.

and agreeable, the colour limpid, the touch elegant and facile. It lacks as yet several qualities which the painter was to acquire later; but already, in more than one respect, his art surpassed that of the elder Janet, whose teaching is nevertheless apparent in it.

I think the date of it should be fixed at before 1545. On the other hand, the portrait of the king must be assigned to quite the end of the reign.

The death of François I. occupied a special place in the artistic career of Janet the younger, as giving rise to some curious works, the like of which is no longer seen in our days; I mean those funeral effigies on which, from the Middle Ages and throughout the century we are speaking of, painters and sculptors in turn were employed. A mask was taken of the face of the dead, and then retouched and painted to appear on the bed of state which was used at the funeral. Perréal had made one on the death of Louis XII.; later, Pierre Biard did the same for Henri IV. On the death of François I. the task fell to François Janet.* I will give no details of it since it is outside my subject, and will do no more than draw this conclusion from it—that the second of the Janets held a most distinguished place in the royal favour, and that doubtless he was looked upon as chosen beforehand in any case where a likeness was required. As this commission could only come from the new king, it is obvious that at the very beginning of the reign he received an earnest of the continuation of favour.

* Laborde: *Renaissance*, p. 62. It is worth noting that in those days they thought these funeral masks worth preserving, and the merit of the art was appreciated. When the famous Cardan came to France he saw that of François I., which, he says, was taken at his funeral to the house of the Cardinal de Tournon. *Revue universelle des Arts*, vol. ii. p. 367.

This is the more remarkable inasmuch as even in those days the family of Janet was no longer alone in winning the rewards of honour and profit from the art of making small portraits. A Fleming, a native of the Hague, whose Christian name of Corneille is all we know, had been settled at Lyons for about ten years, and was building up a reputation in the same branch of art, which was already reaching to the royal family.

Two points in his early history are unknown: the circumstances which brought him to Lyons, and the origin of his relations with the court. The second point would be of interest. We should like to know how, having settled in France without any engagement by the king, and living at a great distance from all the royal residences, he none the less ended by becoming something like an official painter, honoured with commissions from illustrious patrons and living under the protection of the crown. Possibly several visits which the king paid to Lyons in the year 1536 were the occasion of the establishment of those relations. At any rate, that year is the date of the portraits of the king's two children, the dauphin François and Madeleine, later Queen of Scotland, the latter of whom died in the following year, the former in 1536. The portrait of the dauphin is at Chantilly,* unhappily entirely repainted; that of Madeleine, till quite lately known as Marguerite, Duchess of Nevers, is in the museum at Versailles.†

For a long time fancy and probability were the only rules employed in discovering Corneille's portraits. The

---

* Catalogue, No. 244.

† No. 3185. I have restored its identity, *Chronique des Arts*, 1901, p. 268.

very name of the artist was hardly known, and went no
further than a little circle of experts, who, finding him
called Corneille of Lyons, believed him in good faith to
be French. But as the nationality and career of the
painter came to be cleared up, an exact means was discovered of determining which are his works. M. Bouchot *
found that Gaignières, a famous French amateur of the
seventeenth century, had put Corneille's name on several
pieces in his collection of portraits. He was found to
have put the name sometimes on the picture itself, sometimes on the copy which he had had made of it in the
famous albums which have been distributed between the
Bodleian at Oxford and the Cabinet of Prints in Paris.
The author of this valuable discovery decides to put
implicit faith in Gaignières' evidence, for two reasons
which I cannot omit to mention. One is the scrupulous-
ness of the amateur, who was little given to making such
attributions; the other, the certainty of origin which was
assured to these attributions by Gaignières' methods. It
is stated, in fact, that to find Corneilles he went to Lyons
itself and the neighbourhood, where there could be no
doubt that, after a lapse of only a century, and considering
the indifference to this master's productions which soon
arose, a great number might be found. Gaignières picked
them up right and left and in considerable quantities; it
is true that we should not be able to recognise them in
the works he has left us, without the aid of the notes he
added to some of them, which sufficed to distinguish their
very characteristic and also uniform style.

M. Bouchot believes further that these pictures, each
of them separately and by name, were the work of

* *Op. cit.*, p. 44.

Corneille de Lyon, and that Gaignières had the proof of
it in his possession, either in the form of documentary
evidence or in some other form. On this point I cannot agree with my master, because I do not believe in
Gaignières' scrupulous accuracy. This is not the place
to explain my distrust, and I shall, perhaps, give my
reasons elsewhere. Let it suffice for the present to note
this, that the rarity of the occasion on which he does
make any attribution might just as well come from the indifference about the names of painters of a man interested
solely in the persons represented, as from caution and the
critical faculty. It is true that no doubt he never went
so far as to put the name of a painter so obscure in his
time as Corneille de Lyon out of sheer imagination.
Thus we know the origin of the attributions he made,
and therein lies the chief merit of M. Bouchot's valuable
discovery. There can be no doubt that the name of
Corneille was suggested, and quite legitimately, by the
place where the amateur acquired the paintings, not to
mention the fact that the vendors had doubtless attributed
them to him. In distinguishing some of them, purely,
I believe, at haphazard, by affixing the name as I have
mentioned, Gaignières made them models for the attribution of all the others. That does not bind us to accept
them absolutely as more certain and better than the rest;
but at least they bear, among all the others, as it were, a
certificate of the spot where Gaignières found them, which
guarantees their origin.

Thence there sprang an extremely large but very unequal and confused family of little portraits, painted on a
single clear ground, placed three-quarter face and lightly
touched, but unhappily very dilapidated and for the most

I

part repainted in the course of all sorts of vicissitudes, which they have undergone even since Gaignières' time.

To the whole collection, and even to those on which Gaignières put the name of Corneille, I should hesitate to assign any more particular origin than the school and studio of this painter. But on that point our certainty is absolute. If, therefore, it is a permissible and even perfectly strict proceeding in the consideration of the collective works of a studio or a school, to see the personal intervention of the master in the pieces of the greatest merit, nothing could be more legitimate in the present instance than to attribute the best of these paintings to Corneille himself.

Whether this may be done with those I have already mentioned, I cannot say. True, it is hard to believe that one painter, who was then at the beginning of his career and working for the most exalted patrons, should not have been anxious to fulfil all his commissions himself; but since there is nothing to prove that the paintings actually before us are the original portraits and not copies executed later, nothing is absolutely certain on the point. The fact is, that the Madeleine, Queen of Scotland, though fairly well preserved, is but an indifferent work. The portrait of the Duke of Orleans, afterwards Henri II., no doubt painted in the same year, is no better. Gaignières, to whom it belonged, put the name of Corneille to it. It is now the property of Mr. Pierpont Morgan, and is being exhibited at the South Kensington Museum.

The difficulty of being sure that Corneille, after such a beginning, did not make several journeys to the places where the court was, in order to paint its members, prevents us from assigning his portraits to the precise and established dates of the visits which the king paid to Lyons. It is none the less natural to suppose that each occasion on which the king came near that town was an opportunity to prove the power of a painter he valued. He was near Lyons, for short intervals it is true, in 1537, 1538, and 1542. After that, Lyons never saw the court again until the death of François I. In default of better information, we shall be wise to include within these dates all the portraits which the age and costume of the subjects declare to belong to this period.

I will mention only the best, which are a Beatrice Pacheco, maid of honour to Queen Eléonore, in the museum at Versailles *; a man unknown, perhaps the Dauphin François again, belonging to Lord Derby at Knowsley; finally a really admirable work, so much better than all the other pictures of the same kind that at first we shrink from adding it to the list, the portrait of Jean, sire de Rieux, baron de Chateauneuf, which belongs to Mr. Charles Butler.

Within the same period we find the first sign of the favour which Corneille was winning at court: the title of painter to the dauphin was given him on the 7th January 1541 (o.s. 1540).† The dauphin, so styled since the death of his elder brother, was the same as the prince mentioned above, who came to the throne under the name of Henri II.; a famous recommendation against the coming of the succeeding reign.

* Catalogue, No. 3172.

† Natalis Rondot : *Les peintres de Lyon du XIV. au XVIII. siècle.*— *Sociétés des Beaux-Arts des Départements*, 1887. This author believes that the title was attached to the person of the prince, and proved Corneille's residence at court ; but there is no justification for drawing such a conclusion.

It seems that one of the first acts of the dauphin after his accession was to naturalise Corneille. The letters he granted for this purpose are dated 1547.* From that date onwards we find him settled in the king's household, with the title of painter to the king,† which in a way made him equal with Janet.

It must have been, at the latest, near the beginning of the reign that, as Borghini states, ‡ Stradano, or Vander Straet, a Flemish painter, who was afterwards famous in Florence, came to study with him. Corneille's reputation must then have been firmly established, and there is every reason to suppose that his studio was included among the curiosities to be visited on a journey which the king and court made to Lyons in 1548.

They were received there with much splendour. There was a triumphal entry and rejoicings of all kinds, the remembrance of which will long survive. M. Bouchot assigns to this journey the execution of a portrait of the new queen, Catherine de Medici, which is mentioned in Brantôme, and furnished her fifteen years later with matter for the reflections he describes. There is every probability that the date is the correct one. The same learned author believes a copy in chalks at Chantilly § to have been taken from this portrait. Another portrait which was quite certainly painted during this visit is that of Mme. Marguerite, the king's sister and daughter of Francois I., who later

---

* *Ibid.*

† *Ibid.*

‡ *Il Riposo*, edition of 1587, p. 579. Stradano was at Antwerp in 1545, and stayed there three years with Lange Peer (Peter Aartsen), after which he came to France.

§ Hung in the Galerie du Logis.

became Duchess of Savoy. It is now in the Château
de Chantilly,* and is dated 1548. But it has suffered
from being retouched. There are many other portraits
in the same museum, formerly in Gaignières' collection, which were doubtless painted in the same circumstances. It is a fact that fifteen years later, at the
time of the events narrated by Brantôme, the painter
was in a position to exhibit in a large room his own
portraits of "all the great lords, princes and gentlemen,
and the great queens, princesses, ladies and maidens of
the court of France." † I imagine that the Suzanne
d'Escars, Dame de Pompadour, at Versailles,‡ and the
wrongly styled Lorenzo de Medici in the Louvre, § were
part of the great work of the time, for they too date
from this period. I mention them here for the sake of
their merit and their excellent state of preservation.

The quantity of portraits that issued from Corneille's
studio in the costume of Henri II.'s time shows that the
painter's vogue lasted throughout the reign; but we can
give no more details on the point.

Then comes the question, what idea we can form of
the daily work of a painter whose only known subjects are
portraits of the members of the court, and yet who lived,
as I have shown, so far from the places where the court
was usually to be found.

Must it be granted that he only painted his sitters
during the visits which the court of the time, always on
the move as it was, occasionally paid to his neighbour-

* No. 245.
† Brantôme : *Œuvres*, Lalanne's edition, vol. vii. p. 343.
‡ No. 3171.
§ Lately taken from Versailles, where it was numbered 3108.

hood, and that, when once the originals were finished, the
rest of his time was only occupied in multiplying endless
copies of them as the order arose? Or was it Corneille
who was always on the move? Artists used to travel in
those days with astonishing ease, and it is by no means
impossible. There is a third possible supposition—that a
chalk-drawing by some painter with easier access to the
subjects was sent to the master as a basis for the composition of his painting. But two considerations throw
doubt on this last hypothesis: one is the indifferent merit
of Corneille's portraits, so far as we can judge from the
general run of his works, which makes it almost incredible
that any one should have taken so much trouble to have
them; and the other the lack of chalk-drawings to match
the paintings, which according to this supposition ought
to be found in great numbers.

I know only one of the kind, which, for that reason,
I regard as very instructive. It is a portrait of Jacqueline
de Longwy, first Duchess of Montpensier, in the Chantilly
collections,* which was used for a portrait now lost, but
formerly owned by Gaignières, and copied by him in his
collection † with the note that it was by Corneille. I see
no reason for recognising Corneille's hand in this drawing
and many reasons for recognising another's; and therefore I can only explain this attribution on the hypothesis
of a drawing made on the spot and sent to the painter.
But this instance is unique so far.

The foregoing inquiries bring us to the consideration
of Corneille's manner of working, which was different from
that of the Clouets and the painters who were formed on

---

* Case XVI., No. 374.
† Cabinet of Prints, Paris.   Oa. 17, fol. 21.

their style. Corneille, in fact, made no chalk-drawings at all; although, so far as painted replicas are concerned, we find them in no smaller numbers. However, it is not likely that the society of the period should have cared to change its habits in passing from one painter to another, and given the new one a longer sitting in order that he might paint their portraits without preparation. It is wisest to suppose that he completed nothing in the presence of the sitter beyond a chalk-drawing, on which he laid the colour afterwards. Several of Corneille's pictures are certainly painted in distemper on paper, and varnished over like panels in oil.* But, oil-painting or distemper, it would be interesting to know if it is always paper that is found; the knowledge would enable us to have a thorough comprehension of the artist's method of procedure.

I will add here that the idea promulgated by several writers, that Corneille also painted history and figure-subjects in general, is without even a shadow of proba-bility. Neither a Corneille Vander Capelle, of whom Mr. Weale speaks,† nor a so-called Claude Corneille, an engraver, whose name is given by Robert Dumesnil, ‡ can be identified with our Corneille.

A verdict on his talents and his importance is difficult to give, owing to our lack of all information, both on his

* I owe this discovery to the perspicacity of M. Pérraté, assistant-keeper at Versailles.

† *Revue de l'art chrétien*, 1899. He finds the name written in the inscriptions on two pictures of money-changers, of the Flemish school, with the mention of the title of Painter to the King.

‡ On the strength of a monogram, C.C., which is found on the prints issued from the presses at Lyons. Several writers have followed him in giving Corneille the Christian name of Claude.

origin and on any school that could be said to have resulted from him, and also to the impossibility at the
present time of separating his own works from those of
his studio. To those I have mentioned above as the best
of all and therefore to be attributed to him, I will add
the portrait of Mme. de Martigné-Briant at Chantilly *
and Lord Spencer's two portraits at Althorp,† one of
which is wrongly believed to be Mary Stuart. If we
judged Corneille de Lyon only by works of this order,
we should grant him some skill of hand, and decide that
he had trained himself in a formula which he had learned
by heart and repeated pleasantly enough. He under-
stands the three-quarter face, the foreshortening of the
cheek, the eye, the farther corner of the lip; and on the
side towards the spectator, the insertion of the eyelid and
the nostril, the bony structure of the chin and the cheek,
the ear and the roots of the hair. But it is useless to
ask more of him, or expect him to change his method,
or vary the perspective by a hair's-breadth. His knowledge is so scanty that he can scarcely fill in his own
feeble design. In the best of these pictures the bust
and shoulders are like student's work, and verge on the
ridiculous. His texture is delicate, limpid, and absolutely
fresh; sometimes the handling of the jewels is charming.
The total effect of these pictures is monotonous but
pleasant, the result, cleverly attained, of genius of a very
small order. But when we pass suddenly from the works
I have noted to the Baron de Chateauneuf of Mr. Charles
Butler, our opinion is completely changed. This portrait

---

* Catalogue, No. 246.

† Waagen, "Treasures of Art in Great Britain," vol. iii. p. 457. They
are preserved under the name of Janet.

passed with Fountaine for a Holbein, and though the
attribution is certainly mistaken, it is scarcely unworthy
of that great name.    In depth of knowledge, boldness of
execution, and extreme beauty of colour, this little work
is a masterpiece far and away superior to anything that I
have ascribed to the elder Janet, and more perfect in the
sum of its characteristics than anything we can rightly
attribute to his son.    But I see no means of depriving
Corneille of the credit of it.    The drawing in general is
the same as that of those we have noticed, which perhaps are only copies, if we may suppose that the hand of
the master himself has never yet been seen except in
this unique example.    The problem is one that cannot
be stated now, but we may hope that the future will
decide it.

For François Janet too the reign of Henri II. was a
time of prosperity.    We find him enjoying the same
honours and maintained with the same emoluments as
before; and certain extraordinary gifts, like that of the
post of commissary of the king in Chatelet, the revenues
of which were his in 1551,* prove that some ingenuity
was exercised in finding unusual means of enriching
him.

He painted the king's portrait twice at least, once
before 1558, and again in 1559.

The first is proved by a passage in the poet Jodelle,
which has been often quoted.†    Henri II. was painted on

---

* Some writers have stated that he fulfilled the duties of the office; but
they were no work for a painter.   The office was one that could be purchased, and a presentation of this sort, soon resold, was equivalent to a
gift of money from the treasury.

† Laborde : *Renaissance,* p. 576.

a large scale, on horseback, in *court dress*.\*   By means of
this detail and the date, we may perhaps recognise this
picture in an equestrian portrait in the ancient collection
of the Castle of Azay-le-rideau, which has since been sent
into England.   In that portrait the king's face is taken
from a drawing in the Cabinet of Prints in Paris,† which
forms an authentic part of the work of the presumed
François Clouet.   The same chalk-drawing was used
besides for a quarter-length, sold in 1901, with the rest
of the Azay collections.‡   I only know this portrait
in these three examples, the group of which is one of
the most interesting of the century.§   We have here,
in fact, three very different states of the same original,
from the simple chalk-drawing to the great state work
destined for the galleries.   I have remarked above that
an equestrian portrait of François I. must have been put
to the same use ; and there is one circumstance which
enables us to unite these two portraits—the exact resemblance of the horses, and even of the harness, with
the slight difference, that in the portrait of Henri II.
several ornaments have been added.   Perhaps they were
hung in the same gallery, facing each other, and thus
contrasted, for the two horses are going in the same
direction.

---

  \* That I believe to be the meaning of the words, *Henrici equitantis
domi*, which have never yet been satisfactorily explained : they show that
the king was not in armour.

  † Case IV., anc. No. 34.                    ‡ Lot 3 in the sale.

  § It must not be confused with the portrait of 1559, to be spoken of
later, in which the king, much older and notably different in feature, is
posed in the same attitude.   It is worth noting that the text of Jodelle,
which dates from 1558, makes a distinction between them, and that only
the first of the two can be recognised in his lines.

The other portrait is the most celebrated picture of Henri II. Several copies bear the date I have mentioned, which was the last of his reign.* These copies are quarter-lengths, as are several others. None of them deserve to be called originals; but, on the other hand, this quality cannot be denied to the full-length example in the Uffizi at Florence, reproduced in a small copy, of somewhat inferior execution, in the Louvre.† The same face exactly copied appears in any number of illuminations, none of which deserve mention here. But an example which is worthy of all attention from amateurs and historians is the original drawing preserved in the British Museum, a choice specimen of the younger Janet's work, and in every way a masterpiece.

There must equally have been a portrait of Queen Catherine de Medici by Janet, which, in the absence of the original, we cannot positively attribute to him. It reappears in all the collections of second copies and in several enamels, the most celebrated of which belong to MM. Edmond and Gustave de Rothschild, Paris. The Uffizi at Florence still preserves this portrait painted in oils and full-length. There is a copy of the drawing in the British Museum.

Mme. Marguerite, the king's sister, sat several times for drawings by Janet. The Chantilly collections show her at all ages.

Further details on this head would only be tedious. What we have just said will suffice as a type of the master's activity during the period at present under con-

---

* Notably one in the Uffizi in Florence, No. 262, and at Versailles, No. 3175.

† Catalogue, No. 130.

sideration. Shall I add that he was employed by the king to decorate with his devices, *crescents, lacs et chiffres,* a certain coffer called *mect,* the nature and use of which are unknown ? *

Around him other portrait-painters were beginning to show their talents. It may be said that the reign of Henri II. marked the formation of a French school of portraiture.

First of all, there was Bouteloup, who appears in 1548 † in the king's household ; then Germain Lemannier, attached from 1547 to the household of the Enfants de France ; ‡ Nicolas Denisot, who in 1551 painted a portrait of Marguerite of Navarre for the *Tombeau* or collection of panegyric poems on this princess ; § Jean Scipion, mentioned in 1558 ; ‖ finally, Etienne Dumoûtier, the first of a celebrated family of portrait-painters (the father of which I shall have to mention later), who is called in his epitaph ¶ painter and groom of the chamber to Henri II. I will add the most important facts known about each of these artists.

Bouteloup painted in 1560 a portrait of a certain fool of Catherine de Medici's called Thonin,** who indeed appears in a drawing at Chantilly,†† but the identity of this work cannot be certified. He had the title of groom of the chamber to the king and 70 livres pension. We know, moreover, that he was a native of Blois.‡‡

Germain Lemannier painted several portraits of the

\* Laborde : *op. cit.*, p. 93.          † Bouchot : *Les Clouets,* p. 62.
‡ Moreau-Nélaton : *Les Le Mannier,* p. 10.
§ Bouchot : *op. cit.*, p. 56.          ‖ Laborde : *op. cit.*, p. 30.
¶ *Revue universelle des Arts,* vol. i. p. 240.
\*\* Bouchot : *Les portraits au crayon de la Bibliothèque Nationale,* p. 35.
†† Hung in the Galerie du Logis.          ‡‡ Bouchot : *ibid.*

young princes and princesses, the children of Henri II.; that is to say, in 1548 the dauphin, later François II., and his sisters, Elizabeth, afterwards Queen of Spain, and Claude, afterwards Duchess of Lorraine.* He went out of office in 1559.

Denisot is a curious figure in the life of those days. He was wealthy, and a member of a noble family of Perche, and used the title of Comte d'Alsinois. Lacroix du Maine states that he was an orator and a poet, and also drew portraits in chalk. He was thirty-two years of age at the accession of Henri II., and died in the same year as that prince. He had been, for some reason or other, tutor to the three noble sisters Seymour, who composed the *Tombeau* mentioned above.

Besides the portrait engraved at the head of that work, he is represented by contemporary writers as the painter of that of Grévin, physician and poet, of a mistress of the poet Ronsard, and of Mellin de St. Gelais, another poet.†

Jean Scipion, whom M. Bouchot believes to be the same as Scipion Bruisbal, was painter to Catherine de Medici, who commissioned him, at the date given above, for a portrait of Mme. de Crussol.‡

Etienne Dumoûtier was born in 1520,§ which makes

---

* Moreau-Nélaton : *op. cit.*, p. 15. This writer believes that we may attribute to Lemannier several other portraits, which we find mentioned, and some drawings. I have shown the uncertainty of these attributions in the *Gazette des Beaux-Arts*, July 1902.

† Of the last named, according to an epigram unknown to M. Bouchot, the accurate biographer of Denisot. He is there called *Nuceus*. *Revue universelle des Arts*, vol. iv. p. 378. For the rest, see Bouchot, *Les Clouets*.

‡ Mentioned again as living in Paris under the name of Scipion de Brunbal in 1561. *Revue de l'art français*, 1886, p. 309.

§ Calculated from his epitaph mentioned above.

him the same age as the queen. We know really nothing
about him at that time, except that he was already of an
age to practise his art and be talked of.

That is the sum of the information furnished by the
texts concerning the art of portraiture under Henri II.
There were, as we see, five artists, who appear to have
been by no means contemptible. Unfortunately, while
the names of several are accompanied by the mention of
their paintings, there is nothing to enable us now to
recognise the works mentioned among the productions
that survive from that period. We are compelled to
prosecute the study of the latter independently of the list
given above, until new discoveries shall have enabled us
to some extent to combine the factors.

We come now to several important points in regard
to the works themselves.

In the first place, in the cases at Chantilly there
are a number of drawings in the manner of the elder
Janet, which the age and costume of the subjects compel
us to put later than 1540; they are inferior in quality to
the works of the master, and at the same time very different
from those I assign to his son. A Comte de St. Paul *
and a Nicolas de Vaudémont † are instances in point. I
may add that the same hand, that of an imitator of the
master, betrays itself in several works executed during
his lifetime. Can we see in them the work of Clouet
de Navarre?

Later, and under the reign of Henri II., we find a
still more individual manner revealed in a profusion of
works, nearly all of which are to be seen at Chantilly.
Two drawings of this group, however, are in the Cabinet

* Case IV., No. 234.          † Case IV., No. 266.

JEANNE D'ALBRET, QUEEN OF NAVARRE
UNNAMED ARTIST OF 1550.  CABINET DES ESTAMPES, PARIS

of Prints.  They represent King Antoine of Navarre and
his wife, Jeanne d'Albret, still a young woman. *  Among
others at Chantilly are two portraits of François II. in
childhood, which has inclined M. Moreau-Nélaton to
believe that Germain Lemannier ought to be considered
the maker of these drawings.  There is nothing to prove
this identity, nor even to render it probable; and since
all these works come about 1550, I think it better to call
this unknown painter the anonymous artist of 1550.  He
is prolific, but only second-rate; he must have studied
in the school of the elder Janet, and endeavours to imitate
the younger.  He must have been of the same age as the
latter, and no doubt died some fifteen years before him.
Of all the artists of this group whose careers can be dated,
Lemannier and Denisot are the only ones who fulfil the
same conditions; but there is nothing to prevent the
creator of such feeble works having been some unknown
artist, still buried in hitherto unstudied documents,
whence perhaps he will emerge some day.

A very different and much cleverer hand is that of
the chalk-drawings of the Comte de Martigues and M. de
Carnavalet at Chantilly.†  It is difficult to believe that
the author of such works as these is an unknown artist, and
involuntarily we utter the name of Etienne Dumoûtier.
The Martigues is copied in a miniature in the Prayer-
Book of Catherine de Medici in the Louvre, the Carnavalet in a well-painted oil-panel in the Museum at
Versailles.‡

Finally, we cannot bring this chapter to a close with-

* Case I., anc. No. 31 ; and album Na 23 c.
† Both shown in the Psyche Gallery.
‡ Catalogue, No. 3249.

out further mention of the albums of second copies, the importance of which I noted above. Let me turn to them now.

They are all after the sitters of François Janet, whose good fortune seems to have increased the rage for them. The sitters copied are now innumerable. Huge volumes are crammed with the faces of the men and women who composed the court of Henri II., sometimes husbands and wives in pairs, sometimes in two series which divide the sexes. We find them in later albums, copied from older ones which are now lost, like the Valori album at Lille, or that of the Arts-et-Métiers in Paris. Here are the king, the queen, the princes and princesses, M. de Piémont the king's brother-in-law, the Guises, the Chatillons, the king and queen of Navarre, the aged Montmorency, young Balafré, Mayenne, also young, Biron, Brissac, d'Estrées, Mme. d'Etampes in mourning, Diane de Poitiers as an elderly coquette, Anne d'Este, still Duchess of Guise, La Châtaigneraie and Jarnac, the champions of a famous duel, Mme. de Roannez, Mme. de la Bourdaisière, and many others, which bring the total of the fullest of these albums to the number of a hundred and fifty portraits.

A new importance is added to these copies by the services they rendered to the enamellers. The taste for enamel went hand in hand with that for portraits, and the two had to be united to please the society of the time. The practice grew up of painting portraits in enamel, and the faces of celebrated persons provided wealthy houses with ornament more precious than ever. The faint beginnings may be seen in the reign of François I., and the full flower under his successor. The

famous Léonard Limousin, who followed the Italians of
Fontainebleau in the style of his composed pieces, went
to the Janets for his work in portraiture. Albums taken
from the Janets' originals provided him with copies for
models, and about that time we see the appearance of a
new description of these albums, twice as badly drawn, bar-
barously smudged with red chalk, altogether horrible to
look at. These were the enamellers' manuals, the famous
models which inspired the masters of an art so prized
to-day. The unworthiness of the source became evident,
it is true, in the extreme ugliness of the results; but the
fragility which has made them so scarce must be reckoned
among the causes of their advance in price. They were
so much admired in their own day that whole rooms
were filled with them, and the inventory of Catherine de
Medici mentions series of them beyond number.

But this point is outside my subject, and I will dwell
on it no longer. It is enough to have touched on it, in
order to complete the picture of the epoch in all that
concerns the branch of art we are chronicling, a branch
in which succeeding reigns were to see new changes and
developments.

François Janet was commissioned for the death mask
of Henri II., as he had been for that of his father. We
have the detailed accounts of it,* in which the very
repetition of the ceremonies held twelve years before is
striking evidence of the steadiness of his reputation and
the solidity of his position.

* Grandmaison : *Documents inédits pour servir à l'histoire des arts en
Touraine,* p. 82. What is considered to be a fragment of this mask is in
the Louvre ; Catalogue, No. 174.

# CHAPTER VII

The Fontainebleau school under Henri II.—Niccolo dell' Abbate—The
Ulysses Gallery—The Ball-room—Niccolo's part in these two works
—Partial eclipse of painting—Departure and death of some of the
Italians—The new arrivals—The patronage of the Guises—The
Grotto of Meudon—Salviati—Paris Bordone—Death of Henri II.
—Primaticcio directing the Buildings—Consequences of this fact—
The Chapel of the Hôtel de Guise in Paris—Last paintings at
Fontainebleau—Some of Niccolo's works—The Chapel of Fleury-en-
Bière—Unknown works—Death of Primaticcio and Niccolo.

THE accession of Henri II. has been represented as the
period at which the Italians in general and the Fontainebleau artists in particular fell into semi-disfavour.
So far as painting is concerned, this opinion would be
hard to maintain.

Henri II.'s reign, in fact, saw the completion of the
Ulysses Gallery and the entire painting of the Ball-room,
which were Primaticcio's two most important works at
Fontainebleau. The same reign saw the arrival in
France of the famous Niccolo dell' Abbate of Modena,
called Messer Niccolo, who is celebrated in the history of
art for his collaboration with Primaticcio, and was the
third of the Italian painters of importance whom the
patronage of the Valois had induced to settle in France.

Legend, which is innocent of dates, has credited this
artist with being the sole and universal auxiliary of the
Bolognese painter. Not only do the ancient descriptions

invariably give their names in each and all of the principal works at Fontainebleau; but M. Reiset himself, in his study of this painter,* has found no better method of determining his works than an indiscriminate mention of all those known to be Primaticcio's, with the addition of a general remark that Niccolo was responsible for a great share in them. Criticism, however, is not reduced to such vague conclusions. We know the exact date of Niccolo's arrival in France. A contemporary witness † states, against the date of the 25th May 1552, that he had been there some little time. Putting aside all examination of the paintings, it follows of necessity that Niccolo had had no part in the execution of any of the things I have mentioned hitherto, and that the Ball-room and part of the Ulysses Gallery were his first works at Fontainebleau. It is equally wrong to say, as M. Reiset says, that whatever Primaticcio did without Niccolo was executed by his own hand, for before Niccolo he had had several assistants of the same kind. The truth is that Niccolo did not confine himself to painting Primaticcio's designs without doing any original work of his own. It is due partly to the inveteracy of the mistake and partly also to the feeling that so celebrated a name demanded more than the credit of a modest collaborator, that there has even been little hesitation in robbing Primaticcio of some part of his works and giving the honour of them to Niccolo. But the obscurity which historians use to wrap this collaboration is entirely

* *Gazette des Beaux-Arts*, 1859, vol. iii.

† Lancilotto, quoted by Tiraboschi : *Pittori di Modena*, p. 17. Niccolo is represented as intending that his wife and sons should follow him shortly. He was then forty years old.

dissipated by an examination of the drawings used for these works, which were all Primaticcio's.[*]

In general, the false idea which has been, and continues to be, held about Niccolo, starts from the three following false principles: that Niccolo executed all, or nearly all, the works which Primaticcio directed; that Niccolo executed nothing else; and that before Niccolo's arrival Primaticcio himself went on to execute his own designs. Not one of the three is true, and Niccolo cannot be allowed to occupy such an extraordinary place in history. Niccolo did nothing in the Ball-room and elsewhere which Miniato, Luca Penni and the others had not done before him. If it is alleged that, as Primaticcio advanced towards the close of his career, he was obliged to leave more to his new collaborator than he had to the others, it must at least be admitted that he never went so far as to entrust him with the charge of making the designs themselves.

The Abbé Guilbert says that the ornament placed on the walls of the Ulysses Gallery [†] contained the devices of François I., from which I have concluded in my "Primaticcio" that the pictures of the story of Ulysses painted within these ornaments were executed in the reign of that king. Vasari, however, affirms [‡] that the execution of them was Niccolo's; and this author's statements, though vague and subject to contradiction when they concern Rosso, are, on the contrary, extremely exact upon Primaticcio and the works he directed. It is true

---

[*] The conclusion is all the more inevitable because Niccolo's manner of drawing in these designs is as well known as that of the Bolognese artist.

[†] See thereabout, *Le Primatice*, pp. 289 *et seq.*

[‡] *Opere :* Milanesi's edition, vol. vii. p. 411.

MINERVA CARRIED TO HEAVEN

PRIMATICCIO. DESIGN FOR THE CEILING OF THE GALLERY OF ULYSSES AT
FONTAINEBLEAU. BRITISH MUSEUM

that he also gives Niccolo a half share in the King's
Chamber, which was painted twenty years before his
arrival in France, but without insisting on it as he does
in the case of these pictures in the Ulysses Gallery.
In this case he goes so far as to describe the process of
fresco which this painter employed. The testimony of
the Abbé Guilbert, though considered indisputable in
itself, nevertheless does not imply as an inevitable consequence that the paintings are as old as the reign of
François I., since they might not have been executed till
after the ornaments. On the other hand, some of the
drawings of this story of Ulysses on close examination
gave me the impression of sketches, although even so
they were used as the final models. This implies that
Primaticcio did not supplement them with studies from
nature, which come between the first sketch and the
definite design. Now this expeditious method is the kind
an artist has recourse to in the later stages of his career,
and Primaticcio, at any rate in the works he painted
under François I., is never found to have employed it.
These considerations incline me to correct what I have
written in my former work, and on this point to follow
Vasari, at least so far as will allow us to consider Niccolo
as collaborating with the master in the pictures of the
story of Ulysses.

Perhaps some still remained to be painted, and it is
certain that the ceiling was in progress; * but the main
part of this gallery must have been finished under Henri
II. Till a long time afterwards there was still some of

---

* We know this, not only from the king's cyphers contained in the
ornamentation, but from the evidence of the "Comptes." See *Le Primatice*, p. 289, on this and all other points in connection with this gallery.

the ornament left unpainted, and some small part of the figures; but it is only natural to treat the whole gallery as belonging to that epoch.

The Ulysses Gallery, then, now demolished, stood in the court of the White Horse, which it adjoined on one side, while on the other it looked over the Garden of Pine-trees. It was one of the first things to be built, and remained without decoration for ten years. Only after the death of Rosso was the decoration of it first considered. Primaticcio was charged with the work, and put all his most skilful workmen on the task. Their names I have given above. In so glorious an enterprise he appears to have wished to work entirely in his own way, and he abandoned the mixture of stucco and painting which Rosso and himself also had adopted in several places. The relief was less and the ornament smaller. What we know of the stuccos of the ceiling reminds us rather of the Palace of Te than of the gallery of François I. On this ceiling, beside the historical paintings, was scattered a profusion of ornament, painted in a style which had not been seen before in France, and which, twenty years later, was fashionable in Italy under the name of grotesques.*

Primaticcio learnt the practice of them from Giulio Romano, who had it from Raphael.† The success of this style, which was immense in Italy, was to be no less in France, where the Ulysses Gallery was certainly the first example of it. The first collection of Ducerceau, who was famous for inventions of this kind,‡ had not yet appeared;

* Now called arabesques.
† In the Loggias of the Vatican.
‡ Through his two collections, the Small and the Large Arabesques, the former of which appeared in 1550, and the latter in 1566.

NEPTUNE RAISING THE STORM

PRIMATICCIO.  DESIGN FOR THE CEILING OF THE GALLERY OF ULYSSE  AT
FONTAINEBLEAU.  LOUVRE.  COLLECTION HIS DE LA SALLE

and the renown of these arabesques was so great that two
centuries later they had not ceased to be objects of universal admiration.* Not only was the ceiling covered
with them, but the walls below the paintings and in the
embrasures of the windows as well. At the outset, and
for about half the ceiling, the Bolognese Fantose directed
the execution of them under the superintendence of Primaticcio. It seems that this artist stood in nearly the same
relation to his master as Giovanni da Udine did to
Raphael in the work on the arabesques of the Vatican.

To get a proper idea of the total effect of the Ulysses
Gallery we must imagine a breadth about equal to that of
the gallery of François I., and a completely disproportion-
ate length. It ran the whole length of the court of the
White Horse, nearly 150 yards; and was therefore less a
single whole, consisting of mutually supporting and homo-
geneous parts, than a succession of fifteen bays, each
decorated independently, and meant to be looked at
separately. These bays were divided on the ceiling,
according to eight different systems, by pictures varying
in number from five to nine, with the exception of that
of the centre bay, which had only three. This was divided
on a unique system; that of the others was symmetrically
repeated up to either end. Such was the vast and magnificent frame which was to contain ninety-eight mythological paintings in the divisions of the ceiling, besides the
fifty-eight scenes from the history of Ulysses on the walls.

The following is the list, with an indication of what
drawings of them are preserved.

---

* Guilbert: *Description de Fontainebleau*, vol. ii. p. 27, and the
testimony of the Comte de Caylus: Edmond et Jules de Goncourt: *L'art
au dix-huitième siècle*, vol. i. p. 22.

On the walls : the embarkment of the Greeks after
the siege of Troy, Ulysses offering sacrifice (both drawings in the museum at Stockholm); Neptune rousing the
tempest against Ulysses (drawing at Chantilly); Ulysses
defeated by the Cicones; Ulysses with the Lotophagi,
Ulysses with the Cyclopes (drawings of both at Stockholm); the return of Agamemnon; the murder of
Agamemnon and of Cassandra, Polyphemus keeping his
flocks (drawings of both at Stockholm); Ulysses putting
out the giant's eye; Ulysses and his companions escaping
from the cave of Polyphemus hidden under the bellies of
the sheep (drawing at Stockholm); Polyphemus throwing
rocks at Ulysses; Ulysses receiving from Æolus the bag
of the winds; the ship of Ulysses driven on by the
Zephyrs; the companions of Ulysses opening the bag of
the winds; Ulysses with the Læstrigones; Ulysses landing
on Circe's island; Ulysses protected from Circe's charm;
Ulysses leaving Circe; the arrival of Ulysses in Hades;
Ulysses sacrificing the black rams (drawing in the Albertina collection at Vienna); Tiresias drinking the victims'
blood; Ulysses talking with Hercules in Hades; Ulysses
burning the body of Elpenor; Ulysses and the Sirens,
the companions of Ulysses and the oxen of the sun (drawings of both in the Albertina collection at Vienna); Ulysses
torn from the arms of Calypso by Mercury; Ulysses taking
leave of Alcinous (drawing at Stockholm); Ulysses carried
asleep into his own country; * Minerva waking Ulysses;
Minerva appearing to Ulysses in the guise of Telemachus;
Ulysses talking with Eumæus; Ulysses recognised by his
dog; † Ulysses receiving alms from one of his servants;

* Engraved by Philip Galle.
† Poorly engraved by Jean Chartier.

ULYSSES BURYING THE SUITORS

PRIMATICCIO.  DESIGN FOR THE GALLERY OF ULYSSES AT FONTAINEBLEAU, ALBERTINA COLLECTION, VIENNA

*From a Carbon-print by Braun, Clément & Co., Dornach, Alsace*

Ulysses begging at the door of his house, the combat of Ulysses with the beggar Irus (drawings of both at Stockholm); Minerva urging Ulysses to demand the bow; Ulysses drawing the bow (drawing at Stockholm); Antinous shot by Ulysses * (drawing in the Albertina); Ulysses revenged on the suitors; the handmaids condemned to death by Ulysses, Ulysses washing his hands (drawings of both at Stockholm); Euryclea telling the men-servants of the return of Ulysses; Ulysses disguised by Minerva, Penelope and Ulysses embracing (drawings of both at Stockholm); Ulysses and Penelope in bed; Ulysses in bed recounting his adventures; Penelope in doubt whether Ulysses is her husband; Ulysses and Telemachus going to Laertes; Ulysses giving his arms to Eumæus (drawing at Stockholm); Ulysses talking with his father; Ulysses saluted by his kinsmen (drawing at Stockholm); the bodies of the suitors removed (drawing in the Albertina); the revolt of the people of Ithaca, the rebels subdued by the aid of Minerva (drawings of both at Stockholm); Ulysses receiving the homage of his subjects.

All these compositions were engraved in the seventeenth century by the Fleming, Van 'Thulden,† a pupil of Rubens; and though not so badly as has sometimes been declared, at least in a manner too inferior to the model to enable us to judge from these prints the compositions of which the drawings are lacking.

We come now to the paintings on the ceiling. Right

---

* Engraved by Philip Galle.

† Under the title of *Travaux d' Ulysse.* His engravings are of service, at least, in furnishing a general knowledge of the work. A complete set of copies in chalk, after the same compositions, very poorly done, is preserved in the British Museum.

in the middle was the Dance of the Hours, painted in
an oval (drawing at the Staedel Institute in Frankfort);
accompanied by two oblongs representing Apollo and the
Muses on Parnassus, and a Feast of the Gods (drawing at
the Louvre, collection His de la Salle). These three pieces
formed the central compartment, on either side of which
the divisions of the ceiling were repeated symmetrically.
The two adjoining compartments, the seventh and the
ninth bays of the gallery, had a hexagon in the centre accompanied by eight other compositions, four in medallion.
These were Apollo in the sign of Leo (drawing in the
Albertina); then Orpheus, Latona with Diana and Apollo,
Diana and Pan, Æsculapius; Diana entreated by Niobe,
Apollo slaying the Python, Apollo and Diana slaying the
children of Niobe, Io guarded by Argus. The ninth had
a triumph of Minerva, then Religion, Goodwill, Charity,
Prudence; the battle of the Romans and Sabines, Romulus building a temple to Jupiter, the rape of the Sabine
women, the triumph of Romulus. The sixth and tenth
compartments were composed of a rectangle with semi-
circular outlines accompanied by four others with ressauts.
In the former were Jupiter, Neptune and Pluto (drawing
in the Hermitage at St. Petersburg); then Apollo and
Pegasus, Diana, Venus and Mercury; in the latter the
Hours surrounding the Chariot of the Sun (drawing
in the Louvre); then the Nile, the Ganges (drawings of
both at the École des Beaux-Arts in Paris), la Plata
(drawing in the Louvre), and the Danube. In the fifth
and eleventh were four subjects with the corners cut off
surrounding a principal subject, which in the fifth represented Diana with Apollo, Minerva and Cupid, in the other
Neptune creating the horse: the four accessory subjects

APOLLO AND THE MUSES ON PARNASSUS

PRIMATICCIO.    DESIGN FOR THE BALL-ROOM AT FONTAINEBLEAU.    BRITISH MUSEUM

were, in one bay, Spring, Summer, Autumn, and Winter;
in the other, Bacchus (drawing in M. Valton's collection
in Paris), Ceres, Flora, and Saturn (drawing in the
Louvre).* The fourth and twelfth had each an octagon
in the centre with four rectangles with semi-circular
sides and two recumbent ovals. In the fourth were Venus
and the Fates (drawing in the Louvre), Erato, Apollo
and Pan, Calliope, Terpsichore †; France Victorious
(drawing in the Uffizi at Florence), and France the
Fertile. In the twelfth, Bellona borne by two genii
(drawing in the British Museum), the Charity of Rome
(drawing in the Louvre, collection His de la Salle);
Mars and Venus (drawing in the Albertina), Pyrrhus
sacrificing Polyxena; Polymnestor slaying Polydorus,‡
and two subjects unknown. In the third and thirteenth
the central subject was in the form of a cross, and the
accessory subjects were recumbent ovals. The central
subjects represented Juno descending from heaven (drawing in the Louvre), the Graces, Hercules and Pan, Nymphs
and Cupids, Bacchus and Saturn; § the accessories,
Minerva visiting Jupiter (drawing in the Uffizi), and
four subjects of Nymphs and Naiads. An octagon with
four upright subjects and two recumbent ovals composed
the second and fourteenth compartments. Here were
Neptune calming the tempest (drawing in the Louvre,
collection His de la Salle), Vulcan, Æolus, Bellona,
Mercury (the drawings of the two last in the Louvre);
Vertumnus and Pomona (drawing at Chantilly), Venus

---

* These four were engraved in the following century by Ferdinand.
† These four were engraved by Giorgio Mantovano.
‡ Engraved by Ferdinand.
§ All four engraved by Giorgio Mantovano.

and Cupid, in the second; Parnassus with Jupiter (drawing in the Uffizi); the sacrifice of a child, another of a horse
(drawing in the museum at Dijon), another of a ram, and
a fourth of a bull; Diana and Apollo, and Cupid and
Psyche, in the fourteenth.  Finally, the first and fifteenth
bays had a central square supported by four oblongs and
two other subjects, representing in the first, Olympus *
(drawing in the Louvre), Juno and Cybele, Mars and
Saturn, Mercury and Bacchus (drawing in the Amsterdam
Museum), Diana and Ceres, a Cupid with a quiver and
another in a helmet; in the second, Flora, and four
subjects of women and children.

If we add the Four Seasons at either end of the gallery,
five chimney-pieces, one at the end and the others in the
side walls, and a hemicycle above the entrance, which was
painted a little later with the scene of Charles IX.
receiving the surrender of Havre, we reach, for the
whole gallery, the number of a hundred and sixty-one
paintings.

These figures are more eloquent than any amount
of amplification; they raise a vision of so much resource,
of a faculty of invention so various, and so extraordinary
an activity, that the mind remains confounded.  But it
would be a mistake to suppose that the effect of this
facile and pleasing abundance was to obviate any necessity
for perfection in this excessive fertility.  The place did
not lend itself to this kind of illusion; the gallery was
only extreme in its length, the rest of its proportions
were moderate, the figures were small and seen at a very
short distance.  The Ulysses paintings were only eight
feet by six, and most of the pictures on the ceiling were

* Engraved by Cornelis Cort, with a false ascription to Vincidor.

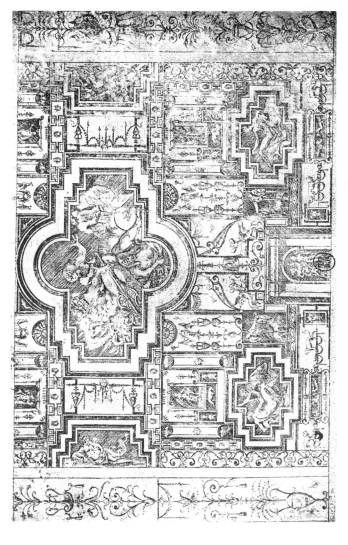

DETAIL OF THE CEILING OF THE GALLERY OF ULYSSES AT FONTAINEBLEAU

PRIMATICCIO. AFTER A PRINT BY DUCERCEAU

still smaller. The ornament took a principal place on it; and all things considered, the best idea that we can form of the whole effect is that it closely resembled the Loggias of Raphael. I speak only of the arrangement.

The arrangement of the Ball-room, which was painted between 1551 and 1556,* is very different, as we may still see on the spot, for this Ball-room has survived.

It is known nowadays as the gallery of Henri II. The name has recently been given, and there is neither tradition nor reason that can justify it. It is not a gallery, in fact, but a room, of extraordinary dimensions, a royal hall, where balls were held, and all the other court entertainments. The life of the court created these fresh needs. The court of the Valois was one that must promptly have felt the necessity of such a place of assembly; the best and most brilliant example of the sort in the French monarchy is the Galerie des Glaces at Versailles. The project of a building of this kind, therefore, came as the consummation of the plans of François I., who in fact began to construct it; and this Ball-room, like the Ulysses Gallery, marks the fortunate continuity that binds the encouragement of art of François I. to that of his successor.

If it were not for the Ulysses Gallery, the Ball-room would be the most important work which Primaticcio carried out at Fontainebleau. And it is true that if it yields to the former in the number of paintings, it surpasses it by far in size. Nowhere has the Bolognese painter covered so large a space. Eight large subjects filled with figures of every kind cover the walls between ten immense windows; a ninth stood over the musicians' gallery. The

* *Le Primatice*, p. 284.

whole was excellently painted, composed in the finest
taste, and carried out with the perfection of figures and
ornament.  Smaller subjects of two or three figures, four
in number round the fireplace and fifty in the embrasures
of the windows, complete this majestic work, which was
truly surprising for the period at which it was executed.
The seventeenth and eighteenth centuries, in which painting was far more widespread in France than in the sixteenth, can show no undertaking of such importance.

The Ball-room was long the admiration of all visitors
to Fontainebleau.  They looked without ceasing at the
crowd of mythological figures, the chief of which were
seen to be painted on brackets originally intended to
receive a vaulted roof, though the design was altered.
Here was Ceres symbolising summer, surrounded by
reapers, and autumn under the emblem of Bacchus.  He
appeared at table, raising his cup with a movement full
of indolence and *abandon*.  Ariadne was seated opposite
him, and all round them Fauns and Satyrs filled the scene
with voluptuous intoxication; two figures of men in the
foreground were leading lions and leopards.  Activity,
effort, and heavy labour were contrasted in the other
picture with this painting of pleasure.  The whole scene
was crowded round Ceres.  Clothed in long working garments, women were cutting sheaves, which young men
were piling into bundles on their shoulders.  One of them
was carrying a sack, and reaching out his arm so naturally
that he might almost be seen to bend under his burden.
But the finest of all were two large figures seated at the
foot of the arcades, drawn with a light and flowing touch,
and completing this scene of rural labour.  Near to
Bacchus was Apollo enthroned upon Parnassus and sur-

rounded by the Muses, while opposite was Venus constraining Vulcan to forge darts for Cupid. There Primaticcio had painted the bellows of the forge and all the poetic accessories with striking simplicity. Further on Phaeton was supplicating the god of the sun; and on the other side were three goddesses dancing before the assembled gods. Below came the story of Philemon and Baucis, and Discord on the way to embroil the gods.

Sixty years ago this beautiful work was no more than a ruin: to-day the very ruins have perished, not by a final stroke of time, but through the impertinence of man and the fault of those who proposed to restore them. It is altogether impossible to recognise, in the paintings with which M. Alaux covered the walls anew, the least trace of Primaticcio. The comparison of the drawings is enough to decide this point; and the substitution he dared to make of encaustic for fresco* is sufficient comment on the exactness with which the colours have been restored. The painter's friends were perfectly right to praise his work in his own time: we may speak the truth freely about it now. Beyond question, the result is as detestable as can be imagined. The offensive crudity of the tones, the absolute want of intelligence in the proportions and outlines, the extreme coarseness of the brushwork have turned this brilliant work into a ridiculous mess, a nameless confusion, a chaos of deformed attitudes, of crippled members, of extravagant and dispirited gesticulations, of reddish flesh and colourless drapery.

---

* On the authority of Jamin : *Fontainebleau sous le roi Louis Philippe*, p. 19. As to the designs, they were recomposed with the help of some imperfect engravings which a certain Bétou made in the seventeenth century of the whole of this decoration.

The visitor casts uneasy glances on these ridiculous cari-
catures.  This, he is told, is Primaticcio's finest work : it
was restored under Louis Philippe.

The wise man will know what this means; and in this
case as in others, he will not neglect to go to the master's
drawings.  Those of Ceres and Bacchus are at Chantilly;
of Parnassus, in the British Museum ; of the Concert
above the musicians' gallery, part is in the Albertina at
Vienna, part in M. Masson's collection at Amiens.  I
will mention here also the fragments which remain in
the embrasures of the windows.  The two pictures of
Diana above the chimney-piece * are preserved intact in
two drawings in the Albertina.  The drawing of the
Charon in the first window is in the Louvre; so is that
of Mars asleep, in the sixth; a naiad and Neptune in
the seventh ; Cupid asleep with a nymph, and Saturn,
in the ninth; Jupiter and Vulcan in the tenth: that of
Pan in the third is in the British Museum.

These last drawings have another advantage besides
that of preserving the master's work; they show us
further the measure of Niccolo's assistance in this undertaking.  They are all taken from the living model, each
contains two or three figures only, and not a single accessory is added.  It was Niccolo's task, therefore, to give
all these figures their proper attributes, and to arrange
them according to mythology.  For instance, the Pan in
the British Museum merely represents an ordinary model,
to whom Niccolo in the painting has given goat's legs.
This is a most certain evidence on this collaboration.

Thus, under Henri II. as under his father, there was
no lack of great works at court.  In fact, the reign of the

* One of them engraved by Bonneione.

latter gave birth to them in such profusion that no comparison on this point is possible.

The decoration of Fontainebleau, which had been all but completed in the space of sixteen years, no longer afforded scope for the variety of application and the constant growth of initiative which had been witnessed in the former period. The display of excessive magnificence, the profusion, the splendour, the expenditure which the late king took delight in, could not be kept up after him. And moreover, Fontainebleau, though not abandoned, ceased to hold the first place in the royal predilection. The favourite residence of François I. saw its prestige diminish under his son. The new king preferred above all other spots Anet,* the property of Diane de Poitiers, his favourite. Finally, a new style of decoration came into favour, in which the paintings of other days were replaced by carved panelling, and marble chimney-pieces ornamented by Philibert Delorme with pilasters and other divisions, according as the architects invented them.

On the accession of the new king, Philibert had been appointed Director of the Buildings, an office held till then † only by gentlemen of the court; so that Primaticcio had enjoyed under them not independence only, but the general authority which his professional abilities naturally gave him. The installation of an artist in the chief position had the effect of throwing in his way an unprecedented rivalry, and of somewhat diminishing his importance.

* On the authority of Philibert Delorme : *Instruction*, published by Berty : *Les Grands Architectes français*, p. 67.

† On the importance of this appointment to architecture and art in general, see *Le Primatice*, pp. 140 and 222.

L

That is the best solution of the difference in the situation of the Italian painters under these two reigns. Several of those I have mentioned went away. I have said * that Bagnacavallo returned to Italy about 1546, and no doubt Cachenemis and Fantose, who are nowhere mentioned again. It must have been about that time that Luca Penni crossed over into England.† Miniato hanged himself in 1548.‡ Others of the same nationality, however, soon appeared; among them, besides Niccolo, Ruggieri, called Roger de Rogery, a Bolognese, was taken into the king's service. We find him at Fontainebleau from 1557 onwards.§ No doubt the case was the same with Prospero Fontana, a friend and compatriot of Primaticcio's, who stayed but a short time; ‖ and no doubt also the king's service would have claimed Lorenzo Sabbatini of Bologna, whose engagement we also find under consideration.¶

There were many rich private people too who joined in occupying what leisure the court might seem to have left the artists.

The favour which at that time was placing the star of the house of Guise in the ascendant could not be without effect on the events I am relating. To the thousand brilliant qualities which seemed to have marked them out for the filling of the highest *rôles*, these princes joined a love of the arts and the ostentatious display of an all but royal magnificence. Their alliances with the

---

* Above, p. 115.
† See p. 116.                                  ‡ P. 115.
§ Laborde: *La Renaissance des arts à la cour de France*, p. 665. Vasari mentions this assistant of Primaticcio's, *op. cit.*, vol. vii. p. 410.
‖ Vasari: *ibid.*                              ¶ *Ibid.*, p. 415.

house of Valois gave them a unique rank at court, and
the presence of their niece, Mary Stuart, educated as
dauphine with the Enfants de France, renewed every day
the material signs of their extraordinary fortune.  Of
the sons of the old duke Claude, the proudest of all was
Charles, Archbishop of Rheims, who was soon to be appointed Cardinal of Lorraine.  He had made his principal
residence at the Castle of Meudon, which had been abandoned by the Duchess d'Etampes after the death of the
last king; and he resolved to decorate it magnificently.
With this design, in 1552, he set his artisans to work on
the famous building known as the Grotto of Meudon,*
which all the writers of the time describe as a marvel,
and which continued to dwell in the memories of the
French long after it had been destroyed.

It was a sort of palace, with but few living-rooms, but
a vast expanse of galleries and staircases, which gave the
exterior a magnificent effect.  But the important part
of it in the present instance is the decoration of the
interior which was entrusted to Primaticcio.

Of this decoration Vasari has left a description, which
is exceedingly magnificent, but void of precise detail.
According to this, there is nothing to prevent our im-
agining an infinity of rooms completely decorated with
paintings, and a second Fontainebleau in this Grotto of
Meudon.  Two at least of the rooms are known for
certain ; one, in the principal pavilion, had numerous
fresco subjects in the ceiling, each revealing a more
violent foreshortening than the others, in an equal number of divisions separated by mouldings.  Below was the
grotto, properly so called, decorated in a style like that

* *Le Primatice*, p. 420.

of the grotto in the Garden of Pine-trees, which, moreover, it eclipsed. It differed from it in several points, principally in the enamel with which it was covered, and a mosaic pavement. Built in a rustic order of architecture, its walls, which were decorated with arabesques and compartments of shell-work mingled with coral, supported stucco fountains, which made a uniquely beautiful ornament. The vaulted roof had the same stucco reliefs.

Further details on the subject are lacking, and we can only make a guess, on such general information as this, at the importance of such a work in the history of painting in France. It is clear that here, as at Fontainebleau itself, ornament and sculpture were mingled with painting; so that after all the changes of fashion that had affected the decoration of rooms, we none the less find Primaticcio, well on in the reign of Henri II., still directing a band of sculptors and painters, mingling stucco and fresco as of old, calling to his aid imagination and the study of rare materials, anticipating Palissy in this use of pottery, working boldly in the most various branches of art, and hazarding in mosaic the delicate grace of his design and the poetry of his invention.

One other point to be recorded about this work is the great favour which it shows Primaticcio to have enjoyed with the Guises ; and there are several other signs of this still to be noticed.

Another celebrated painter worked for these princes, and was engaged by this same Cardinal de Lorraine, no doubt on the introduction of Primaticcio. This was the Florentine Salviati, who came to France in 1554.* The prelate set him to work at Dampierre, near Chevreuse,

* Vasari : *op. cit.*, vol. vii. p. 33.

another castle which he wished to beautify; but the details of the work are unknown.

The town of Lyons had had from this painter, before his arrival in France, a "Doubting of St. Thomas," painted for the Chartreux, which is now in the Louvre.* He painted an "Entombment" for the Célestins in Paris, which is now in the Church of St. Marguerite in that city.

A little later there came Paris Bordone, a Venetian,† equally no doubt brought over by the Guises, whose niece, Mary Stuart, he had painted, and who had employed him for several works. Vasari asserts ‡ that he painted a picture of Venus and Cupid for the duke himself. The Cardinal de Lorraine had from his brush, on the one hand, an "Ecce Homo," and, on the other, a "Jupiter and Io." For the King of France the same painter painted several pictures, and the portraits of several ladies. Neither of these painters stayed long in France. Salviati was only there twenty months, and Paris Bordone has left no traces, so that there is no occasion to dwell on him longer.

Meanwhile King Henri II. had died, in the year 1552, and this event had been the cause of a small revolution, the consequences of which were to be felt by the history of painting.§ On the morrow of this king's death, the architect, Philibert Delorme, resigned the

---

* Catalogue, No. 1484.

† Federico (*Memorie Trevigiane*, vol. ii. p. 41) holds that he arrived in 1559 at the summons of François II. Vasari gives the date as 1538; but Vasari's own account of the people he worked for compels us to prefer the other date.

‡ *Op. cit.*, vol. vii. p. 464.

§ Laborde : *Comptes des Bâtiments*, vol. i. p. 333.

office of Director of the King's Buildings, and Primaticcio took his place. There can be no doubt that this new appointment left our artist no time whatever for directing the painters. The last ten years of his career were spent, thereupon, in duties slightly different from those which we have seen him fulfilling till now, and foreign to the subject of this book. Thenceforward his part was to build, and to direct the works in bronze and marble which the queen-dowager, Catherine de Medici, was ordering for the various tombs of her husband and children. Continually we find Primaticcio giving evidence of his perfect aptitude for such tasks. His talent as a painter did not prevent him from being a very clever architect. He had already given some proofs of it at Fontainebleau under François I.; * under Henri II. the Guises entrusted him with Duke Claude's mausoleum at Joinville,† a perfect preparation for those which he was to erect in St. Denis at the royal command. Thus, by the agency of unforeseen events, the career of this artist as painter proper comes to an end precisely at this epoch. It is only fair, however, to note that, completely lost though they were to painting, his merits as painter went with him everywhere, and did not fail, when employed in other fields, to exercise the influence of that art over the others, and to turn to the profit of painting the hierarchies which an architect like Philibert Delorme had carefully regulated to the sole profit of architecture. ‡

* In the fountain mentioned above, p. 112, and perhaps in the grotto of the Garden of Pine-trees.

† *Le Primatice*, p. 334. The monument is destroyed, but several fragments and the drawings, which were Primaticcio's work, have survived.

‡ See above, p. 161, note †.

The following is an account of all the paintings that Primaticcio can be found to have executed between 1559 and his death in 1570. I will pass over the Ulysses Gallery, for the little that remained to be done was put into the hands of Niccolo,* and seems to have dragged on to an interminable length.

First of all, before 1564, the Guises employed him to decorate the chapel of their hôtel in the Rue St. Avoye in Paris,† which has since been replaced by the hôtel de Soubise, where the Archives of France are kept. These decorations have perished. They consisted of a vast construction, in which the ceiling,‡ which represented the Eternal Father beneath a canopy (the drawing is in the Louvre), and Angels pointing to the Miraculous Star (drawing at Chantilly), made a single composition with an Adoration of the Magi painted as an altar-piece (drawing at the Uffizi in Florence), and their long train of attendants, copies of which are in the Staedel Institute at Frankfort. On the walls were David and a Prophet; then the Journey to Emmaus, the Resurrection, Jesus walking on the waters, and Jesus appearing as the gardener to Mary Magdalen. This was Primaticcio's last great work; all that he painted thereafter at Fontainebleau was but of little importance and only what the circumstances demanded.

The circumstances in question consisted of a new

---

* Only the ornaments and five pictures over the fireplaces remained to be finished.

† *Le Primatice*, p. 324.

‡ Engraved by De Pooter, a Flemish engraver, known in France as Le Poutre. *Le Primatice*, p. 504. This work, of inestimable value for information about a painting of which only fragments are preserved by the drawings, was lost, and has not yet been found.

building raised under his direction, which blocked up
two windows of the old chamber of the Duchess
d'Etampes.* The two spaces had to be covered with
paintings, and Niccolo was entrusted with the execution
of them, after the designs of Primaticcio. They may
still be seen on the spot, though completely repainted,
like the rest of the chamber. One represents a
subject unknown, with a nude woman by the side
of Alexander; in the other the conqueror is employed
in collecting the books of Homer. The period was
between 1568 and 1570, shortly before the master's
death, as if it had been decreed that, in spite of his
new occupations, his last years were to be accompanied
by painting.

Meanwhile, however, Niccolo, freed from the subjec-
tion which the proximity of Primaticcio had imposed
upon him, had not failed to wield his brush in a manner
that must be admitted to be brilliant.

I regard this master, first of all, as the author of the
paintings that decorate the chapel of the Castle of
Fleury-en-Bière, near Fontainebleau, the ceiling of which
had a Resurrection, with the four Fathers of the Church
and some figures of children painted in a most agreeable
manner. They are commonly ascribed to Primaticcio
on the evidence of the engravings of these made by
Garnier in the following century; but his claim to them
cannot be upheld. Everything points to the attribution
I have given.

The engravings, by preserving some parts of this
decoration which have been destroyed, are of service in
authoritatively fixing the date. The proof is that the

* *Le Primatice,* p. 271.

painting contains a St. Côme, the patron saint of Côme
Clausse, the owner of the castle, who died in 1558.
Moreover, the "Comptes des Bâtiments du Roi"* give
Niccolo as the painter of a picture on the chimney-piece
of the King's Chamber in the Pavilion des Poèles at
Fontainebleau, and of four large landscapes in the corner
of the vaulted roof of the Cabinet des Bagues, on the
second storey of St. Louis's Tower.

But the principal evidence of Niccolo's fertility is the
large number of drawings, evidently made as designs for
decoration, which are found in several galleries, notably
in the Louvre. In default of documentary evidence,
these reveal a most important part of the career of a
man who is barely known at all under his true colours,
and whose reputation future discoveries must certainly
increase. These drawings show what is nothing less
than a very individual style, which was destined to
make its way beyond official commissions and the royal
residences.

Niccolo survived Primaticcio only one year. Primaticcio died between the 2nd March and the 14th September 1570.† His rival and collaborator followed him
in 1571.‡ With Niccolo's death came the extinction of
the line of the great Italian artists of Fontainebleau,
whose glorious history Rosso had opened forty years
before. A year later, again, François Clouet died, and
there followed, in another realm, the momentary eclipse

* Published by Laborde, vol. i. p. 285 ; ii. p. 51. Lancilotto, quoted
by Tiraboschi, adds that he had painted the portraits of the king and
queen soon after his arrival.

† *Le Primatice*, p. 210.

‡ Laborde : *Renaissance*, p. 774.

of the arts which France had been maintaining. But before we go on to conclude the history of François Clouet, and with it that of the second and principal epoch, we must embark on the critical consideration of Primaticcio's gifts and a full account of his school.

# CHAPTER VIII

The School of Fontainebleau—How it was formed—Style and manner of
Primaticcio—His difference from Rosso—Their common elongation
of the figures—Extent of this characteristic—Geoffroy Dumoûtier—
Other French painters—Jean Cousin—His authentic works—True
beginnings of the school—Comparison of Primaticcio and Niccolo—Oil-
paintings by these two—The former's poetic style—The Fontainebleau
School in the provinces—Bouteloup—The Artemisia series—Antoine
Caron—Pierre Quesnel—Their mediocrity—Painting difficult to establish in France.

THE simple story we have told so far has shown the importance of Primaticcio to the French Renaissance. The
fact is generally recognised, but the reasons given are
not always sufficiently cogent for the clear understanding of it.

The most striking of all is the extreme duration of
his residence and his influence. He survived Rosso thirty
years and preceded Niccolo dell' Abbate by twenty. In
all the forty years during which, as I have said, the first
studio of Fontainebleau was at work, he was in charge of
it for all but two, the first and the last. All the rest of
its long career was maintained and filled by his presence.

His influence, which was shared at first and even
slightly surpassed by a rival of greater weight, had not
ten years to wait before it reached the throne from which
it was never to fall, and which the cleverest of the newly
engaged artists was only to enlarge and strengthen still

further. We have observed the deep mark left by Rosso on ornament, by motives borrowed from his stuccos which Primaticcio himself imitated. With that exception, it must be acknowledged that all the direction exercised on art by the studio of Fontainebleau had its principal and almost unique source in Primaticcio. I am speaking here of the figure, and exclusively of what concerns my subject. If the question is asked, why the great work left by Rosso did not equally form a school, the point is reached at which we can no longer escape a comparison between their respective manners.

Great and able as are the paintings which cover the gallery of François I., they have scarcely a single merit that is not to be found in Primaticcio, with the addition of something more of attractiveness, of balance, of pleasantness, with which it is not surprising that imitators were much taken. Poetry, learning, a fine intellectual equipment, and noble and fertile invention are found equally in both these artists: there is an ease and a grace and a more delicate feeling for nature in the second, which distinguish him from the first.

Three influences went to form Primaticcio: Giulio Romano, Michael Angelo, and Correggio. From the first he took his poetic form, the calm majesty of his faces, and a real and very vivid feeling for the antique; from the third his undulating and flexible line, the roundness and fulness of his drawing, his happy contrasts, his pleasant nonchalance, his loose and floating drapery, all his tenderness and all his grace; finally, from Michael Angelo he took his good sense, the grandeur of his outlines, the delicacy of his transitions, the vivid display of anatomical science, the unexpected in action, his grandeur and his vigour.

Such a combination composes a style very different from that of Rosso and decidedly superior to it, which could only pass unrecognised by a hurried observer, or one who knew nothing of the drawings of the two masters.

It is the opinion of such observers, however, that has commonly been accepted; and nothing is so common as to hear these two artists spoken of as if they formed part of one and the same school. They are bracketed together for the same praise and the same blame; the lucubrations on Fontainebleau combine their names and the history of their influence; the catalogues suggest them both as possible painters of the same works. When it comes to defining their styles, it appears that one can scarcely be distinguished from the other, and that their most individual characteristics are nothing more than varieties of the same style.

The features of this style are dinned into the ears of all who seek for information on these subjects. It has but one characteristic, and that has become so much a matter of popular knowledge that not a man but thinks himself entitled to bring out the name of one or the other at will, and even to assign works to them off-hand. Ask any amateur the decisive mark of these painters, and scarcely one will hesitate to say that it consists in a singular elongation of the figures, which is at the same time the characteristic of the school of Fontainebleau. Such is the easy authority assumed; an authority which has resulted, from one end of Europe to the other, in the attribution to this school and the sixteenth century in France of any number of works, either in drawing or in painting, that are obviously dubious. Now I do not deny that this elongation is found in Rosso and in

Primaticcio; nor that it is, as a matter of fact, a characteristic sufficiently unlike nature to tempt us to retain it as a distinguishing feature. But that would only be possible on one condition : the total oblivion of the number of other painters who equally adopted it, a number so large that a school constituted on this basis would run the risk of including all the countries and all the indefinite periods imaginable. The most striking example I know of this, is a passage in Waagen's "Treasures of Art,"* concerning the illuminations of Godofredus Batavus in the manuscript of the Gallic War. "The over-slender proportions," he says, "the free, often graceful, but sometimes extravagant attitudes, show that they already belong to what is called the Epoch of the Renaissance in France, which attained its highest perfection in the so-called School of Fontainebleau." These illuminations date from 1519. I have shown what the French School was like at that time, and these productions are the work of a Hollander. How, before a school is formed, can a foreigner possibly be chosen to represent a characteristic of style which was the special note of that school ?

The truth is that the elongation we are speaking of, which is found at such a distance from Rosso and Primaticcio in what is here called the French School, is met with in a hundred other places too. To begin with, is it not present in Botticelli and Mantegna, and any number of primitive painters ? It acquires later, I admit, another character, which derives from the influence of Michael Angelo; and I believe that, as a fact, that great artist was the source from which sprang the proportions of the figure maintained by the Fontainebleau artists; but that

* Vol. i. p. 119.

is a common character, which it would be quite erroneous
to discover only in the artists who worked in France, like
Cellini again, and Niccolo, and, I will add, Luca Penni.
For we do not find that all these painters differed in that
respect from those who stayed in Italy. Bronzino, for
instance, or Parmigiano had this elongation quite as
strongly. If anything more was wanted, surely the Libyan
Sibyl in the Sixtine,* or the group of Victory in the
Bargello, and some other figures by Michael Angelo, were
quite enough to spread the taste and the imitation, without assigning the mysterious inception of this feature to
the mutual approximation of the painters in the pay of
the court of France.

There is another point to notice, and that is, that
there is no school worthy of the name which can take its
title from Fontainebleau, at least during the whole of the
reign of François I. and the first half of the career of
Primaticcio. In fact, it is impossible to combine Rosso
with Primaticcio in any common definition of style, since
both had been completely formed by different schools
before their residence in France, and could do no more
than approximate their different styles to each other.
The word school, which is used to join these two men, can
signify no more, therefore, than a studio, in which their
works were mingled. Rosso belonged to the Florentine
school, Primaticcio to that of Parma; Luca Penni, whose
works were widely different from those of the other two,
was almost exclusively Roman. Then what part can be
played by Fontainebleau and the unity imposed by the
name, in defining the manner of these painters?

* The one with the bust facing sideways, turning over the leaves of a
book.

It is true that the conjunction of their teachings
ultimately gave birth to a school; but time was needed
for this result, and the passage of several years at least.
From looking at these models side by side, the eyes of
the French painters, like those of the less able Italians,
came to be accustomed to mingling their styles; and it
may be said with truth that out of that combination,
towards the end of the reign of Henri II., there grew
the type of figures and compositions which was to remain in favour throughout the whole century. Only
thus is it correct to speak of a School of Fontainebleau.
The characteristics of this school I shall come to very
shortly.

If, therefore, we go back first of all to the reign of
François I., and seek for the first effects of the lessons
of Fontainebleau, we must expect no more than individual and distinct instances. A Frenchman, Geoffroy
Dumoûtier,* comes to hand as a good example.

I have mentioned before his son Etienne, a distinguished portrait-painter. Geoffroy comes under the
heading of the stylists formed by the influence of Italy.
He was a native of Rouen,† and we find his name in the
" Comptes des Bâtiments du Roi "‡ about the period of
1538 to 1540. The latest date of some etchings assigned

---

* I prefer this way of spelling his name to *Dumonstier*, the contemporary form, because the use of the latter has resulted in spreading
among French connoisseurs a false pronunciation. In his time it was
certainly pronounced *Dumoûtier*. Moreover, this form was universally
used in the seventeenth century in speaking of the last of the family
(Daniel, mentioned in chapter xii.), which justifies my preference of it,
as less likely to lead to false readings.

† *Société des Beaux-Arts des Départements*, 1884, p. 381.

‡ Edited by Laborde : vol. i. p. 137.

LIFE OF THE MAGDALEN

GEOFFROY DUMOUTIER.  DESIGN FOR A WINDOW.  LOUVRE

to him by very ancient evidence is 1547.* We know
nothing more of him, but these etchings, twenty-two in
number, make us acquainted with the style he practised.
To these we must add a design for painted glass preserved
in the Louvre, from which the latest catalogues have
incorrectly removed his name.† It represents in several
episodes the life and ascension into heaven of Mary
Magdalen. I am inclined also to attribute to him the
drawing for two celebrated pieces of pottery made at
Rouen in 1542, now at Chantilly.‡ In the absence of the
pictures which we have the right to suppose he painted,
this is sufficient indication of his scope. The most unmis-
takable feature is a decided imitation of Rosso, carried
out with but moderate though skilfully managed ability.
Hence he fits exactly into the epoch that produced
Leonard Thiry; and there is every reason to suppose that
the other Frenchmen then at work, like Claude Badouin
and Charles Dorigny, who were employed in the execution
of the master's designs in the gallery of François I., were
subject to the same influence.

It is true that we cannot be certain that they painted
pictures on their own account, for we know scarcely
anything of them but their names. But it may be
added that Badouin was employed on the Fontainebleau
tapestries,§ and possibly painted some part of the glass

* Reiset : *Catalogue des dessins du Louvre*, part ii. p. 290.

† No. 2076.

‡ These famous pieces, on which the date given above was placed by
the potter's own hand, were the ground of countless conjectures, until it was
discovered that they came from the furnace of Masséot Abaquesne. Their
style, a corruption of Rosso's, is exactly that of the engravings and the
above-mentioned design by Geoffroy.

§ Laborde : *Comptes*, vol. i. pp. 190, 204.

M

in the chapel at Vincennes,* which was begun under
François I.

I have mentioned in their places others of these
Frenchmen who worked under Primaticcio after Rosso's
death: Carmoy, Musnier, and Rochetel. Of Charles
Carmoy we know that he was a native of Orleans.†
Musnier and Rochetel are given by name as painters
of the wardrobes in the King's Closet, the former for
Temperance and its fellow-figure, the latter for Zaleucus
and Justice.‡

For want of a better time, I will choose the middle
of the century for the mention of an enigmatical artist,
who has been talked of far and wide, but of whom very
little indeed is known for certain; I mean the famous
Jean Cousin.

Every detail about this painter, his life, his works,
even the branches of art he practised, have yet to be
verified. He is referred to on all hands as a glass-painter,
and unsupported tradition certainly affirms that he was.
There is no proof that he did the famous windows of the
chapel at Vincennes, and the opinion that assigns them
to him is no older than the eighteenth century.§ It is
acknowledged now that he did not make the statue of
Admiral Chabot, and that his part in his tomb could not
have extended beyond the accessories and the ornaments

* Félibien : *Entretien sur la vie et les ouvrages des plus fameux
peintres*, 4to edition, vol. i. p. 704.

† Laborde : *Renaissance*, p. 551.

‡ On the Chartres enamels, which M. de Laborde assigns to Rochetel ;
see p. 110, note *.

§ Félibien makes no mention of it. Lépicié, in his *Vies des plus
fameux peintres du roi*, and Florent Lecomte, in his *Cabinet des singularités*, were the first, I believe, to ascribe this work to him.

and fortifications which accompany it. Further, in his case, there is always a possibility of confusion among writers on the subject, no less than in the " Comptes," between this artist and some other, from the common-ness of his name, which was shared by several artisans of the time. It is true that he came unquestionably from Sens; but there is no reason to suppose that that town had fewer people of the name than any other. He had no official title to distinguish him, and his whole biography suffers from this uncertainty. For instance, must we admit that the accounts of works executed in Sens Cathedral in 1530 * have anything to do with him? He is credited with a grown-up son in 1542 † and an elder brother, a jeweller, who, like himself, was also named Jean. After 1542 we find him a citizen of Paris, where he appears to have lived, with the exception of a few visits to Sens, till his death, which took place between 1583 and 1595.‡

A point to be remembered is that this famous painter, who appears in nearly all the manuals as a great ancestor of French painting, is never mentioned in any con-temporary document as commissioned for any work, nor granted any distinguished post. That means that all the current ideas on this subject are in need of refor-mation. No doubt, what made his fortune with posterity was the surname of the " French Michael Angelo "; and that name was given him by those who had only studied his " Last Judgment" in Pieter de Jode's engraving.

---

* *L'Art*, 1883, vol. i. p. 112.     † *Ibid.*, 1884, vol. i. p. 106.

‡ The first of the dates is that of a licence to print Domenico da Sera's book on Linen, which contained drawings by Jean Cousin; the second is that of the mention of his heirs in the census of Saint-Germain-des-Prés.

The following is a list of his authentic works, which are
very few in number and of trifling importance.

The "Last Judgment" in the Louvre,* engraved under
his name in 1615, may pass as sufficiently guaranteed by
this old ascription.  The " Book of Perspective," published
in 1560, also bears his name, like the " Book of Lace," with
additions by Domenico da Sera, which appeared in 1584.
A print of the "Brazen Serpent," engraved by Etienne
Delaune, is lettered *Cusinus Senon. inven.*  Another
anonymous print of the " Conversion of St. Paul " has
*I.C.S. in.*, which, considering the style of the composition,
is equally convincing.  A third, engraved by Léonard
Gautier in 1581, which represents the " Forge of Vulcan,"
has these words : *Johannes Cusinus Senon. inv.*  I pass
over several instances of less obvious signatures, in which
there is nothing at all to indicate that Cousin was more
than the engraver.  That is the whole of the authenticated
output of this artist ; enough to give a sufficient idea of
his style, and at the same time to enable us to credit him
with other works which may some day be classed together.
Meanwhile, the duty of criticism is to see that all the
rest is forgotten, and to prevent the return of fabrica-
tions which make the supposed biography of this artist
tend to falsify all the present history.   His manner
reveals but indifferent knowledge, taste of little refinement in spite of considerable care, and an imitation of
Primaticcio, which compels us to include Jean Cousin
in the number of those in whom the School of Fontainebleau became at last a real thing.

Primaticcio is not the only artist I find imitated in
this work : a few notes of Rosso still survive, and some

* Catalogue, No. 155.

THE LAST JUDGMENT

JEAN COUSIN. LOUVRE

signs of Roman influence which may have been drawn from
Luca Penni, or from the drawings by Giulio Romano
brought by Primaticcio from Mantua,* or from the same
artist's tapestries which filled the storehouse of the royal
furniture.  But all this was set in motion and carried
forward by the purely Parman style, imposed by the
constant study of Primaticcio's works and his living influence.  This style, in fact, united all the others, and
this unification marked the establishment of what at
length we may rightly call a school.

If I were asked for a precise date, I should give
the year 1552, when Niccolo came to settle in France.
Niccolo so soon caught the manner of Primaticcio, for
which his education at Parma had admirably prepared
him, that his enamels in the Sainte Chapelle,† which
date from 1553, show him already in perfect enjoyment
of it.  Most of the drawings that are classed under
his name are of the same style, which is easy to recognise, and though distinct from the master's, are
none the less evidently an emanation from that admirable model.

This is the natural place for a comparison between the
two, in which their common features will be the first consideration.  These common features consist in rich and
emphatic drawing, in prettily contrasted attitudes, in all
the correction that delicate taste could administer to the
decadent fashions born of the time, and of those collective

---

* For proof of this, see p. 64, and the number of prints engraved by
Fantose and other Fontainebleau masters after Giulio Romano's compositions.

† Preserved in the Louvre, Nos. 282 to 327.  A portion of the original
drawings is in M. Valton's collection in Paris.

impulses to which the members of an aristocracy are
always subject.   Like all imitators of Michael Angelo,
Primaticcio is decidedly mannered; but his mannerism is
of a peculiar kind.   It is composed of contrary elements
artistically united, which, though they miss being perfectly
natural, attain none the less some sort of balance.   The
same may be said of Niccolo.   This balance and good taste
are what attaches them to the Roman school, though
they cannot make them part of it; as M. Reiset has
justly remarked.   "Their principles," says this excellent
writer, " were precisely the opposite of those of the clumsy
imitators of the great Michael Angelo.   The examples
they gave to the French artists were those of an elegant
and lofty taste, and could have borne nothing but good
fruit, if they had been faithfully followed."   What dis-
tinguishes one from the other is the excess of manner, or
rather of practice, in Niccolo's works, which no amount of
study could correct.   In Primaticcio, it did not hold so
complete a sway, nor absorb his whole talent; on the
contrary, it was incessantly refreshed by the imitation of
nature.   Scarcely ever with him did design degenerate
into a formula, or miss the reward that came of impres-
sions born of looking at things as they are; and although
his eye gave to natural objects too much refinement and
selection, at least it was always open.   We have a proof
of that in the large number of studies after nature
which have survived among his compositions, especially
in the early part of his career.   Among Niccolo's, on the
other hand, we find nothing of the kind.   Nearly all his
drawings are mere exercises: the stroke of his pen is
more abstract and his attitudes less natural.   His ideas
are as ordinary as his hand is easy and intelligent.   But

THE CHASTITY OF SCIPIO
NICCOLO DELL' ABBATE.   LOUVRE

such as he is, he is among the artists who can do much for the glory of a school, because the manner in which their talents were formed has fitted them to multiply unlimited examples of a single style, to circulate, as it were, the coin of the masters. What in Primaticcio is rare invention, profound thought, racial or natural characteristics, with Niccolo takes on a popular and *banal* air, though still giving evidence of the promise of extraordinary fertility. Nothing is so valuable as this kind of talent when it follows in the footsteps of a veritable master. At the head of a school such men are incapable of imposing on art anything but a rapid decadence; if they fall into the rank of assistants, they are wonderfully helpful. Invaluable workers in the field of industrial art, they give without measure what they conceive without pain, and contribute to the spreading of good taste, which they could neither invent nor maintain.

It must be added that Niccolo brought to Fontainebleau an art of which Primaticcio no doubt knew nothing, the art of landscape-painting. His " Rape of Proserpine," at Stafford House,* is admirable in this respect. Till the present moment this was the only picture painted in his Fontainebleau manner that was known to be his. I have ventured to add a " Continence of Scipio " at the Louvre,† and I am now prepared to add the picture of " Achilles with the daughters of Lycomedes," in Lord Pembroke's collection at Wilton House, which has quite erroneously been ascribed to Salviati.

For a long time I despaired of finding anything of the same kind of Primaticcio's; I mean any oil-painting, the preservation of which, being more certain than that of a

* Waagen : *op. cit.*, vol. ii. p. 62.    † Catalogue, No. 1014.

fresco, might provide the opportunity of judging his
talent from something else than his drawings. The
examination of two pictures in the most famous collections
in England has enabled me at last to add what I sought.
One is a " Helen Swooning," at Wilton House ; the other
a " Ulysses relating his adventures to Penelope," at Castle
Howard.* I regard them both as absolutely authentic, and
can only regret that the first has been damaged. The second
is copied from the principal part of one of the compositions
in the Ulysses Gallery, and the only difference is in certain
accessories which have been altered to suit the needs of
the case. It settles what might well be suspected, that
Primaticcio sometimes took studio - pictures from his
frescoes, and so made double profit. These two pictures
enable us to form an idea of the softness of his execution,
his bold and pleasant touch, and at the same time of his
colour, which is darker than we should be led to suppose
by certain old copies of the frescoes, as it lacks the dis-
coloration which was possibly Niccolo's work and is
repeated in his oil-paintings.

The actual subjects of the pictures with which these
two masters conquered the admiration of the French must
not be omitted, for Primaticcio is one of those artists in
whom the poetic meaning of a composition is of some
importance. In that he resembled his master, Giulio
Romano, and a yet greater painter who was to arise to
the glory of the French school, Poussin. Mythology and
fable provided him not only with hackneyed motives for
the grouping of his characters, but with inspiration and
counsel. In his historical paintings he was imbued with
the spirit of the ancients whose stories they told, and

* Waagen : *op. cit.*, vol. iii. p. 322.

THE RAPE OF PROSERPINE

NICCOLO DELL' ABBATE.   STAFFORD HOUSE

with the most delicate aspects which the Muse had given them.

In this respect nothing can be more striking than the long series of the story of Ulysses, in which the painter has followed the " Odyssey " so closely, and supplied, as it were, the most faithful and complete commentary on the poet that has ever been seen in painting. It is true that there is a great difference between the studied art of Primaticcio and the simplicity of Homer; but it must not be forgotten that the painter's mannerism does not touch the composition of his subjects, and that, though mannered in his drawing, he is not mannered either in his arrangement or his choice of accessories, the sobriety of which brings him into perfect accord with his author. In Primaticcio as in Homer we are surprised and charmed to find all but barbarous manners represented in so elaborated a style. The direct, the familiar, the un-civilised elements in Homer's characters are rendered more exactly than we can express. We see jaws that eat, fists that strike, mouths that cry, represented with that frankness of gesture and accent which give such striking beauty to the works of the ancients. On the side of mythology we find the same agreement. He introduces the gods as boldly and as freely as the Greek. They appear in the midst of mundane events, mingled with the men they govern and the elements they let loose, and with the appropriate action which the Ionian Muse assigned them. On the ceiling of this Ulysses Gallery the illusions were still greater. A vast number of different subjects, collected from all points of antiquity, composed a whole of which the like was never seen. Passing from allegory to legend and from fiction to history, Primaticcio seems to have exhausted the whole field of poetic invention in a series of paintings which had no bond of union but his imagination. Or rather, it was a work after the fashion of the " Metamorphoses," in which episodes, by turns amusing, grave and terrible, formed a single whole by means of the wonderful unity of their style and the ingenious and constant resuscitation of interest.

These were the characteristics which put the School of Fontainebleau so closely in accord with the times, and made the masters of this branch of art stand out as historical personages, proclaiming the taste for classical antiquity which the court of the Valois possessed as no other did. In that court the love of ancient literature made its influence felt outside the narrow circle of a few scholars. The learned men who lived at court had inspired the knights and ladies with the taste. Rosso, Primaticcio and Niccolo were their painters, the painters of the humanists, just as Poussin was said to be the painter of the *gens d'esprit*. What pleasure in seeing, in the newly-built palace, the succession of their brilliant paintings, giving visible beauty in an instant to the stories which poetry alone had recounted till then! * Who can express the delicate delight bred by this evocation, in minds illuminated by the sun of the Renaissance in all the beauty of its rising? They might fancy old Olympus alive once more. It would have been well if this paganism had known its own limits; if, in the

* This is the merit which Dufresnoy sees in Giulio Romano :—
     *Graphicaque poesi*
  *Quae non visa prius sed tantum audita poetis*
  *Ante oculos spectanda dedit.*

ULYSSES RELATING HIS ADVENTURES TO PENELOPE

PRIMATICCIO.   CASTLE HOWARD

innumerable subjects on every side, no excessive licence had debased this admirable artistic aim.

Established finally on these models, the School of Fontainebleau held sway, not only in the royal residences and in Paris, but also, naturally enough, in the provincial houses of the great. I have mentioned its production in this period at Ancy-le-Franc. But it is not only in the Chamber of the Arts that we must note its effects. All the paintings by different hands, with which this castle is filled, bear the mark of the same style. Unhappily, some of them have been so entirely repainted that it is impossible to express any opinion about their original creators. A few pieces preserved in the Hall of Diana and the Emperors' Closet, on the first floor, are, next to the Chamber of the Arts and a long way after it, the best of all. At Tanlay, in the same neighbourhood, a vaulted roof at the top of a tower is decorated with figures of divine beings in the same style. At the Constable de Montmorency's house at Écouen there are numerous chimney-pieces painted with cartouches, cameos and mythological figures,* several of them excellently done, which bear the vivid imprint of the examples spread abroad by Primaticcio and Niccolo.

At Oiron in Poitou, in the house of the Boisy family, we find, in the Æneid Gallery, obviously painted under the influence of the pictures of the story of Ulysses, a long series of large compositions, enclosed in imitations of frames in relief, which repeat the ideas of Rosso's stuccos. At Troyes there are several pictures which bear witness

---

* For details, see Gallet : *Peintures murales au Château d'Écouen.—Société des Beaux-Arts des Départements*, 1882.

to the extent of a similar influence : one of them, the
" Treachery of Judas," is in the Church of St. Pantaléon.

It is remarkable that in all these works the ornament
required to frame them is invariably in imitation of relief.
The owners were afraid of the great expense of the stuccos,
even when they appear to have paid a large price for
paintings of some merit.  The object was not always attained, and a clumsy bungle is most frequently the result
with these provincial paintings.  Most of them must have
been executed on the spot by local artists, with the aid of
prints, or occasionally by the lowest rank of assistants in
the decorations of Fontainebleau, on their return into their
own country.  Sometimes they confined themselves to
copying engravings.  Thus the Gallery of Jason and Medea
at Ancy-le-Franc is taken from plates by Leonard Thiry.*
From all these signs it may be understood that, whether
from want of funds or want of readiness to incur an expense which was still only newly in fashion, France was far
from responding, so far as the development of painting
was concerned, to the brilliant example set by the crown.
And so it is to the crown that we must return and confine
ourselves in the main, if this history is to be pursued to
any advantage.

It has not been possible yet to date the works I have
mentioned with the necessary precision.  On the other
hand, we know the moment at which Bouteloup's paintings appeared, though it is true that nothing survives of
them but references to them.  The date was 1556, and
the work consisted in scene-painting.  I have already
mentioned this artist among the portrait-painters of the
period ; but there is nothing surprising in his being

* Mentioned above, p. 117.

GREEKS FEASTING WHILE SACRIFICE IS OFFERED

DRAWING OF THE SCHOOL OF FONTAINEBLEAU.   COLLECTION OF M. MASSON AT AMIENS

bespoken for large compositions, since he had taken some part in the decoration of Fontainebleau. Catherine de Medici engaged him for a tragedy played at Blois.*

A very interesting work of this epoch has happily been preserved, and aptly presents in a convenient form, foreshortened, so to speak, a summary of the second and third rate talents which France produced in historical painting; in some respects an invaluable document on the School of Fontainebleau. I refer to the famous series of the story of Artemisia, dedicated to Queen Catherine de Medici, which may be seen in the Cabinet of Prints in Paris.† The story of this series is a curious one. It is composed solely of pen-drawings, touched with Chinese white, and accompanied by indications of frames in parts only. The drawings number thirty-nine, of which two appear to have been added later. It is true that the Louvre has two others, doubtless taken from the same series, which would bring the total up to the same figure. The idea of the collection was due to a courtier, for whom Artemisia was but a pseudonym for Catherine de Medici; and the intention of the man who bore the expense, as the preface modestly explains, was that some day they might be woven in tapestry. This, in fact, was done, and there are in existence several pieces of a set of hangings of Artemisia executed after this series; all, it is true, very inferior to the composition of the series itself, with which we are concerned here.‡

It is dated 1562, and was ordered, says the preface,

---

* Bouchot: *Les portraits au crayon de la Bibliothèque Nationale*, p. 35.
† Album, Ad 105.
‡ It is minutely described by J. Guiffrey: *Nicolas Houel.—Mémoires de la Société de l'histoire de Paris*, 1889.

"of the first men of Italy, as of France." But there is
no drawing in the whole of the series that can be attributed either to Primaticcio or to Niccolo, who were both
then living.  To begin with, then, nothing more should
be seen in this account of its production than the habitual
exaggeration of such dedications to princes.  One point
at least it decides, that several artists were employed on
the series, which is borne out by the evident difference
of styles, and that some were French, some Italian.  I
will add that one and all were of indifferent ability; the
result being that this work is an accurate representation
of the School of Fontainebleau, in its middle and ordinary
regions, where Italians and French were mingled.

At least one of the latter can possibly be named,
Antoine Caron, whose name appears in an old inscription
on one of the two drawings in the Louvre, and whom
old inventories give as the sole creator of the cartoons for
the Artemisia tapestry.*  M. Reiset reckons thirty-one
out of the thirty-nine drawings as his.  I cannot assent to
so large a number, and believe this artist's part to have
been about equal to those of the rest, who remain unknown, though occasionally of superior merit.  Antoine
Caron came from Beauvais.†  Like so many others, he
had worked on the decorations at Fontainebleau, where
his name appears among the second-rate men before
1550. ‡  Later we find him employed on work which distinguished him further—the restoration of the paintings
in the King's Closet, which was ordered by Primaticcio,
the designer of these paintings, in person, as Director of

* Guiffrey : *Le Mobilier de la Couronne sous Louis XIV.*, pp. 333 *et seq.*
† Laborde : *Renaissance*, p. 789.
‡ *Id., Comptes,* pp. 192, 194.

ARTEMISIA IN BATTLE

ANTOINE CARON.   CABINET DES ESTAMPES, PARIS

the King's Buildings.* The Artemisia series marks a period in his life at which he must have attained to some reputation, but to no excellence, which, indeed, was never to be his. Nevertheless, he must count for something in the history of French painting in the sixteenth century, as being one of the few artists of that country and that age concerning whom we are not reduced to the vaguest of conjecture. He was a contemporary of Jean Cousin, and the acknowledged works of both give precise indications of the level of the national artists in that branch, following those of Geoffroy Dumoûtier, which do the same service for the preceding epoch.

In truth, that level was a very low one, and we have no authority for believing that there were any others who could raise it. In 1557 Pierre Quesnel, whose works are unknown, gave the Augustins of Paris a design for a painted window, which represented the Ascension. He came, strangely enough, from Scotland, whither Maria de Lorraine, the wife of James V., had taken him, and, according to the Abbé de Marolles, presented him to her husband.† Sprung, like Geoffroy Dumoûtier, from a family of portrait-painters, he practised, as Dumoûtier did, historical painting, and no doubt with as little success. No other French artists of the period can be found; so that, from what has just been said, we may judge of the effect produced on the French workmen by the teaching of Fontainebleau in that epoch of 1571, when the death of the great Italian masters left them to their own devices.

Some suspicion of elegance, some rudiments of com-

* *Id., Comptes,* vol. ii. p. 33.

† Reiset: *Catalogue des dessins du Louvre,* part ii. p. 412.

position, and an effort to equal the too lofty models, by which, nevertheless, their restricted and feeble talent was exalted: that is the whole round of these works. The result was a number of drawings, which no doubt looked pleasant enough in windows and hangings, but nothing whatever on the side of painting, which must have greatly excelled the anonymous works in the provinces, the chief of which I have noted.

In that respect the Artemisia series remains a monument of the feebleness of the whole school. Everything is wrong at once, but especially the figure, which displays so much ignorance that there is no room left for even a superficial dexterity. That was the case with nearly all the French artists of the time; Ducerceau himself, whose paintings reveal such perfect mastery of ornament, comes off with no more honour when he attacks figures of a certain size. One only deserves exception in this respect, Etienne Delaune, who was an engraver also, and who, though not belonging to this period and working after the time now before us, heralded, in the correct drawing of his figures, several excellent artists whom we shall meet quite at the end of this history, as ornaments to the reign of Henri IV.

Meanwhile, the soil remained all but barren; a condition that will very likely be attributed to the resistance made by the genius of France to the teachings of Italy. This resistance is by no means mere imagination, and I am quite willing that the idea of it should be retained; but solely on the condition that it is not made a cause of reproach against Italy. It cannot be said that any other kind of painting had flourished in French hands before that date. It is true that François Clouet was just then showing high abilities in another branch of the art; but

ALLEGORY OF RELIGION
ÉTIENNE DELAUNE, LOUVRE

there are other circumstances to be reckoned with in his case, among which the fact that he was the son of a foreigner must not go for nothing. A certain facility in this kind of painting, too, may be added, since several artists of rather more merit than the pupils of Fontainebleau, Frenchmen and the sons of Frenchmen, were revealed in that branch of the art. But composition, allegory, style, offered too many different parts and too many difficulties to be overcome so quickly by a school that was still only in its infancy.

A palpable proof of the justice of these observations may be taken from the history of French sculpture, which, unlike painting, was in an extremely flourishing condition at this period, though completely imbued with the Italian influence. The difference sprang from the prosperity which had not ceased to attend the art since a time before the Renaissance in this country. The Italianisation of sculpture, far from stifling it, was the determining cause of its brilliant progress, which may be sufficiently recalled here by the names of Colombe, Goujon, and Pilon. The two last are the direct outcome of the influence of Fontainebleau, and Pilon is even something of a Primaticcio in sculpture. For Primaticcio's influence stretched out on all sides; and those branches of art in which France was better prepared show how she could respond to teaching such as his.

# CHAPTER IX

WE must now complete the symmetry of our picture of
what has gone before, by returning to François Clouet and
the painters who were partly formed on his style and
distinguished themselves at his side in the last period
of his life.

Catherine de Medici had become mistress of the
kingdom by the death of her husband; and he enjoyed
her favour no less than that of preceding rulers. In
fact, in view of the increasing number and beauty of
his works during his epoch, we are almost tempted to
declare it the apogee of his career. It is remarkable that
though the queen's predilections were entirely in favour of
Italian art, and though she had made the first efforts of
her power to be felt in this domain by the appointment
of an Italian to the direction of the King's Buildings, the

kind of passion she had for portraits, which is amply
attested by the details in her inventory, inclined her
to be equally favourable to the school of which Clouet
was the leader.

We have now reached the date at which the fashion
of having galleries of portraits arranged by series, and
in their proper order, became rife. It seems probable
that Catherine de Medici wished to appear to some
extent in accord with the fashion.

The portraits she possessed * were arranged partly
according to a plan which implies more than a mere
chance arrangement. It reveals some study of symmetry,
and a deliberate design. For instance, portraits composed of two figures, which we find her to have possessed
in considerable numbers, could only be the results of
express orders. This idea is borne out by the portraits
of Charles V. and his wife, Isabella of Portugal, of
Edward VI. and Queen Mary, of Charles VIII. with Anne
of Brittany, of Louis XII. with the Duchess of Ferrara,
and many more of the same kind. There are others, it
is true, which seem to have belonged rather to a family
collection than to a historical gallery, and it will not do
to push our observations too far. But this is certain,
that a like scheme was growing up on all sides. Un-
mistakable signs prove the existence of a taste for acquiring a collection of portraits of the most celebrated
people not only of the time and the country, but of other
times and other peoples, for looking for any authentic
representations and having them copied to equal sizes
so that they might be kept together.

This taste was widely different from that which gave

* See p. 28.

birth to the albums of chalk-drawings made in France. It appears to have come from Italy, which since before 1521 had been filled with the fame of a notable example, the museum of Paolo Giovio.* It is not surprising that an interest so superior in quality to any of this kind that had been seen before, should have found imitators on all sides. We have palpable proofs of it at a later period; and are justified in seeing in the same source the origin of the following signs of it in the epoch now before us.

In 1550 we find Admiral de Coligny sending to England to look for a portrait of King Henri VIII.† Apparently he was forming some collection of this kind. In 1566 Claude Gouffier de Boisy, lord of Oiron, orders of Guillaume Jacquier, professional copyist, portraits of Louise of Savoy, the mother of François I., and of Claude his wife, who had died thirty years before.‡ We know from Gaignières' correspondence § all the ancient portraits, prior even to the sixteenth century,‖

---

* Müntz : *Le Musée des portraits de Paul Jove.—Mémoires de l'Académie des Inscriptions et Belles-Lettres*, 1900. This museum contained at least 240 portraits, collected at great expense from all quarters, and sometimes the work of the most famous masters. All the potentates of Europe might be seen there, to the sultans and the king of Abyssinia, men of letters, popes, &c. Paolo Giovio died in 1552 before completing it to the full extent of his wishes.

† *Archives de l'art français :* Documents, vol. iv. p. 138.

‡ Benjamin Fillon : *L'art de terre chez les Poitevins*, p. 69. Elsewhere we find Jacquier occupied in painting tracings, made by other artists, for the entry of Charles IX. Douet d'Arcq : *Devis et marchés pour l'entrée solennelle de Charles IX. en* 1571.—*Revue Archéologique*, 1849. This time he was painting historical subjects. That he was a general copyist is clearly proved by those two facts.

§ Grandmaison : *Gaignières, ses correspondants et ses collections de portraits.—Bibliothèque de l'École des Chartes*, 1892.

‖ Among others, the famous portrait of Jean le Bon, dating from the

MARY QUEEN OF SCOTS

FRANÇOIS CLOUET.   CABINET DES ESTAMPES, PARIS

that there were at Oiron. Thus in the next reign, that of Charles IX., France was already in possession of great lords who loved portraits, and they were to go on increasing in number day by day, till the end of our history.

A fashion of this kind, while it provided the copyists with bread and butter, could not but be favourable to the production of originals; and we imagine that Catherine de Medici cherished Clouet with all the ardour that she put into the formation of the collections I have mentioned.

After the beginning of the new reign, we find him commissioned for four portraits at least, of which we still have the chalk-drawings. Catherine herself as a widow,* the young king François II.,† his brother Charles IX. in infancy,‡ and Mary Stuart,§ are brilliant signs of this outburst, a magnificent testimony to talents that were constantly improving and a favour that was constantly renewed. Once more a new set of patrons was substituted for the old without disturbance or loss of favour. In both branches of painting, what had been enjoyed before continued to be enjoyed and sought after. The protection of the great was still extended to the masters of Fontainebleau, and at the same time the painters of Flemish blood kept the privilege of delineating the royal features.

The new portrait of Catherine is the one of which history has preserved the memory. It has been copied

fourteenth century, and contemporary with that prince, now in the Bibliothèque de Paris.

* Cabinet of Prints, Paris, Case II., old No. 23.
† Case IV., old No. 22.      ‡ Case II., old No. 25.
§ Case V., old No. 110.

a thousand times and reproduced on all sides; and to it
we owe the idea we have of Catherine and of her face.
That is how we can see her: in widow's weeds, aged about
forty, though her face is still young; already an old hand
in statesmanship, complete mistress of the affairs of a
nation which she was to rule for twenty years, playing
her double *rôle* of Artemisia, inconsolable for the death
of her husband, and directing, to the best of a woman's
ability, the interest of her royal sons. The "Mary
Stuart" is known all over Europe by the copy in
miniature at Windsor, which the inventory of Charles I.
attributed to Janet.

When the young king died, Mary Stuart sat once
more for a portrait in chalks by the master. This is the
portrait in white mourning of which there are so many
different copies. The original painting is lost, but the
drawing is happily preserved near the first in the Bibliothèque de Paris.* To the same date belong the portraits
of the young king, Charles IX., quarter-length, aged
about ten, authentically dated on the drawing and the
picture, of which the painting is at Vienna,† and the
drawing again in the Cabinet of Prints in Paris.‡

Such was François Janet's introduction to the last
reign he was destined to see, and under which he died.
An absolutely unrivalled work made its first year illustrious. I mean a washed chalk-drawing, exhibited in the
Psyche Gallery at the Castle of Chantilly, which represents Marguerite, afterwards Queen of Navarre, at the age

---

* Case V., old No. 25. There are copies of the original painting
in England, at Windsor, and in Scotland, in the National Portrait Gallery,
Edinburgh.

† Museum, No. 628.                 ‡ Case II., old No. 125.

MARGUERITE OF FRANCE, AFTERWARDS WIFE OF HENRY IV.

FRANÇOIS CLOUET.   CHÂTEAU DE CHANTILLY

of six; a work so perfect that we scarcely wish to recover the painting; if, indeed, it is true that there ever was one, and that so perfectly finished a work was not composed for its own sake.

Before long the same princess, at sixteen, was to sit again for a chalk-drawing by Janet;* and the king also, no doubt on the occasion of his marriage with Elizabeth of Austria, which was celebrated in 1570.

That marriage was a great occasion for the exchanging of portraits. We have two of Charles IX. himself, full-length, one copied from another, and of different sizes. The life-size portrait is at Vienna;† the other, which is reduced nearly to the proportions of a miniature, is among the most precious ornaments of the Louvre.‡ It is one of the two works in this museum which are attributed to Janet without reserve. The Vienna portrait has this inscription: *Charles VIIII. très chrestien roy de France en l'aage de XX. ans peinct au vif par Janet.*§

These two examples, both held to be original, and the signature, which is unique in the history of this master, make this portrait the principal work of his career; and since it did not appear till 1569, it holds almost the last place in it. At the same time as a painting now so famous set out from France for Vienna, no doubt Austria, for her part, was despatching the chalk-portraits of

---

* Drawing in the Cabinet of Prints in Paris, Case V., old No. 15.
† Museum, No. 627.   ‡ Catalogue, No. 128.
§ The date 1563 appended to this inscription is obviously false. M. Engerth explains it by a retouching, and restores it as 1569. A portrait so signed is a genuine Janet, and will serve on all occasions as a check in the attribution of other works to him. But it must be remembered that, in the case of these portraits, satisfactory assurance is only to be obtained from the chalks, and that, so far, the drawing of this portrait is missing.

Maximilian II. and his wife, the parents of the young betrothed princess. These drawings are, indeed, in Paris; * and it is noticeable that the style, which is extremely unlike anything that was then being produced in France, proves their foreign origin. No doubt the intention was to have them executed in oils by some French master; for the Maximilian, copied after the crayon with the greatest care, but only an indifferent resemblance, is still to be seen in the Versailles Museum.†

Two years later came the portrait of the new queen, another jewel in the French collection, the pearl of the sixteenth-century room in the Louvre.‡ The preparatory study in chalks of this famous work is in the Cabinet of Prints in Paris, § and marked with a date which fixes its period, 1571. This admirable drawing shows the face only; and it is remarkable that, in completing the painting, Janet made use of the hands in the portrait of Princess Marguerite, mentioned above, which is at Chantilly. Taken thus from two perfect studies, the picture in the Louvre is more perfect yet, and adds the charm of colour without losing any of that peculiar to the original drawings. After this masterpiece, I can add nothing but a so-called Duchesse de Bouillon, which is only known from the drawing,‖ and the excellent last portrait of Charles IX. The painting of the latter is only known from replicas; but there are two examples of the drawing, both from the hand of the master himself, in

---

* Cabinet of Prints, Cases VI., old No. 1, and V., unnumbered.
† Catalogue, No. 3215.       ‡ Catalogue, No. 129.
§ Case III., old No. 120.
‖ Cabinet of Prints in Paris, Case I., old No. 40. There is a copy in the British Museum.

ELIZABETH OF AUSTRIA, QUEEN OF FRANCE

FRANÇOIS CLOUET.  LOUVRE

the Cabinet of Prints in Paris.* Here we see the king,
already ill and melancholy, portrayed with a sureness of
touch and a breadth of execution which prove the un-
ceasing progress which the master was making in his
art. It is his last known work, and the end of the new
period.

So far as the painter's life is concerned, this period is
no fuller of authentic details than the one that preceded
it. We know that he lived in the Rue Ste. Avoye,† in
the Temple quarter, close to the hôtel de Guise. Moreover, a document which some day may prove to be of
great importance‡ shows that in 1568 he was under the
protection of Claude Gouffier de Boisy, whom I have
mentioned above, and his then wife, Claude de Beaune.
Both were famous for the number of marriages they suc-
cessively contracted.

What I have said of the husband, and the place he
held among the great lords and patrons of art of the
time, shows his protection must be held to have been of
some importance in the life of a man like Janet.§ It is
possible that his portrait in the Versailles Museum ‖ was
copied from some original by Janet; but I hold that of
his wife in the Louvre ¶ to be his beyond question. It is
an admirable piece of work, and the Louvre does not

---

* Case XII., old Nos. 27 and 28.

† *Nouvelles Archives de l'art français*, vol. ix. p. 77.

‡ *Revue de l'art français ancien et moderne*, 1891, p. 144.

§ This document proves it, by the gift of 450 livres a year to François
Clouet from the de Boisys, out of a yearly sum of 4200 livres paid to the
lady by the town of Paris.

‖ Catalogue, No. 3225.

¶ Catalogue, No. 1026. Gaignières, who owned it, wrote on the back :
"Original by Janet." The drawing is at Chantilly, Case XVI., No. 388.

seem to be aware of its importance, for the catalogues
place it among a crowd of anonymous works, though
it is one of the portraits in which the manner we take
to be that of François Janet is most pronounced, no
less in the painting of the face than of the clothes and
accessories.

Another important episode in the life of this painter
was the taking of his opinion in 1571 on the likeness
to the king of a portrait struck by the mint.  We have
the text of the deliberation,* which shows that Janet was
"summoned to the office of the Court of the Mint" at
the same time as Claude de Héry, Graver-General, and
declared himself satisfied with the new coin.

Several writers have made out from this that Janet
was controller-general of the king's coinage; but the
document does not say so, and it was merely a case of
a single day's engagement.   Still, it serves to confirm
the fact that these painters of small portraits found
themselves credited with competence to deal with any
matter where it was a question of a likeness.   This commission on the matter of the coinage should be combined
with another that was entrusted to Janet, that of mould-
ing the faces of the two kings after death, for their
funeral ceremonies.

This consideration allows us to penetrate the contemporary idea on these subjects.   One other must be added,
which is more difficult to understand, the employment of
the same men on trifling works which are now entrusted
to the commonest artisans.   We have seen an example
of this before, in the coffer which François Janet was

* Laborde : *Renaissance des arts à la cour de France,* p. 583.

CLAUDE DE BEAUNE, DAME DE BOISY

FRANÇOIS CLOUET.   LOUVRE

charged to paint with the device of Henri II.* Once
again, in 1570, we find him mentioned † as simply painting two trumpet-banners for the king's stables, and a coat
of arms for a pursuivant. He had merely to decorate
these different objects with fleurs-de-lis.

After this, we shall not be surprised to learn that, as
we suspected of his father, the younger Janet painted
miniatures. Formal proof of this is found in the mention
of a payment ‡ for a "portrait of the queen which he
painted in a little plate of gold." Unfortunately the
work is lost, though the discoverer of the document believed that he had found it in a miniature in the imperial
collections at Vienna, which represents Catherine de Medici.
But he has evidently forgotten that in 1572, the authentic
date of the commission, another queen was reigning, and
Catherine de Medici could only be called the queen-
mother.§ What is really to be discovered is a portrait
in miniature of Elizabeth of Austria, which would probably be found to be taken from the same chalk-drawing
as the oil-painting in the Louvre.

Meanwhile, in expectation of the day when all these
questions shall be settled and all these toothing-stones
find their places in a more complete edifice, I should like
to enumerate here the works which I regard as Janet's,
on the same evidence as those previously mentioned.
They are, the portraits of Anne d'Este, Duchesse de
Guise, ‖ at Versailles; and that of Jeanne d'Albret.¶

* See p. 140.                    † Laborde : *op. cit.*, p. 121.

‡ Printed by M. Mazerolle : *Miniatures de François Clouet au trésor
imperial de Vienne.—Revue de l'art chrétien*, 1889.

§ The author adds that Catherine was of far more importance in the
State than her daughter-in-law ; but that does not alter the case.

‖ Catalogue, No. 3212.             ¶ No. 254.

Both should be detached from the promiscuous crowd of works so prodigally attributed on all sides to François Clouet, without regard to the study of the chalk-drawings, which are the source of far more precise conclusions than any that can be drawn from the paintings. After giving this list, which is composed of picked works, nothing remains but to draw from it as just an idea as possible of the master's talent.

François Janet died on the 22nd September 1572, shortly after the massacre of St. Bartholomew.* M. Bouchot believes that he was a Protestant, and that he died of the terror caused by the events of that day. As a matter of fact, however, his will contains a declaration of the Catholic faith, though perhaps it may merely be ascribed to the fear of persecution. But this is no proof of M. Bouchot's statement, nor any convincing reason for believing it. With François Clouet came the end of the glorious days of portrait-painting which France had received from his father, and the close on all sides at once of the period of the great influence on painting of the French Renaissance.

Let us add without hesitation that in a more restricted way, it is true, and with more confined means, the gift of the Clouets to the nation was no less precious a gift in its way than that of the Italians of Fontainebleau. With them came the foundation of a school of portrait-painting, which, though afterwards taken up anew under other responsibility in the same way as the great art of historical painting, none the less marks the origin of the whole of a famous current of French art. The results in both cases

* *Revue de l'art français*, vol. i. p. 117.

alike owed their importance to the long reign of the masters from which the two branches started. The Clouets, no more than Primaticcio, left any one the legacy of their authority; but they maintained it for nearly half a century, and we cannot be surprised if the school they founded blossomed anew over their graves.

The master we have just spoken of left it in the right road, instructed both by precept and example how to win from history a rare renown.

The second Janet excelled the first considerably in science. His drawing in reality is extremely profound, and as exactly calculated as any known. In tracing the human face and all the parts presented by the model, he has the ability of a specialist, whose long practice of an art that is deep rather than wide has enabled him to accumulate a mass of information and experience. He reaches perfection in the proportion of the features, in the exact placing of all the fine fugitive, mobile parts of the face, in the careful study of the extremely subtle relations from which the mass of form draws its solidity, and in skill in constructing the unity of impression of a face and of a type. He has nothing of the captivating boldness, the seductive brilliance professedly sought by Italy. To bring in Holbein once more, Janet has nothing of his beauty of style, and he offers no better comparison with painters like Moro, Adriaan Key, or Pourbus—Pieter Pourbus, that is, the first of the family, who was born at Gouda. For while he lacks the Italian grace, he is equally without the joy and solidity of the Flemings. It is among the Flemings, however, that we must look for resemblances to his work, if we wish to understand his qualities. For

example, he must be ranked high above a Schoorel or a
Marten de Vos, in spite of the fact that he uses much the
same *pâte* as they, though it is drier and smoother in the
case of the French master. The fact is, that the correct-
ness of his drawings endows all his work with a power
which, though less fitted to dazzle, is capable of giving a
more lasting satisfaction to the taste. We come back to
him again and again to learn the form of a thing so
complicated in a small space, and so interesting in its
commonness, as the human face. With very little fascination and a beauty that only reveals itself upon analysis,
Janet is one of the painters we are least prone to become
tired of. Attentive examination will even discover har-
monious qualities in his colour. The features of the face
are lightly touched, the lips are well folded, in the best of
his portraits the edge and shading of the eyelids are put
in without dryness; in the portrait of Queen Elizabeth of
Austria the hands are perfect marvels of pleasant and
delicate execution; and throughout his work the accessories, the folds of the garments and the feathers, are
copied with considerable charm, and the jewels touched
in with deliberate care and some art. All these details,
in short, inferior though they are to what the greatest
masters can show, are nevertheless clear signs of a serious
element in his genius, of vigorous penetration and intelligent study, which have won for him a special place with
heedless posterity. They offer a rare, though not unique,
example of an art that is deeper than it appears to be,
an art from which the extreme of painstaking has not
banished its innate ability.

At the opposite end of France, we must remember,
Corneille de Lyon was pursuing his career. This was

the date of that famous journey, of which Brantôme reports that Catherine de Medici found her own portrait in his house dressed in the fashion of years before.* Her three daughters were there too: the Duc de Nemours looked at them, as she did; but we do not hear that the duke or the queen or any one of the party had recourse on this occasion to the painter's skill. However, in that same year, Corneille and his wife received a donation from the king.† Five years later, in 1569, we find Corneille, as we find all the Huguenots of Lyons, abjuring the Protestant religion with his wife, his daughter and servants.‡ Finally his name appears in the registers of his native town up till 1574, and his death must have occurred soon after. Thus he quits the scene almost at the same time as the second Janet, whose popularity he had shared. He left a son, named Corneille like himself, and a daughter who, according to Vauprivas, "painted divinely well." We know nothing of the results of this gift; but to go no further than Martellange, another Lyons painter, whose name is found on a small contemporary portrait in the museum at Versailles,§ we can only form a low estimate of the school that grew round Corneille in Lyons. I shall not refer to it further.

The younger Janet never married, and left only natural daughters, who later became nuns; ‖ but a son of his sister Catherine, the wife of one Abel Foulon,¶ sur-

* See above, p. 132.
† *Archives de l'art français*, vol. v. p. 142.
‡ Weale: *Le peintre Cornelis Vander Cappelle.—Revue de l'art chrétien*, 1899.
§ Catalogue, No. 3269.
‖ See the document cited, p. 34, note ‖.
¶ The same document.

vived him and carried on his art. M. Laborde wrongly
imagined that the young Foulon, who used his Christian
name of Benjamin, was the son of a certain Pierre Foulon
of Antwerp who painted for Claude de Boisy. I believe
Abel Foulon to be the same as a poet and mathematician,
groom of the chamber to Henri II., whose name appears
in Lacroix du Maine's dictionary.* He would have been
the son-in-law of the elder Janet, and died in 1563, so
that Benjamin Foulon, who is not mentioned before
the year 1577, was early entrusted to the care of his
uncle, and brought up in the same profession. It is
not the time yet to speak of this artist, whose career
comes a little later. Others who flourished in the last
year of Francois Clouet claim our attention for the
present.

I need do no more than mention Bouteloup and
Etienne Dumoûtier, who so far are no more than
names; but the Protestant, Marc Duval, who is usually
left out of *résumés* of this kind, deserves important
notice.

Lacroix du Maine † says that he was a native of Mans
and lived in Paris. He was known as Le Sourd, and also
as Bertin, which was the name of his step-father. He
was an engraver and a painter in oils, and Van Mander
states that the famous Flemish painter Spranger worked
under him.‡ The same author adds that Marc Duval
had been a pupil of Clovio. The best known of his works
is the engraving called "The Three Colignys," which

* *Bibliothèque française.*                                    † *Op. cit.*
‡ *Le Livre des peintres*, Hymans' edition, vol. ii. p. 126. Van Mander
does not definitely name Duval. He says : "The painter of the queen-
mother, a good miniaturist, named Marc." I follow Hymans for the
interpretation.

THE THREE COLIGNYS

ORIGINAL DRAWING BY MARC DUVAL.  CABINET DES ESTAMPES, PARIS

represents the three brothers, Admiral Coligny, Dandelot, and the Cardinal de Châtillon, standing close to one another in a landscape.

This print is dated 1579. Forgeries of it were scattered all over the Protestant countries, and great paintings were taken from it, one of which is in the museum at the Hague, another in Lord Sackville's collection at Knole. A bad chalk copy, touched, is shown at Chantilly, and the original drawing is in the Cabinet of Prints in Paris.* As I see no reason against assigning this drawing to Marc Duval, the engraver of the plate, I think too that a head of Coligny, a study for this drawing, also in the Cabinet of Prints,† must also be his work. If this example may be taken as a type and model, I know of several others in the same place from which I can reconstitute the work of the artist I presume to be Marc Duval. To him belong, among others, a chalk-drawing of Antoine, King of Navarre, which is at Chantilly.‡ The manner is firm and backed by some science, but gives little enjoyment.

A contemporary of his was Georges Vénitien, mentioned in the memoirs of De Thou,§ whose portrait he painted at the age of seven years. Mariette identifies this painter with a Georges Bombare, a Fleming, made known to us by some manuscript notes.|| It seems true,

* Hennin Collection, vol. vii. fol. 52.

† Case II., old No. 49.

‡ Shown in the Psyche Gallery.

§ Michaud and Poujoulat's edition, p. 272, col. 1.

|| *Abécédario*, vol. i. p. 152. The notes quoted by Mariette do not appear very trustworthy. But the existence of Bombare, at least, is no invention. There is a portrait of him, with his name and calling, in the Cabinet of Prints in Paris (Album Na 21, fol. 108). M. Bouchot believes

at any rate, that he is the same with a master named Georges, painter to the Cardinal de Lorraine, a portrait by whom is still in the museum at Rheims,* for Georges Vénitien was painter to the Cardinal according to De Thou. The catalogue of the Rheims museum goes further, and states that this master Georges is no other than Georges Boba, a pupil of Frans Floris who is mentioned by Van Mander.† It would follow from this that all we know of Boba must apply to Georges Vénitien. I cannot go quite so far as that, and am content to identify the latter with the Georges of the Rheims museum, and to attribute to him, besides the portrait mentioned above, a lost portrait of the Cardinal de Lorraine, of which there are three copies in the town. The same Georges, again, was painter to Renée de Lorraine, the Cardinal's sister and abbess of St. Pierre-les-Dames. We know nothing more of this master.

Still less is known of the unnamed artist of a now famous collection, on which I regret my inability to agree with the learned keeper of the Cabinet of Prints in Paris, M. Bouchot. I refer to the chalk-drawings, at present dispersed from a single album, which was bought a century ago for this famous collection from a certain M. Lecurieux, and which therefore I shall style simply the Lecurieux album.‡

him to have been an Englishman of the name of Bunbury, but assigns no reasons.

* Catalogue, No. 8, signed *Me Georges pinxit anno* 1593. The portrait is believed to be that of P. C. Clicquot, Master of Bombardiers at Rheims.

† *Op. cit.*, vol. i. p. 349. Boba is also known by some print in the style of Fontainebleau, signed with a monogram made up of the four letters of his name.

‡ Now separated ; the fragments have been mounted and put in cases.

It consisted of fifty-six parts, thirty-eight of which, recognisable as the work of a single hand, were of superior merit to the rest. M. de Laborde was the first to discover that one of the remaining eighteen had a signature, that of one *Fulonius*, who was quickly seen to be the same as Benjamin Foulon, Clouet's nephew. The portrait so signed is that of an infant prince, César, Duc de Vendôme, the son of Henri IV. and the fair Gabrielle. Now there was no doubt that among these eighteen there were several works by the same Foulon, of exactly similar execution to this portrait of César de Vendôme. So much had been discovered, when M. Bouchot took the matter up. It is well that it should be known, outside the borders of France, how much this learned authority, who is as conscientious as he is acute, has done for the progress of the studies we are now following. His is the honour, if not of actually creating them, of having so directed them that those who come after him have only to prosecute these studies on the same lines, to see them go forward of their own accord. The knowledge and classification of French portraits in chalk is entirely due to him; and only those who follow faithfully in the track of his labours, which are the determination of the whole science, can hope to make a step forward. Now the advance which he has won for it is due to one thing only, his constant care to direct it towards one chief end, the establishment of a series of works that can be ascribed with certainty to the first and second of the Clouets. Around that object, which was carefully thought out at the start, are grouped all the classifications and all the discoveries which the science has received from his hands. Struck by the inadequacy of the proofs adduced on this subject, he became possessed with the design of finding other and firmly-based evidence, drawn from some palpable circumstance. Such a circumstance as the existence of several authentic works by Foulon * in a series which contained a number of others from a more able hand, seemed to be exactly what was needed to bring his task to completion. From that M. Bouchot infers that the better among these drawings were the work of François Clouet; that they covered several pages of an album, the remainder of which were blank when this artist died; and that, when the album so compiled had descended to his nephew Foulon, he filled the empty spaces with his own drawings, and even added to those he had inherited the names of the sitters they represented. For M. Bouchot, who is an expert in Benjamin Foulon's handwriting, knows that the names of the sitters are in his hand. Everything in the scheme seems natural, on condition that the album, which the nephew completed and annotated, is attributed to the uncle. And so we have found the desired presumption that will help us to attribute to Clouet something more than hypothetical works.

The great obstacle, however, to accepting it is the sensible difference revealed by examination between the chalk-drawings in the Lecurieux album and those commonly attributed to Janet. The drawing of Catherine de Medici, that of François II., the two of Mary Stuart, the Marguerite in infancy at Chantilly and the rest, make up a family of works uniform in manner and absolutely

---

* M. Bouchot has pushed to its furthest extent his strictness of identification between Fulonius, the signatory of the drawing, and the Foulon we find in the documents. *Les portraits au crayon de la Bibliothèque Nationale*, p. 49.

DUGAST

ANONYMOUS ARTIST OF THE "RECUEIL LÉCURIEUX"
CABINET DES ESTAMPES, PARIS

alike, which M. Bouchot still leaves to François Clouet.
But I am convinced that we must choose between the two.
There is no absolutely certain evidence to compel us to
assign these works to him, nor the Elizabeth of Austria
or the Charles IX. in the Louvre that go with them ; and
perhaps there is no objection to preferring the probabilities opened up by the palpable circumstance of Foulon's
annotations to general likelihood and universal tradition ;
but by no possibility can the two be combined.   To look
first at the merit of the work alone, it is certain that
the Lecurieux album is far inferior to the drawings elsewhere which are presumed to be Janet's.   They have
not the sureness of drawing, nor the knowledge of the
difficult features, nor the sound execution of the drapery
and jewels which are so admirable in these latter.   The
drawing is weak, the bony structure uncertain, the perspective of the face sometimes ridiculous; in the three-
quarter faces the farther eye is always very badly drawn,
the delicate anatomy of the eyelids is lost, the hair is
badly planted and hatched in with little strokes which are
meant to be clever, but which are here stiff and mechanical
and there go flying wildly anywhere, and so succeed in
giving the impression of self-conscious ignorance and
sterile painstaking.   Add the minute care with which the
details of costume and the jewels are represented, like the
illustrations in a catalogue, without the least idea of
nature, the vague and unpleasant tone of all the shadows,
the trivial and sometimes execrable lightening of all the
eyeballs, and you have a summary of the most remarkable
features that distinguish the chalk - drawings in the
Lecurieux album from the works which were previously
ascribed to Janet.   I suspect, however, that M. Bouchot

realised something of the sort, when he affirms that François Clouet detracted from the quality of his best portraits by excess of work upon them, and when, in comparing them with his father, he holds the balance even by giving the elder Janet what these Lecurieux drawings certainly have not, simplicity and a pleasant effect.

But, in point of fact, why should the annotation by Foulon be considered as evidence that the drawings are François Clouet's? It is true that M. Bouchot does not give it as a proof, but is it so much as a presumption? In the first place, besides the drawings of the nephew, the album does not contain only those which this theory presumes to be the uncle's. Then whence comes that third or that fourth hand, which M. Bouchot has not failed to distinguish, and which may equally be considered to be certificated by Foulon's notes?

Their presence is sufficient to destroy the most alluring part of the hypothesis of a family album, which could have contained nothing besides the drawings of the great master except those of his heir. Again, there is nothing to prove that the series was originally one, and not bound together later. In the latter case, we have nothing left but some chalk-drawings by different hands, which belonged, it is true, to Foulon, who added his observations; but why must we suppose that the works of his uncle make up the principal item in what survives of this painter's collection? Finally, to cut short this already lengthy discussion, I believe the evidence that these drawings cannot be François Clouet's to amount to proof positive. In one of them, in fact, which bears the name of Mme. Forget-Dufresne,* the head-dress is in a style which I find

* Case III., old No. 56.

was never used before 1575, or 1574, when this painter was
dead ; and a chalk portrait of a woman in the Louvre,*
obviously by the same hand as these drawings, is dated
by the dress she wears at about twenty years later.

And therefore we must keep the artist of all these
works separate from Janet, under the title of the unknown artist of the Lecurieux album, till the day comes
when some discovery will enable us to restore his real
name.

The thirty-eight drawings just mentioned, together
with several others in the Cabinet of Prints and in the
Louvre, make him up a large body of work, on which we
may judge his qualities. I will add two pictures in the
Louvre, one of a woman unknown,† which answers to
a drawing of his,‡ and the other representing Diane
d'Angoulême, natural daughter of Henri II.§ Two
miniatures at Hertford House are also in all probability
his. One is an exact reproduction of the so-called
" Duc de Retz " in the Lecurieux album ;‖ the other is a
woman whom I cannot identify.

What I have said above will relieve me from the
necessity of entering a second time on a lengthy criticism
of the powers of this unknown artist. All I need do
is to correct the unfavourable portions of it by acknow-
ledging the presence in all these portraits of a certain
generally pleasant quality, a finesse and charm which
conceal the secret flaws, and in one or two happier efforts
imitate a master-piece so well as to deceive even eyes

---

* Exhibited, No. 1369.              † Catalogue, No. 1027.
‡ Cabinet of Prints, Paris, album Na 23a, old No. 102.
§ Catalogue, No. 1024.
‖ Case VI., old No. 11.

forewarned by the observation of glaring inequalities and mistakes that are little short of abominable.

It only remains now to say a word on certain Flemings, visitors and even residents in France at that time, who are known to have practised portrait-painting, and therefore may have contributed to this country's output in that art.

First comes Cornelis Ketel and Hieronymus Franck, whom Van Mander * notes as being in France in 1566; Ambroise Francken or Franck, brother of the latter, whose name is found in several French documents † in 1567; and lastly Lucas de Heere, a native of Ghent, who again, according to Van Mander,‡ worked for Catherine de Medici between 1559 and 1565. All these artists painted history, and there is nothing to prove that during the time, in some cases short, which they spent in France, they had occasion to paint any portraits. Still it was necessary to give their names, in order to complete the picture of the epoch, and enable my readers to see the exact state in which France was found at the death of François Janet.

The painters whose names have appeared in this chapter were then in full activity; and the list of them alone is enough to show that the court, in default of the one great master, was in no lack of artists. They were to give birth to an imitation, as it were the small change, of the precious treasure that had just been lost.

---

* *Op. cit.*, vol. ii. p. 147.     † Laborde : *Renaissance*, p. 927.

‡ *Op. cit.*, vol. ii. p. 2. The date is taken from two facts : first, that he married on his return from France, and that he was married in 1565; secondly, that he put the date 1559 on his picture of the Queen of Sheba, which he painted, and which may still be seen, at Ghent.

# CHAPTER X

THE twenty years that elapsed between the Massacre of St. Bartholomew and the conversion of Henri IV. in 1593 formed one of the most troublous periods, and the most notorious for disasters of all kinds, that France had ever known. The disorder spread throughout the country by the religious wars, and the daily increasing troubles which ended in driving the king from Paris and installing in his place the Estates of the League, are matters of common knowledge. But at least the consummation of this anarchy marked the period of the worst of these calamities. The complete downfall of power was followed in a few years by the re-establishment of authority in the person of Henri IV. Only a short time was needed to restore order and bring back into the minds of all a calm which heralded a new century, the century which was to be the most wonderful in every way that the country had ever seen.

We must embark now on the history of those twenty
years from the point of view of the arts.  The period is
the least brilliant of all, as much obscured by the lack
of documents as it was hampered by the violence of the
times.  Nevertheless it contains several signs of a very
sure vitality, and of a persistent production which was
occupied, during this momentary eclipse, in preparing an
honourable revenge.

Niccolo died, as I have said, in 1571; and there were
no Italians of any importance left in the king's service
except his son, Giulio Camillo, and Roger de Rogery.
To these we must add Cristoforo, also called dell' Abbate
or Labbé, who was probably, like the first named, a
relative of Niccolo.*

Giulio Camillo was certainly in France from 1561
onward,† already married and a father, and of full age
to exercise his powers.  It is true that we only find him
in the *Comptes des Bâtiments* between 1568 and 1570‡;
but other documents mention him at a later date, and it
is almost certain that he was employed on the schemes
of painting which the court continued to carry out.
Unhappily, the remnant of the "Accounts of the Buildings"
which has survived goes no further than 1570, and after
that date we enter upon a profound obscurity, which a

---

* M. de Laborde regards him as his second son, on what evidence I
cannot tell.  He adds a third, under the name of Camillo, whom, for my
own part, I believe to be the same as Giulio Camillo.

† Laborde: *La Renaissance des arts à la cour de France*, p. 671.
The first time he is mentioned he is stated to be dead, but the later
references to him make it obvious that this was a mistake.  M. de Laborde
adds, on what evidence I know not, that he was in France at the same
time as his father.

‡ Edited by Laborde, vol. ii. p. 179.

few side-lights from other sources only enable us to pierce here and there.

One thing is certain, that on his father's death, when the succession to Primaticcio was, as it were, divided, Giulio Camillo dell' Abbate inherited the direction and superintendence of the paintings of Fontainebleau, with a salary of 300 livres.* Later he drew 400,† from which we conclude that he took a high place. A last mention of this painter, at the date of 1577,‡ proves that he lived longer than has been supposed § and into the reign of Henri III. These few facts are the sum of our information about the son and successor of Niccolo.

Cristoforo dell' Abbate worked for the king from 1560,‖ and we meet him again more than twenty years later, still living in 1585.¶ His talent, no doubt, was exercised throughout that period, but for what reward, and on what kind of work, we have no means of knowing.

We are a little better informed about Roger de Rogery. I have given his dates above, and have said that he was alive during the lifetime of Primaticcio. The period now before us is the right one, I think, to which to ascribe what seems to have been his greatest work—the decoration of a room in the Pavilion des Poèles at Fontainebleau, on the same floor as, and adjoining, the hall which Rosso had decorated in times gone

* Jal : *Dictionnaire critique de biographie et d'histoire,* p. 11.
† Thoison : *Notes et documents sur quelques artistes se rattachant au Gatinais.—Société des Beaux-Arts des Départements,* 1900.
‡ *Nouvelles Archives de l'art français,* 1876, p. 27.
§ Among others, Jal, *op. cit.* On his misreading, see Thoison, *op. cit.*
‖ Laborde : *Comptes,* vol. ii. p. 58.
¶ *Revue de l'art français,* 1885, p. 86.

by.  Father Dan * and C. del Pozzo † have both described
these paintings.  They represented the story of Hercules
in thirteen pictures, the subjects being as follows: Hercules at table with Deianira; Hercules discharging an
arrow at the centaur Nessus; the centaur wounded to
death; Deianira receiving the shirt from Nessus; Deianira sending the shirt to Hercules; Hercules receiving
the shirt; Hercules vainly attempting to cast off the
fatal gift; Hercules on the funeral pile; Hercules slaying
the dragon that guarded the garden of the Hesperides;
Hercules haling Cerberus out of Hades; Hercules carrying off Proserpine; Hercules surprising a satyr who
thought to deceive him, taking him for Deianira; the
satyr punished by Hercules.  Nothing remains of these
works, which were effaced in various restorations even
before the pavilion which contained them was pulled
down ‡; but the importance of the commission shows in
general that Rogery was much esteemed at the court of
the King of France, and assigns him a place of no small
importance in the period we are now reviewing.

He had, like Camillo dell' Abbate, a pension of 400
livres, increased after 1577 § to 600.  In 1582 we find
that he had succeeded him in the superintendence of the
paintings at Fontainebleau.‖  Even during Primaticcio's
lifetime he had been in charge of works of some import-

* *Le Trésor des Merveilles de la maison royale de Fontainebleau*,
p. 130.

† *Diarium*, published by Müntz: *Mémoires de la Société de l'histoire
de Paris*, 1886.  Del Pozzo ascribed them to Dubreuil; but we can hardly
accept this theory in the face of the testimony of Father Dan.

‡ Guilbert, who describes the castle before the destruction of this
pavilion, takes his account of them (in 1731) from Father Dan.

§ Jal, *op. cit.*, p. 1095.                    ‖ Thoison, *op. cit.*

ance at Fontainebleau and St.-Germain-en-Laye.* After this epoch, in 1581, he was still working for the queen-mother, no doubt in the hôtel de Soissons.†

Meanwhile, Antoine Caron, safe thenceforth from comparison with the most illustrious of all these artists, continued to advance in the royal commands. In 1573 we find him combined with Germain Pilon in the management of the fêtes at the entry of Henri III., King-elect of Poland, into Paris.‡ His importance increased during this period, less, perhaps, as an effect of his ability than of certain family connections which he contracted. He had married his three daughters to three men of importance in the world of art of the day, more celebrated now for their engravings than many other artists for their paintings; certainly in the case of the first two, Thomas de Leu and Léonard Gautier. The third, Pierre Gourdelle, is far from sharing their celebrity. Caron and his three sons-in-law appear to have composed a solid and resisting body in the midst of the artists of the time, which was strengthened by a very definite political attitude. All four were on the side of the League, and therefore opposed to all the Protestant artists we have spoken of.

We know that Thomas de Leu was primarily celebrated as an engraver of portraits. May we believe that Caron snatched a moment or two from historical painting, in order to furnish him with models for this kind of work? The fact is, that Thomas engraved the portrait of his father-in-law himself, after a chalk-drawing now

* Laborde: *Comptes*, vol. ii. pp. 3, 69, 96.
† Jal, *ut sup.*
‡ Laborde: *Renaissance*, p. 790.

in the Cabinet in Paris,* the style of which is so markedly
superior to that of the rest, that it might well be the
work of Caron himself. It must be noted also, that in
the Pinakothek at Munich there is a portrait in the
French manner, dated 1577,† which is signed with the
monogram A.C., possibly the signature of our Caron.

Another painter of the day is Henri Lerambert,
doubtless a member of a family of sculptors who flourished
from this time until the reign of Louis XIV. We find
him at Fontainebleau in 1568,‡ occupied on the King's
Closet. After that, history is dumb concerning him,
until he reappears later. Pierre Quesnel and Cousin
were still living, and must not be omitted from our
sketch of this epoch.

Charles IX. died in 1574, two years before the
Massacre of St. Bartholomew, and his brother, Henri III.,
returned from Poland to succeed him.

This is not the place to discuss the shameful life and
the extravagances of this monarch; but we are compelled
to point out that a taste for the arts had a place in his
extraordinary nature. A feature of the commencement
of his reign was a unique circumstance in this long story
of the French Renaissance, his passing through Venice on
his return from Warsaw. Henri III. was the first of all
the kings of France, and in general of all who were to
have any influence on the arts in this country, to be
acquainted with the magnificent school maintained in the

---

* Album Na 21a, fol. 129.

† No. 1316, lithographed by Strixner. M. Gustave Gluck proposes
the attribution to Caron. The suggestion of the Museum Catalogue, that
it is the work of Adrien Crabeth, who died in 1554, cannot be entertained.

‡ Laborde: *Comptes*, vol. ii. p. 179.

city of the Doges. That the spectacle did not leave him
indifferent is proved by an authentic document. Actually
while he was in Venice, he ordered of Tintoretto three
pictures at fifty crowns.* It would be pleasant to be
able to reinforce this episode with others of the same
significance, that might enlighten us on this king's ideas
upon this subject, and on the influence which possibly he
exercised upon the arts. He was the first of the Valois
since Henri II. from whom something of the sort might
have been expected. His two elder brothers were too
young or too sickly ever to have had the time to bestow
on the arts, and their mother's initiative in these matters
was paramount throughout their reigns. With Henri III.
it was different; but unhappily our knowledge is very
fragmentary, and apt only for general reflections.

One of the objects of his patronage was Jacques
Patin, known to amateurs of prints by his drawings of
the celebration of the marriage of the Duc de Joyeuse,
the king's brother-in-law, in 1581. The engravings of
these drawings give an interesting picture of the mythological masquerades of the time. He held the position
of painter to the king, to which he added a more
singular title, that of painter to the king's stables.†
We have seen François Janet employed on work which
implied that he held the same post. In the same way
Patin painted, in 1577, some escutcheons,‡ which must
have been connected with this strange office. He was
at work from 1567 onwards; and the authentic accounts

---

* *Revue de l'art français*, 1888, p. 116.
  † Roman : *Dépouillement du Registre des requêtes présentées au roi de
France en* 1586 *et* 1587.—*Société des Beaux-Arts des Départements*, 1885.
  ‡ *Nouvelles Archives de l'art français*, 1876, p. 26.

mention that he had left examples of his art at the Château du Louvre, at the Cordeliers in Paris, and at the Château de Bois in the Vincennes.* I cannot say where another writer † came upon the mention of still further works of his, painted at Chaillot for the queen-mother. Of all the list nothing has survived.

As the reign of Henri III. advanced, new historical painters made their presence known in various ways, and renewed the aspect of the epoch. The Italians I have named above were joined, after 1585, by two others. One is a certain Giacomo Romano, who is said to be " engaged by his majesty," ‡ and of whom we know no more. M. Roman wishes to identify this painter with Jacopo Rocca of Rome, who was a pupil of Daniele da Volterra; but the reasons he gives are feeble, and, if none better are forthcoming, it is wiser to wait for further information. The other Italian I referred to may perhaps be called upon, some day or other, to take a place of very considerable importance in the history we are now pursuing.

The man I mean is Jean Labbé, that is to say, Giovanni dell' Abbate, who was unknown to M. de Laborde, and so is missing from his genealogical sketch of the family. We find him mentioned in documents of very little interest, but, at least, they establish a relationship between him and the Cristoforo mentioned above, the presumed son of Niccolo. We find him a father two years running during this epoch; and this fact, combined with the lack of any previous mention of him, seems to

* *Nouvelles Archives de l'art français*, 1876, p. 26.
† Müntz: *La peinture française*, vol. i. p. 268.
‡ Roman, *op. cit.*

SCENE FROM THE LIFE OF ST. BARTHOLOMEW

UNKNOWN MASTER.   CABINET DES ESTAMPES, PARIS

imply that he was then young, and only at the outset of his career. His two children were born in 1585 and 1586.* To add one more hypothesis to several already suggested, I take this Jean Labbé to be a son of Cristoforo, whom we find to have been already married in 1567, and the father of an eldest son who died about that time.† What leads me to dwell in this manner on Jean Labbé is the existence among the surviving drawings of that time, and dating from the very end of the century, of a large number of works by a clever hand, in which the imitation of Niccolo is extraordinarily evident. The quality is much lower; but the style is so obviously a heritage from Niccolo that now and then there is a risk of confusion between the two. I do not allege this as an absolute proof; but there is nothing surprising in my making use of it to connect these works with the name of Jean Labbé, who was possibly their creator.

These drawings are all done with the pen, and touched, sometimes with bistre and more rarely with violet. The artist, so far anonymous, owes a certain celebrity to a collected series, now in the Cabinet of Prints in Paris,‡ which represents the life of St. Bartholomew in several scenes. The suite is after the manner of the Artemisia series, and is accompanied by designs for frames; it may perhaps have served for tapestry, though the frames are no proof of this. The drawings show little serious art, but a great display of cleverness. The same collections contain others by the same hand, wrongly ascribed by the Cabinet to Lerambert, which represent scenes from the Old and New Testaments.§

\* *Revue de l'art français*, 1885, p. 86.     † *Ibid.*
‡ Album Ad 103.                                § Album B 5.

Finally, the picture of the Italian and French historical painters under Henri III. will be completed by the mention of an artist of whom several authentic drawings have recently been discovered.* They consist of eight parts in a single suite, representing the Tournament of Sandricourt, which was held in 1494 under Charles VIII., King of France. Two of these are signed Baullery. The style declares them to be sixteenth century work, and therefore we may identify this Baullery with Jérôme Bollery, father of a certain Nicolas Bollery,† who was the uncle of the painter Jacques Blanchard.

Jérôme Bollery was settled in Paris and practising his craft of painter in the year 1561.‡ We find him there also in 1586.§ Félibien ‖ gives his name, but without mentioning any works of this period that could be attributed to him. His biography is still to be written. But we are more fortunate in his case than in the case of several other artists, of whom we have fuller details, in being henceforth able to some extent to judge of his powers, very ordinary as they were, from his works.

Such, then, was the state of historical painting throughout the reign of Henri III., according to the faint picture which the extant evidence allows us to draw. Such were the masters, mediocre indeed according to what we know of their works, whom the history of the

---

\* By M. Jean Guiffrey, assistant conservator of the Louvre, Nos. 23,703 to 23,710.

† The relationship is shown by Jal: *op. cit.*, p. 243.

‡ *Revue de l'art français*, 1886, p. 309.

§ Herluison: *Actes d'état civil d'artistes français*, p. 42.

‖ *Entretien sur la vie et les ouvrages des plus fameux peintres*, 4to edition, vol. i. p. 713. For Van Mander's account of a Bollery whose Christian name he does not give, see below, p. 282.

THE TOURNAMENT OF SANDRICOURT

JÉRÔME BOLLERY.  LOUVRE

arts presents as succeeding those of the studio of Niccolo and Primaticcio.

Félibien, whom at first sight we are tempted to believe, because he had the lost series of the "Accounts of the Buildings" to rely on, gives an apparently far completer picture,[*] and one more worthy of the men whom these artists succeeded. He states that, from the reign of Charles IX., Roger and Toussaint Dubreuil took on the direction of the paintings at Fontainebleau under the superintendence of Bullant, who was in charge of the works at the castle. This division of authority between two painters, one of whom is well known by his work and will be assigned a deservedly important place further on, is a neat way of joining the thread of a story which we have seen broken; but it cannot be reconciled with chronology. The fact is, that the date of Dubreuil is settled by a drawing in the Louvre, with an indubitably genuine inscription,[†] which makes him thirteen years old in the year of Niccolo's death. The twenty years of this period, therefore, are none too long to wait before coming to speak of so consummately able a man, the first French artist who can be greeted with all the honours befitting the early stages of so illustrious a school as that of France.

Meanwhile, though it is true that the new home-grown art of France was but indifferent and obscure, the treasures, with which forty years of successful activity had dowered her, continued none the less to illuminate the world.

Nowadays we can scarcely form any idea of the brilliant fame with which the works at Fontainebleau

---

[*] *Op. cit.*, vol. ii. p. 711.

[†] Reiset: *Catalogue des dessins du Louvre*, part ii. p. 296.

resounded throughout civilised Europe. Fontainebleau
was a colony of Italian art recognised by the capital and
celebrated by Vasari; and, from the reign of Henri II.,
its famous decorations began to attract all eyes, with as
much right as any place on the Peninsula, where a famous
school had flourished. In the studio and in the attention
of artists, the palace of the kings of France ranked with
the Vatican and the palaces of Mantua, Ferrara, and
Florence. Vasari has preserved the memory of the time,
when the influences which France had drawn from Italy
were flowing back to Italy from France. The reflux first
became observable in the importation of prints * engraved
or ordered by the masters of Fontainebleau. Some were
historical, some ornamental. The success of the latter
was so great that the Venetians made forgeries of them,
and sculptors showed extraordinary eagerness to imitate
them.† Later we find Italians who came in person to
Fontainebleau, as the famous Giorgio Mantovano ‡ did
about 1550, and made engravings with the burin. Eight
plates by this artist, indeed, were reproductions of paintings on the ceiling of the Ulysses Gallery; and it was no
small honour for this gallery to have its fame and its
charm spread far and wide by a burin inherited from
Marc Antonio.

But it would be harder still to imagine the ardour excited in the countries of the north by the unprecedented
accessibility of models, which till then had had to be
sought in Italy. We know the eagerness with which,
since Mabuse and Schoorel, since Van Orley and Lambert
Lombard, the artists of the Low Countries had striven

---

* Vasari: *Opere,* Milanesi's edition, vol. v. p. 433.
† *Le Primatice,* p. 139.  ‡ *Ibid.,* p. 524,

to imitate the Italians. The sudden transportation of the
subject of their imitation to their very doors must have
increased their emulation and attracted them in a mass.
That, indeed, is what occurred. M. Hymans, the learned
translator of Van Mander, is fond of repeating that from
that moment Fontainebleau was the Italy of Flanders, at
any rate for all the Flemings who were prevented by one
obstacle or another from journeying to Italy itself.

It is worth noting that from the outset we find among
the actual executants of the decorations which were to be
so eagerly studied, men of this nation, as important as
Leonard Thiry, whose career I have described. He died
at Antwerp in 1550,* but not without having excited all
round him, doubtless as much by his precepts as by his
works, an admiration for the style emanating from the
studio that produced him.

In the matter of ornament, this style soon made such
progress among his fellow-countrymen that it lost its
original category in history, and took on that of Flanders.
Those characteristics of the inventions of Pieter Koeck van
Aelst and Vredeman de Vriese which pass for the most dis-
tinctly in conformity with the Flemish genius, contain all
the elements of the ornament of Fontainebleau. In figure-
painting and historical painting, the imitation, though
less complete and less universal perhaps, is none the less
incontestable.

I have shown Stradano in France about 1548,
and Sprangher shortly after 1565.† Besides these two

---

* According to Ducerceau in the preface to his views of the ruins of
Rome. See p. 117, note †

† This is the date of his departure for Paris, reported by Van Mander.
*Le Livre des peintres*, Hymans' edition, vol. ii. p. 125.

painters, any number of others of the same nation made the same journey in the sixteenth century. Lambert Lombard was in France somewhere about 1540,* during the first blossoming of the School of Fontainebleau. Five years later Augustin Verburcht landed in Paris for a stay of five years, from 1547 to 1552.† Adriaen Crabeth, after a like stay, died at Autun in 1553.‡ The elder Breughel was also in France about this time.§ Pieter Vlerick came before 1566.‖ All this carries no precise mention of any studies made at Fontainebleau, and so is only loosely connected with my purpose; but the following fact is more explicit. In 1566 five young Flemings, Aper Fransen, Hieronymus Francken or Franck, Jan de Maeyer, Dionysius van Utrecht and Cornelis Ketel, settled near the royal residence in order to perfect themselves in their art.¶ Two of them I have dealt with in the preceding chapter. What is of interest here is the avowed intention of a whole body of painters to come and study at Fontainebleau. M. Hymans, and all the other biographers of these painters after him, have stated that they were employed on the decorations there. That was not the case; and Van Mander, who chronicles the event, adds a detail which expressly forbids the misconception; that is, that the court came to enter into residence in the castle, and our friends were obliged to depart, which proves that they were not there as artists employed by the king and charged to carry on the decoration of his dwelling, but as foreign guests and, above all, students. The Flemish author only names one Franck, Hieronymus;

* *Les Livre des peintres*, Hymans' edition, vol. i. p. 207.
† *Ibid.*, vol. i. p. 243.   ‡ *Ibid.*, vol. i. p. 254.   § *Ibid.*, vol. i. p. 298.
‖ *Ibid.*, vol. i. p. 387.          ¶ *Ibid.*, vol. ii. p. 147.

but it is certain that his brother Ambrosius was at Fontainebleau soon after, and perhaps at the same time, for his name occurs in the documents that emanated from that spot.* Another Flemish writer, M. Vanden Branden,† shows that in 1568 Cornelis Floris, a nephew of the famous Frans Floris, was studying with Hieronymus Franck in Paris. That makes seven Flemish artists, and those not the least famous, at one time and in one band, seeking from France and from her new school of painting the instruction which till then had universally been looked for in Italy. Nothing could be more definite than the case of the last named. It was by his father's wish that he was sent to Paris to perfect himself in the art.

I have spoken also of Lucas de Heere. The same remark applies to him. During his stay in France, says Van Mander,‡ he frequently went to Fontainebleau to study on the spot the works of art contained in the castle. And in like manner Thierry Aertsen, a son of the famous Lange Peer, settled at Fontainebleau, and, according to the same author, died there.§

As to the effect of these visits on Flemish painting in general, the only difficulty is to select from the wealth of examples. In whatever way the influences of Fontaine-bleau passed into Frans Floris, they were incontestably present in him; his manner of drawing the nude is as like Rosso as could be. Sprangher and his pupil, Van Aachen, carried the imitation of the same style to the farther end of Europe and well into the seventeenth

---

* Laborde : *Renaissance,* p. 675.
† *Geschiedenis der Antwerpsche Schilderschool,* p. 341.
‡ *Op. cit.,* vol. ii. p. 2.          § *Ibid.,* vol. i. p. 358.

century, and the engravings of Goltzius are completely
impregnated with it. Van Mander himself, if it is true
that a "Woman taken in Adultery," at Brussels, is his
work,* became a propagator of it. So did Cornelis
van Haarlem. Lambert van Noort, Jan van Hemessen,
Sustris, and Wierix the engraver have left plain prac-
tical proofs of the same conclusion. So much so, that
for the last quarter of the century it is with Fontainebleau, rather than with any school in Italy itself, that most
of the Italianising artists of Flanders must be connected.

An interesting verification, and one, I think, that
would not be hard to demonstrate practically, would
be to count, through the whole of Europe, the Flemish
works, both drawings and paintings, dating from this
last portion of the century, which have been attributed
either to Primaticcio himself, or more generally to the
School of Fontainebleau.

A word must be added about England, though England has but little to contribute to the study of historical
painting at this period.

Some of the English monuments, however, show evident signs of an influence drawn directly from Fontainebleau at that time. I am not speaking of those
that came in great numbers by way of Flanders. Certain large decorations in stucco, like those which may be
seen at Hardwick Hall, and some marble chimney-pieces
in the same place, are obviously derived from the lessons
of Primaticcio, which were communicated, no doubt, by
means of engravings. A consideration which I cannot

* In accordance with M. Hymans' opinion. Van Mander, *op. cit.*,
vol. i. p. 15.

omit, and one which no one, so far as I know, has yet remarked, is the trade in prints in the French style, which was established in London at this time. We have already seen Luca Penni practising his art in this way in the country. There were certain engravers settled in Paris, in the rue Montorgueil,* who produced large plates in relief framed with ornament in the style of the Artemisia and the St. Bartholomew: whether some of these did not print in Paris a number of series with English letters intended for England, I cannot say; but it is certain there were more besides, for we find about this time one Gilles Godet settled in London and selling this sort of work there. These prints are now very rare, but a few examples may be seen in the Cabinet of Prints in Paris,† and are lettered " Imprinted at London by Gilles Godet in the Blackfriars." They compose two series, of six plates each: one of the Prodigal Son, dated 1566, the other of the history of St. Paul.

All these considerations combined will help us to realise the sphere filled, between the death of Primaticcio and the establishment of Henri III. on the throne, by the school of historical painting newly founded in France. It is probable that those who only saw it from afar had no suspicion of the sort of interregnum which the names mentioned in this chapter barely succeed in covering.

---

* No one has written the history of these engravers, nor yet distinguished their signatures, but they were imitated by some in other quarters of Paris. Their productions compose an extremely valuable volume in the Cabinet of Prints in Paris, which is indispensable to any one writing a history of the Renaissance in this country. It is numbered Ed. 5 g.

† In the volume above-mentioned, fol. 80 to 82 and 92 to 94.

The deceased masters continued to spread their precepts,
and the mediocrities, whom we seem to see swarming
in those twenty years of obscurity, helped to give an
impression of life around their famous tombs. Brilliant
or not, the School of Fontainebleau was alive. There was
still an enduring tradition in France, dim, it is true, but
uninterrupted, and serving, at least, in default of able
artists, to maintain an artistic atmosphere and a public
for those who were to come after.

I am referring to the revival of painting which came
with the reign of Henri IV. In that revival the school
of the sixteenth century, which was soon to end its
career, reached the honourable close of a history of
seventy years.

This last period is known as the second School of
Fontainebleau; and there is not a single historian of
art who has not plumed himself on displaying his knowledge by casting at it, in passing, remarks which prove
how completely he misunderstands it. But it is clear
that the choice of this second school as the victim of
vengeance for the respect which the detractors of Italianism
have been compelled to pay to the first, was due to nothing
but complete ignorance of it. It is only now that a few
grudging works on genealogy and museography are beginning to throw a little light on this epoch. And yet
it is certain that, though not in the first rank of excellence, it is rendered extremely interesting by its fertility.
I shall deal with it in a succeeding chapter, but must
warn my readers at once, that if the history of this
school is not to be found in this volume so fully developed as it deserves to be, the fault lies with the
scanty knowledge we have of it. This, again, will be

the first occasion on which the attempt, whatever it may amount to, has been made; and that fact will serve as a sufficient excuse.

At present we are only concerned to emphasise a singular and unexpected feature, which what has been said above will in a measure explain: the important part played by the Flemings in this revival of French painting. It is a remarkable fact that Italianism was to bloom anew at the court of Henri IV., not, indeed, by the sole efforts of painters of the Flemish nation, because it is certain that there were Frenchmen of great ability who contributed to that result, but with their important assistance. They occupy several of the highest places, and what is more, we do not find among them the name of a single Italian. Indeed, since the early days of the School of Fontainebleau, the fashion in painting had changed two or three times on the far side of the Alps. The destinies of the colony which France had drawn thence followed an independent course. It is true that French soil was still too rebellious to maintain it, so that foreign aid was naturally demanded; and it came from Flanders, because Flanders during recent years had undergone the influences I have described. Various causes had turned part of the Flemish school into a sub-colony of the School of Fontainebleau; and since these causes had found material there infinitely richer than any in France, nothing was more natural than that the second birth of Fontainebleau should come from the pupils the first Fontainebleau had trained.

How these Flemings formed their determination, we do not know. Scarcely any of them appear in France before 1595, which proves that the cause of their coming

must have been the initiative of the king. It is no less
true that everything combined to attract them, and that,
after the close study given by their nation to the decorations of François I., it must have been thoroughly prepared, by continuing them, to satisfy a prince whose
keenest desire seems to have been the resuscitation, for
his own pleasure, of the old splendours of Fontainebleau.

I find, indeed, a promise and a sort of prophecy of
the productions of the future in the presence in Paris at
this time of a painter who stands for the historical link
between the Flemish students of 1570 and the Flemish
painters to the king in 1600. I mean Hieronymus
Franck, who settled in France after his visits to Fontainebleau.

He was then twenty-six years old,* and the whole of
the rest of his life was to be spent in France. Henri III.
appointed him painter to the king†; and the Cordeliers
of Paris, who issued several important commissions about
this time, had from him in 1585 the altar-piece of their
chapel.‡ Hieronymus Franck there chose for his subject
the Nativity of Jesus Christ. We have no further knowledge of this painter beyond a few genealogical facts,
which are very precise, but have nothing to do with the
present history. The picture I have just mentioned has
perished; and so we must leave the matter for the
present, until the arrival of other painters from his

---

* Vanden Branden, *op. cit.*, p. 340, puts his birth in 1540.

† According to the inscription on his portrait, engraved by Morin.

‡ Mentioned in the old guides to Paris under that date. See in
particular Dargenville : *Voyage pittoresque de Paris*, p. 320. I do not
know whence M. Vanden Branden drew the information he adds, that the
picture was paid for by the first president of the parliament of Paris.

native country enables us to give the story its natural continuation.

I am speaking of historical painters only; for there were a large number of Flemish portrait-painters then living in France. The following chapter will return to this branch of the art, and will acquaint us with their names and their significance.

# CHAPTER XI

AFTER François Janet's death, the office of painter to the
king, which he had enjoyed, was given to Jean Decourt,*
whose name must therefore come at the head of this chapter.

It is not absolutely certain that this painter is the
same as one who signed that name to an enamel representing Mme. Marguerite, Duchess of Savoy, as Minerva,
in the Wallace collection. The enamel dates from 1555.†
But it is difficult to believe that he was not at least a
member of the same family, and the like is the case with
Susanne Decourt, whose name is found on other enamels.

If it is true that he himself practised this art in his
earlier years, it seems that he found portrait-painting
more profitable, for he appears to have done nothing else
after his appointment. He was celebrated as a clever

---

* Laborde : *La Renaissance des arts à la cour de France,* vol. i. p. 224.

† The name of Jean Decourt is familiar to all amateurs of enamel.
The pieces of this date, marked I. D. C. or I. C., are all ascribed to him.

DUKE OF ANJOU, AFTERWARDS HENRY III.
ATTRIBUTED TO JEAN DECOURT.  CHÂTEAU DE CHANTILLY

painter in his own day, and the little that remains of his work, executed at the date we have now reached,* only tends to confirm the verdict on his talent.

His first painting after his appointment to office is a portrait of Henri III., then only Duke of Anjou, which Papyre Masson, a contemporary author, makes the subject of a touching and singular story. According to him,† King Charles IX., when on his death-bed, was struck with remorse for having ill-treated his brother all his life, and asked for his portrait in order to pay it his farewell. Henri III. was then in Poland. They were obliged to look for the portrait in the studio of the painter, who was keeping it, no doubt, in expectation of being able to deliver it. On the strength of this, I believe that this portrait may be identified with one at Chantilly,‡ which was long held to be that of François, Duc d'Alençon, the fourth son of Henri II., but which really, as I have shown,§ represents Henri III., and was painted in 1573 at the moment of his departure for foreign countries. The chalk-drawing of this portrait is happily extant, in the Cabinet of Prints in Paris.‖ Thus we have good reason for supposing, in this drawing and in all the others of similar execution, the hand of a painter, none of whose works had hitherto been supposed to have survived. Meanwhile, pending the production of a critical list, too dry a matter for the present volume, I will content myself with observing that a spurious Louise de Lorraine in the same

* In particular by the poet Desportes. See below.

† Quoted in the Memoirs of Castelnau, 1731, vol. iii. p. 20.

‡ Catalogue, No. 256.

§ *Un portrait méconnu de Henri III. et le peintre Jean Decourt,—Gazette des Beaux-Arts*, 1902, vol. ii.

‖ Case I., old No. 29.

Cabinet,* and the famous Henri III. engraved by Wierix after Thomas de Leu,† may be attributed at once, on internal evidence, to the presumed Jean Decourt.

Besides the Henri III., still Duke of Anjou, which we have mentioned above, we hear of two other portraits painted by Jean Decourt, the recovery of which perhaps may some day confirm my conclusions. One is a portrait of the beautiful Châteauneuf, the prince's mistress, which was highly praised by the poet Desportes‡ in his poems published in 1573. The other comes twelve years later, in 1585, and is a portrait of the Duchesse de Guise, Catherine of Cleves, wife of le Balafré, for which he was paid ninety livres.§

This high price shows how his talents were valued. I would gladly reinforce it with the relatively high pension which we find him drawing as painter to the king; but that matter calls for a reflection of a different kind. The salary amounted to 400 livres,‖ 160 more than was ever received by the two Janets. But we must be in no haste to conclude that Decourt was more highly prized than they. The difference must have depended on other causes; for about the same time we find Foulon, Clouet's nephew, in receipt of 600,¶ which is as much as Primaticcio himself had drawn under previous reigns. The increase of salaries, therefore, was general, and since it is impossible to attribute it to a better condition of the royal finances, we must ascribe it to greater liberality on the part of the king

* Case V., old No. 125.

† There is a chalk-drawing of this also in the same cabinet, Case IV., old No. 131.

‡ Laborde: *op. cit.*, p. 224. § *Ibid.* ‖ *Ibid.*

¶ Jal: *Dictionnaire critique de biographie et d'histoire*, p. 593.

Other facts equally show Decourt firmly settled in the royal favour. A son of his, Charles Decourt, appears in 1575 with the title of groom of the chamber to the king, and even in his father's lifetime obtained simultaneously with him, in 1582, the title and functions of painter to the king.

The presumed age of this son at that time compels us to believe that Jean Decourt was no longer young when he was appointed to the office, and that he did not live long after the reign of Henri III. If I had to judge him from the chalk-drawings which, as I have said, I presume to be his, I should commend his wisdom, the great neatness of his method, and the pleasant knowledge which he inherited from Janet, but deplore his lack of freedom, a certain feebleness in the perspective of the more delicate features, and his mechanical treatment of costume, which is scarcely more supportable than that of the anonymous artist of the Lecurieux album, whom, nevertheless, he surpasses in every respect.

The name of another painter connected with the beginning of this period has been preserved by Hilarion de Coste * in the following story.

The queen-mother, Catherine de Medici, who feared the union of her son Henri III. with Louise de Lorraine, the lady he ultimately married, sent an artist to paint the portraits of the princesses of Sweden and Denmark, with the object of submitting them to Henri III. as possible brides. During that time, the young king had a portrait painted of Louise, and, to contrast her beauty better with that of the ladies they wished him to choose

---

* *Eloges et vies des reines, des princesses et des dames illustres,* vol. i. p. 118.

from, he had the portrait of these princesses secretly copied, with the addition of the French costume worn by Louise de Lorraine. Of this complicated series of portraits, we know the painter of the first two, Nicolas Belon, whose name is given by the chronicler. He, then, painted Elizabeth of Sweden, the sister of King John, and no doubt also the Princess of Denmark. That is all we know for certain about him. M. Laborde tried to recognise him in a certain Nicolas Belliard, of whom more hereafter; but there is no evidence for any such variant of the name.*

At most we may ask if he is not the same as a Nicolas Leblond,† probably a brother-in-law of Germain Pilon by marriage with his sister, whom the "Journal of Héroard" ‡ cites as a portrait-painter. In that case we must attribute to Belon the part belonging to the painter of that name in the obsequies of Catherine de Medici in 1589.§

Side by side with these painters in the king's service, we find others employed by a court which, though poorer and far less brilliant, is nevertheless worth some consideration in view of the future allotted to its monarch, the King of Navarre.

---

* This author, in his *Renaissance*, p. 122, has defaced the evidence till it becomes unrecognisable. In the first place, he starts by calling the painter mentioned by Hilarion de Coste *Béliard* without indicating that he is responsible for the change of spelling; and then makes him paint "the princesses of Sweden," and generally all the pictures mentioned in connection with this matter.

† Mentioned by Herluison: *Actes d'état civil d'artistes français*, pp. 219, 327. Laborde: *op. cit.*, p. 854. Jal: *op. cit.*, p. 751.

‡ Edited by Soulié and Barthélemy, vol. i. p. 222.

§ Müntz: *La peinture française*, vol. i. p. 268.

Before he became king, Henri IV. had several painters in his employment, who bore also the title of his grooms of the chamber. That is the style under which some of his accounts of the period mention a painter we have already named, Marc Duval; and another, Bunel, a Protestant like the former.

The exact date of Duval's death is not known, and it may be that he did not live to see his master's accession to the throne of France. However, we find him in 1578 painting a small portrait of him.* In 1575 some verses, which are supposed to be by Mailliet, an officer of Jeanne d'Albret, had urged him to paint two portraits of women, whose names are not given.† In short, there is no reason to believe that he was less active in the reign of Henri III. than he had been in that of Charles IX., or that the close of his career, which was crowned with a new office, holds less material in reserve for criticism, against the day when important discoveries shall enable us to render to all those painters the things that are theirs out of the large number of anonymous works of which this period is full.

Of Bunel, who is called for convenience by his Christian name of François, to distinguish him from a son whom we shall soon come to, we know that he lived in Blois, which probably was his native place. We have no mention of him after 1590, and all his known works date from after 1583, so that no one could be more appropriately placed in the period before us.

---

* Benjamin Fillon : *La galerie de portraits de Duplessis-Mornay au château de Saumur.—Gazette des Beaux-Arts,* 1879.

† *Revue universelle des Arts,* vol. xiv. p. 401.

Chance has preserved evidence of a large number of commissions given to him,* as follows :—

Two chalk-drawings of his master, the King of Navarre, and a miniature and an oil-portrait of him, in 1583 ; a large and a small portrait of the same king in 1587, and two more in 1590. One of these last is stated to have been destined for the Duc de Roquelaure ; a fact which, taken in conjunction with this repetition of portraits, points to the conclusion that they were copies made in small numbers after certain originals ; and this is still more strongly implied by a commission he received in 1583 for a portrait of Henri IV. at the age of three. No doubt his task was to repaint the face after some original work which had been damaged or was not to the taste of the prince when he grew up, and to make a fresh copy of it which should be suitable for new designs.

The late date of this portrait inclines me to believe that the famous Henri IV. in infancy, inherited by the Versailles Museum † from the gallery of the Duc d'Orléans at the Palais-Royal, is no other than this work of Bunel's. It has been engraved and mentioned over and over again ; it even served as a model for the silver statue which the Bourbons ordered of Bosio on their restoration, and which has never ceased to be very popular in France ; but for all that it remains an indifferent piece of work, conceived in the style of a state-copy, and giving little evidence of talent in the artist. If we judge Bunel solely on this portrait, which we presume to be his, we can form but a low idea of his value ; an idea which,

* Lafond : *François et Jacob Bunel peintres de Henri IV.—Société des Beaux-Arts des Départements*, 1897.

† Catalogue, No. 3282.

nevertheless, is highly probable, in spite of the number
of works for which we find him commissioned.

In the seven years I have mentioned, he painted also
the Prince de Dombes, the Cardinal de Bourbon, the
deceased Cardinal d'Armagnac, St. Gelais, M. de Vaudoré,
M. du Fay, M. du Vas, M. de Fonteraille, M. de Favau, a
child, and a comedian; and finally, it is worth noting, in
1590, a portrait of James VI., King of Scotland, and
another of the famous Drake. The renown of the latter
had penetrated by then into France, and secured him a
place in the common collections of portraits in this
country.

I have described the form which these collections had
assumed since the preceding period. It is not yet time to
revert to them; but, before passing on, it is well to notice
that several other novelties began to appear after the
reign of Henri III. in this lasting vogue of portraiture.

The most important is the preponderance thenceforward of chalk-drawings over paintings. I have shown
that it is doubtful whether the Janets ever executed
portraits in chalks except with the intention of making
paintings from them; at any rate, it is quite certain that
it was not their common practice. But at the period now
before us, there is no doubt that it was the common
practice. It is very remarkable that, of the fifty portraits
which make up the Lecurieux album, barely one or two
are found reproduced in painting. The huge albums
inherited from Gaignières and now in the Cabinet of
Prints in Paris * contain not a single drawing of this date
that has been so reproduced. I confine myself to giving
precise evidence of a fact that must strike all who take

* Na 21 and Na 21 a.

up the study of this subject. The taste for chalk-drawings
had been quickened in the public mind to an unprecedented
extent. Till that time they had been merely handmaids
to the painter's art, and only sought after in special cases;
now they became one of the branches of art, which the
clients of painting were anxious to possess. " Let it be a
chalk-drawing," says Catherine de Medici somewhere in
her correspondence,* " so that it may be finished sooner."
Thenceforward, it seems, that was the cry of the century;
so much so that there quickly followed the appearance of
artists solely devoted to these drawings, of makers of
portraits who knew nothing of the brush or the proper
craft of the painter. Matters had not reached that stage
as yet, and we find that men like Decourt, Belon, and
Duval had not yet abandoned painting; but we have seen
Bunel, at any rate, supplying the king with chalk-drawings, which were ordered of him for their own sake;
and there is no saying how many unnamed artists were
definitely in the same case.

Thence comes that air of finish which we find in the
chalk-drawings of this period, and the carrying through
of the complexion and accessories. They are due to the
intention which produced these works, and which led little
by little to the perfect form of which the last of the
Dumoûtiers were soon to give the most famous examples;
a particular variety of art, very French in character,
and the consequence of which I propose to conclude by
describing.

A second characteristic of the period, which seems
almost a contradiction of the former, is that the vogue of
second copies in chalks, collected, as before, into albums,

* In Bouchot: *Les Clouets*, p. 13.

was over.   Not that albums of this kind had ceased to be
compiled at this time, but there was no new creation of
originals.   The figures which composed the old volumes
of Méjanès and the Cabinet were supplemented by large
numbers of portraits of the court of Henri II.; then came
those of the time of Charles IX., and after that scarcely
any.   The last portraits of this king are found to have
been very rarely copied; Queen Elizabeth of Austria not
at all; and there is not a single Louise de Lorraine or
Catherine de Medici as a widow.   A Henri III., later a
Henri IV. and one or two of the Duc d'Alençon, scattered
among the crowd of faces of thirty or forty years before,
are the only means we have of dating the albums ordered
during the reigns of these monarchs.   And so we owe it
to chance that those which have perpetuated the court of
Henri II. belong, as I have said, to this epoch.   This is
the case with the Valori de Lille album, the Courajod
album, and the album in the Arts-et-Métiers in Paris,
which is the richest of all; as it was also with the lost
Fontette albums.   It is as well to mention them here
in order to avoid any further reference to them, since it
is sufficient to have noted their support of the remark
I made above.

The taste for clumsy copies, which had satisfied the
world so far, appears to have given way before the more
delicate fashions of engraved portraits, like those which
Thomas de Leu and Léonard Gautier, Gourdelle, Rabel
and others had then begun to produce.   These men were
the earliest practitioners of an art which was to mingle its
destinies with those of the school founded by the Clouets.
The first three were, as I have said, sons-in-law of Caron.
A detailed account of them would fall outside my subject,

but I cannot omit a passing word of praise for the cleverest of the three, Thomas de Leu. He was, no doubt, Flemish in origin ; he was a friendly rival of the excellent Wierix, and his name forms a perfect opening for the history of portrait engraving in France.

The intervention of these masters had a second effect on the productions of chalk-drawings, of which I must speak precisely. They caused the creation of a large number with the special object of being engraved. We know of several that were utilised in this manner, from which no painting was ever taken. The execrable copies which these engravings ousted could never have held their own, or occupied the painters in tasks which aimed only at such results. Whether the engraver always made a reduced drawing of the chalk-portrait he proposed to reproduce, before going on to engrave it, is a question on which various considerations make a decision very difficult ; and there is nothing to justify our attempting to decide it here. We have material proof that the system I speak of was practised ; on the other hand, it is hard to believe that it was universal, and that is all that can be said for certain.

The substitution of the new practice of engraving for the old albums of chalk-drawings did not fail to benefit the taste for historical galleries. In 1575 the museum of Paolo Giovio was engraved at Basle by Pietro Perna, and the collection may be regarded as the most important of its class. Twenty years earlier, the Lyons publisher, Rouville, had put forth on a small scale an excellent work conceived on the same plan, the celebrated *Promptuaire des Médailles*, which was engraved by Reverdi. Thevet's series of illustrious men, published

in 1584, which M. Bouchot takes to have been engraved
by Léonard Gautier, was the most important of those
produced in France. A little later the same engraver
was responsible for the appearance of the famous but
indifferent *Chronologie collée*, a collected series of small
prints. The scope of it is confined to France, and it
completely fails to represent the exotic and fanciful taste
of the people of that time, which induced them to find
pleasure in combining Roman with Byzantine emperors,
and German kaisers with Muscovite czars, and jumbling
together pell-mell, in poor but multitudinous present-
ments, sultans, sofies, sheriffs, Tartar chieftains, medieval
theologians and Italian humanists.

This will be the proper place to introduce a characteristic of the epoch we have reached, which is far more
interesting since it touches directly on its art: I mean
the presence at the court of France, and in the employ
of Catherine de Medici, no less than of the kings and
queens of the time, of several Flemish artists who were
skilled in portraiture.

I need do no more than mention Hieronymus Franck,
as all that we know exactly about him has been given above.
But it is certain, and Van Mander definitely states it,*
that besides his historical pictures he painted a number
of portraits. Science, no doubt, will some day distinguish some of his works from among the crowd of anonymous paintings of the time.

Vander Mast is in like case. We know nothing of
him except from Van Mander,† who states that he lived

first of all in the household of the Archbishop of Bourges,[*] possibly Beaune-Semblançay, and then passed into the service of the Procureur-général de la Guesle, who introduced him at court. The queen-mother singled him out for favour, and he stayed nine years in France, after 1570, according to M. Hymans' calculations.

No work of Vander Mast's is known in France, and for a long time historians of art could find no work of his at all. M. Van Riemsdyk has recently discovered what may help to fill the gap, in two authentic pictures signed by this master.[†] They belong to M. Nérée de Babberich, who has lent them to the Amsterdam Museum, where all may study them. The remarkable thing about them, in spite of its feeble realisation, is their imitation of the Venetians. The painter was evidently one of those artists of the Low Countries who was then under the influence of this school, the most famous of them, after Moro, being Thierry Bernard, Gilles Coignet, Willem Key, and Frans Pourbus the elder.

There is no saying whether we may suppose that Cornelis Ketel, a portrait-painter also, who, as I have shown, passed through France in 1566, left any of his works behind him. But the connection between him and Vander Mast is not only due to their presence in this country with so brief an interval between them; they are thrown together also by their manner of painting, which in Ketel himself was quite as strongly imbued with the imitation of the Venetians.[‡]

* Not at Bourges, as some have believed.

† One with his monogram only. They also bear the dates 1587 and 1589.

‡ The authority of an old inventory compels us to add also Hieronymus

SUPPOSED PORTRAIT OF ELIZABETH OF FRANCE, DAUGHTER
OF CHARLES IX

If we add to this list several portraits of French
persons by Frans Pourbus the elder, which were clearly
ordered of him and are mentioned in his inventory,*
we have a complete idea of the whole of this distinct
branch of the Flemish school, which worked for the
court of France in a style very different from what would
have been expected. We commonly imagine the Flemings to have resembled rather the manner of the Clouets;
and that perhaps was the style of some others of them.
Indeed, I cannot help thinking that four chalk-drawings
in a similar manner, now in the Cabinet of Paris, which
have hitherto been wrongly combined with others from a
different hand, and show a style very different from that
of the followers of the Venetians, are really the work of a
Fleming.

I will enumerate them here, with all the particularity
they deserve. Elizabeth of Austria, Queen of France,
as a widow, evidently made after the king's death, which
took place in 1574.† A young princess, painted about
the same time, who is stated by an ancient letter to be
Marguerite, daughter of Henri II. and later Queen of
Navarre, though her costume and her age together
compel us to find another name for her. I believe her
to be the daughter of Charles IX. and the queen mentioned above, who, like her mother, was named Elizabeth,
and died at the age of only six years.‡ A supposed

---

Franck, whose picture, painted for the Cordeliers, is said to be "in the
taste of the Venetians." Stein: *État des objets d'art placés dans les
monuments de Paris au début de la Révolution*, p. 53.

   * Vanden Branden : *op. cit.*, p. 283.

   † Case III., old No. 31.

   ‡ Case III., old No. 84.

Louise de Lorraine, termed anonymous by M. Bouchot *;
and a spurious Marie Touchet, mistress of Charles IX.†
These four portraits show the talents of an artist, who
not only surpassed the other painters of the time of
Henri III., but, after full consideration, ought to be
placed above François Clouet himself, in the highest
rank of all the painters who served France in portraiture
throughout the whole century. The knowledge of drawing is perfect, and the execution far superior to any we
have seen hitherto. The master is not content with
exactly placing all the parts of the face, and superbly
modelling the features of his sitter. He goes on to see
that the matter of his work shall express the flesh in all
its transparence and delightful softness. In his hands,
simple chalks achieve this result, which is familiar in the
Flemish painters. On reflection, I see no master with
whom this extraordinary anonymous painter may be
better compared than the elder Pieter Pourbus, so many
of whose admirable works may be seen in the churches
of Bruges, and so well fulfil our ideas of a perfect
portrait-painter. The artist of our chalk-drawings has
the limpidity and graceful play of his touch, the same
beautiful softness, the same relief and almost the same
texture. There is an extreme freshness about these
touches; the ball of the eye is rounded with infinite
sweetness in the curve of the lids, while the lower lid,
which is translucent, seems to shine with real moisture
held in by the meeting of the lashes, which are light as
feathers. The tender colour of the cheeks, which is
heightened towards the cheek-bone, is placed with extraordinary truth and precision, and the light of the eye-

---

* Case V., old No. 2.         † Case III., unnumbered.

PORTRAIT OF A LADY

UNKNOWN ARTIST, PRESUMABLY FLEMISH.   CABINET DES ESTAMPES, PARIS

balls is enchanting. The careful art of the touch and
of the foreshortening imitate the further parts of the
three-quarter face till the illusion is complete. The
sprouting of the hair is rendered with perfect truth to
nature. In short, we may say that what is commonly
known as the *crayon français* can show in these portraits
four masterpieces worthy to stand near the greatest
masters of this art, and to shine in history among the
choicest specimens of the art of drawing.

It is to be regretted that it is impossible to guess
to whom these perfect works are due. Pieter Pourbus
never came to France, and we know of no pupil of his
who visited this country.* Nevertheless, once more, the
style of the work is such that, in the absence of all other
information and of the artist's name, prudence compels us
to believe him a Fleming.

But we have not yet mentioned all the painters of
that country who flourished then in France. There is
still another, recently discovered in the obscurity of the
" Accounts," who had previously succeeded with difficulty
in winning a shadowy existence from the mention of his
name by Van Mander. I have said in a former chapter
how difficult the critic finds it to distinguish between
the several painters named George. To the pupils of
Frans Floris we must add George of Ghent, who is
mentioned by Van Mander,† and stated by him to have

---

* The second Frans Pourbus, his grandson, cannot be considered to
have been his pupil, and, moreover, did not come to France till twenty
years after the date of these drawings. It is true that we find a painter
named Jacques Pourbus in Paris from 1571 to 1580. None of the historians mention him, but he must have been a member of this family.
Jal : *op. cit.*, p. 990.

† *Op. cit.*, vol. i. p. 348.

come to France. M. Hymans asks what his surname was, and proposes, in default of a better, Vander Rivière, a painter from Ghent, who lived about this time and had the same Christian name of George. An extract from the contemporary " French Accounts " enables us to settle the question. Van Mander says that George of Ghent had in France the title of " Painter to the Queen." Now the document I spoke of * gives this title in 1572 to George Vander Straeten; whence it follows that George Vander Straeten was the name of the George of Ghent, a pupil of Frans Floris, and, according to Van Mander, originally painter to Philip II. of Spain, of whom we are speaking. We find him mentioned a second time, in 1578, under the title of Maître Georges only, but with the addition of the same title, in circumstances which are rather interesting, inasmuch as other painters were engaged on the same work.

The discovery and the story we owe to M. Bouchot; † and this will be an auspicious occasion for the introduction of new names into our history.

The Duc and Duchesse de Nevers, in the year 1578, made a deed of gift for the dowries of girls on their marriage, and wished to have the deed written on parchment in the best characters they could find, and with woodcuts of their portraits. The design was supplied by one Maître Bernard, another contemporary portrait-painter. When it came to be engraved it was found unsatisfactory, and George of Ghent was asked to put it right. But it seems that George of Ghent succeeded no better, for they called in finally an Englishman (his name unfortunately

* *Bibliothèque de l'École des Chartes*, 1892, p. 619.
† *Ibid.*, p. 615.

is not given), who achieved the honour of completing the work. One of the portraits that were to be recut was removed from the wood of the block that formed the title, and a small piece of boxwood, on which the English artist engraved his design, was let into the notch made to receive it. The complete impression has come down to us, with marks that enable us to recognise the notch, and, more especially, the portrait of the duke and that of the duchess as the Englishman engraved it.

We know no more of this English artist than what this story tells us, but he seems to have been held in high esteem, and the document from which these details are drawn adds that he was considered to be "one of the most excellent of whom there is any memory, at least in small works." On the strength of this, the author of this statement, the secretary of the Duc de Nevers, laid before his master a project for a collection of the praises of the famous men of the time, to be ornamented with portraits by the same artist. The collection never saw the light; but we should none the less be glad to know the name of the clever artist who was considered worthy to carry it out.

The name of Nicholas Hilliard has occurred to M. Bouchot, and it seems not impossible, when we consider that this painter was renowned not only in his own country, but in France itself, where we find Blaise de Vigenère * composing a triumphant eulogy on him about this time. But to make the suggestion a probable one, we should first have to prove that Hilliard worked in France. M. Bouchot regards it as certain that he did, because he has discovered in the Accounts of the Duc

* Walpole: *Anecdotes of Painting,* 1786 edition, vol. i. p. 255.

d'Alençon the mention of one " Nicolas Belliart, Anglais,"
painter to this prince in 1577 at a salary of 200 livres.*
That this was Hilliard himself cannot be doubted; but
his appearance in the Accounts of a French prince by no
means proves, considering the customs of the time, that
he ever so much as visited France.  It is true that M. de
Laborde tried to identify Belliart with the Nicolas Belon
mentioned above ; and if Hilliard is turned into Belon,
he may definitely be accepted as having actually spent
a very long time in this country.  The only objection
is that, as I have pointed out, this link is wanting.  So
that we must defer for the present the settlement of the
name of this gifted Englishman, just as in the case of the
Maître Bernard, the artist of those first portraits of
the Duc and Duchesse de Nevers, with whom we may
conveniently bring to a close the list of portrait-painters
who worked in France under Henri III.

To that list I will only add a few works of foreign
origin, which occur so naturally here that it would be
difficult to omit them.  They consist of several portraits
of French subjects, principally of the above-mentioned
Duc d'Alençon, which were made during this period
outside the borders of France.  In 1571 this prince was
to have married Queen Elizabeth of England; and in
view of the match a chalk-portrait of him was sent to
her.† This portrait is probably the one which Hilliard
copied in the miniature with which he ornamented a

---

* Laborde : *Renaissance*, p. 230.

† Bertrand de Salignac-Fénelon : *Correspondance diplomatique*, vol.
iv. p. 186.  The ambassador reports a remark of Queen Elizabeth's on
this portrait : " That the prince's complexion seemed good, although his
face was only scribbled in with charcoal."  M. Bouchot interprets the

"Book of Hours" for Queen Elizabeth, which was formerly in the collection of Dr. Jeffery Whitehead.

Another circumstance in the life of the same prince gave occasion for a similar exercise of foreign art, his proclamation as Duke of Brabant in 1582, which had been preceded by several journeys into Flanders. Van Mander definitely states that Pieter Pourbus painted him; * and among the portraits by Frans, Pieter's son, which were finished in 1581, we find a chalk-drawing of this prince, a painting of his favourite, Bussy d'Amboise, one of his coachmaker, and one of the Prince de Condé.† Finally, the Cabinet of Manuscripts in Paris has a valuable little work by Hans Bol,‡ a Mechlin painter, painted by command of the same prince. It is a Prayer-book of minute dimensions, which contains the triumphal entry into Antwerp and the prince himself on his knees in a church, executed with a perfect likeness and in an exquisite manner. The work dates from 1582.

Thus the intervention of the Flemings was propagated at that time in French art in several ways. Portraiture had come originally from Flanders, and from Flanders, after the lapse of three-quarters of a century, the art

words as a criticism on the portrait, and supposes that the queen took the shadows for smudges. But "charcoal" means nothing but "chalk," and I take the meaning of the speech to be : "The prince's complexion seems good, although he is drawn here almost entirely in black chalk."

   * *Op. cit.*, vol ii. p. 22. I notice that this portrait was included, 150 years later, in the inventory of Cardinal de Polignac, No. 113. *Revue de l'art français*, 1889, p. 269.

   † Vanden Branden, *ut. sup.*

   ‡ Fonds latin, 10564.

R

received anew a quickening and fertile impulse. We shall see how, under Henri IV., the genius of Italy herself borrowed from the stream of the Flemish masters to recruit and sustain the historical painters, who, after so many years, were at last to arise in France.

# CHAPTER XII

WHAT remains to be told of the history of French painting at the Renaissance is not the most illustrious period treated in this book ; but if only for the play of cause and effect which we have consistently kept before us, no period excels it in interest or importance. It was actually the last of all, and only precedes by a few years the establishment of Vouet in the public favour and the lessons of an artist who is rightly regarded as the father of the modern school of French painting.

But although that title, which is bestowed with perfect justice, excludes the idea of dependence on tradition or of an education drawn from the artists of the preceding age, it is none the less out of the question that the very numerous and busy painters of Henri IV., or the large number of their works which were still to be seen in the royal residences throughout the seventeenth century, could

have remained unconnected with the succeeding portion
of the history of painting, or failed to mingle their lessons
with those that Vouet was to bring from contemporary
Italy.  The late Marquis de Chennevières, now unfortunately lost to us, who was hard at work upon this
period and very anxious to prove some continuity in
the succession of these schools, considered that he had
found some trace of Vouet's origin in Dubreuil.  That
is obviously impossible, and the present state of the
science, I think, puts it out of the question; and the
problem I propose here is that of the extent to which
the examples of recent masters, whose paintings were still
fresh, and their descendants still living, masters whose
names were collected and their lives put on record by
Félibien and the abbé de Marolles with the assistance of
contemporary authors, succeeded in influencing a school
formed elsewhere.  Now to that question, with our present
knowledge, we can give no answer at all, or only a very
unsatisfactory one.  Too few of the works of the painters
of Henri IV. have left traces of any importance, to enable
us to form an idea of the period in all its variety, though
the large number of painters and the quantity of various
evidence we have of them imply that its variety was considerable.  And thus, without the knowledge of all its
circumstances, we cannot hope to distinguish its effects.
The following explanation will make this clearer.

Between the date at which Henri III., besieged by the
League, was forced to leave Paris, and the date at which
Henri IV. returned to the capital, lie four years of so
much civil disturbance that it is impossible to follow the
progress of the fine arts, and there comes a break in our
history.  And further, it is not surprising that, after the

conversion of the king and the pacification of France, a certain time was necessary to take up the thread of the past in the domain of painting. The lost Accounts, of which only the headings are extant, show the marks of their interregnum, and it is only in 1595 that we find the text set on foot again and continued in the old way.* None of the great works, therefore, that were to render the reign illustrious, can be considered to have been begun before that epoch; and this is confirmed by our knowledge of the dates at which several important painters entered the service of the king.

But there is this to be said: that we find from a number of documents that the revival came all at once, so that, after the eclipse we have described, painting appeared with more brilliance than ever, and, at any rate, so far as quantity is concerned, in a degree which it had never attained before, even under the reign of François I.

François I., in fact, had only lavished expense upon Fontainebleau: Henri IV. not only planned the restoration and enlargement of Fontainebleau, but devoted equal care to the Louvre, the Tuileries and the Castle of St. Germain-en-Laye. All the old writers, in their descriptions of the works of art of the period, consistently mention those four residences together, and we find them united and detailed side by side in the headings of the lost Accounts. When I add that twenty important artists, whose names I shall give, without counting their assistants, were all at work together on these undertakings, we may form some idea of what was in progress, and the position which, if only it were better known, this period ought to hold in the history of art. Unhappily we know but little

* Laborde : *Comptes des Bâtiments du Roi*, vol. i. p. 43.

of the decorations of St. Germain and the Tuileries, and thus half this chapter is shorn off at a blow. Of the Louvre and of Fontainebleau we know more, verbally at any rate; and also in actual fact, for a number of works have survived, which may give us an idea of what was to be seen there.

The first painter to be engaged on these undertakings was one I have mentioned before, the admirable Toussaint Dubreuil. A drawing in the Louvre * proves that he was already at work on his art in 1588; and therefore, at the date we have reached, he was ready to accept the commissions with which he was to be entrusted.

The work at Fontainebleau was in the Pavilion des Poèles, next to the room decorated with part of the story of Hercules by Roger de Rogery. These rooms, which at one time were part of the lodging of Henri II. and, after his death, of Catherine de Medici, were occupied under the new reign by Gabrielle d'Estrées,† Duchesse de Beaufort and de Monceaux, the famous mistress of Henri IV., who had divorced Marguerite and had not yet taken another wife. The following is a list of the compositions painted in this second room by Dubreuil, the subjects being in keeping with those in the adjoining apartment:—

"The birth of Hercules." "Jupiter freeing the new-born hero from his mortal element." "Hercules in his cradle strangling the serpents." "Hercules learning to draw the bow." "Hercules armed by Mercury and Minerva." "Hesione saved from a sea-monster by Her-cules." "His combat with Antæus." "Hercules carry-

---

* See p. 227, note †.

† Cassiano del Pozzo : *Diarium*, edited by Müntz. *Mémoires de la Société de l'histoire de Paris*, 1885.

ing off the Pygmies." "His fight with Achelous transformed into a serpent." "His fight with Achelous
transformed into a bull." "Deianira married to Hercules." "Hercules receiving the glory of his works."
"Hercules held back by the nymphs when coming out
of the water, in two parts." *

According to Guilbert,† Dubreuil must also have
painted the free views of the royal palaces which may still
be seen, though repainted, on the ground floor of the
Queen's Gallery. Finally, Félibien ‡ adds that he gave
his attention to the restoration of the damaged paintings
in the Ulysses Gallery.

Lestoille in a famous passage § states that he was the
painter of the decorations at St. Germain, and the details
of these works are extant in Bailly's inventory of the
King's Pictures.|| There were seventy-eight subjects,
some of which covered the ceiling; but it is impossible to
enumerate them here for want of any explanation of them
which would enable us to give their titles. The description
of each work, however, we have, and no doubt it will enable
us hereafter to identify several of the master's drawings.

At the same time he was at work in the Louvre, on
the famous Small Gallery, which was burnt down under
Louis XIV. Its sumptuous restoration resulted in the
Apollo Gallery.

Its appearance under Henri IV. seems to have struck

* Dan : *Trésor des Merveilles de la maison royale de Fontainebleau,*
p. 129.

† *Description de Fontainebleau,* vol. i. p. 183.

‡ *Entretiens sur la vie et les ouvrages des plus fameux peintres,* ed.
4to, vol. i. p. 711.

§ Quoted below, p. 268, note †.

|| Edited by Engerand, p. 287.

the contemporary imagination with delight. Félibien, Sauval, and several others never mention it but to praise it highly, and the accident which destroyed it was regarded as a catastrophe. The ceiling is all we are concerned with in this chapter, for the walls were entirely hung with portraits. And as we have no precise description of the subjects of which it was composed, we are unable to assign it here a place in proportion to its importance, either in the history of French art or in the life of Dubreuil, whose masterpiece it seems to have been.

One composition only, the "Battle of the Giants," in which Jupiter striking the Titans with his thunder-bolt stood for an allegory of Henri IV. defeating the League, is mentioned by contemporary writers; though it is true that they dwell on it with such emphasis that, destroyed and unknown as it is, it must be counted among the famous productions of the French school. Sauval even gives some important detail about it;* describing its bold foreshortening, and the great knowledge displayed in the drawing. He adds a general statement that the subjects were taken from the "Metamorphoses" and the Old Testament; so unusual a combination only increases our regrets for the absence of a precise description.

Such were the paintings by Dubreuil, of which the memory has survived to our time. We know of no other works of his; and, in fact, since he died in 1602 † at a comparatively early age, after serving the King of France for only seven years, we could not expect to find more. But it is important to note that Dubreuil was a painter of the kind who direct large schemes of decoration with

* Reiset: *Catalogue des dessins du Louvre*, part ii. p. 293.
See below, p. 268, note †.

facility; and that in thus repeating on a smaller scale the features of the first school of Fontainebleau, he is, of all others, the artist who most recalled Primaticcio in easy fertility and in method. Various sources agree in declaring that he painted as little himself as Primaticcio and Rosso had done. Sauval assures us that the gallery of the Louvre was only painted after his designs, and Van Mander, who mentions him as an interesting contemporary,* writes: "He often has recourse to Flemings to paint his works, and then strengthens them himself by adding vigorous shadows, sometimes using pure black." To that we may add the evidence of Dan, who, in describing † his story of Hercules in the Pavilion des Poèles at Fontainebleau, singles out the picture of Hercules drawing the bow as painted by Dubreuil, "all with his own hand"; which proves that the rest were painted by other people. Dubreuil, therefore, had something of the genius of the great designers and managers of painted decoration, and the drawings of his which have survived prove that he was not without the possession of some of their ability.

And now, who were these Flemings, whom Van Mander mentions so definitely? Sauval gives the name of one,‡ "Artus Flamand," whom we find nowhere else, at any rate under this name. It was he, according to Sauval, who was charged with the painting of the "Battle of the Giants." M. Hymans has made a slight mistake in turning in this connection to the names of the Flemings whom Van Mander gives as travelling in France in 1566. The difference in the dates forbids the identification. Still, we may name Hieronymus Franck,

---

* *Livre des peintres*, Hymans' edition, vol. ii. p. 300.
† *Ut. sup.*                    ‡ In Reiset: *ut. sup.*

who was then, as I have said, settled in Paris. And when we turn to Fontainebleau, we find an excess of men to choose from; and the names of Jean Dhoey, Josse de Voltigeant, and Ambroise Dubois, of whom I shall speak later, come at once into our minds. We may add also Thierry Aertsen, the son of the famous Lange Pier, whom Van Mander again * states to have died about this time at Fontainebleau, and who may perhaps be no other than the "Artus Flamand" of Sauval.

It is practically certain that Ambroise Dubois worked at the time in conjunction with Dubreuil on the decorations at Fontainebleau. He came after 1595 †; and painted the king's favourite, the Duchesse de Monceaux, as Diana, with hounds and cupids,‡ over the chimney-piece of her chamber, which was decorated, as I said, by Dubreuil.

Dubois was a native of Antwerp, but we know nothing of his origin there. What is important to note is that, with the knowledge at our disposal, we must place him with Dubreuil in the first rank of the painters of Henri IV. Dubreuil, it is true, on a comparison of the drawings of the two artists, comes out far above Dubois; but besides the fact that sufficient of Dubois' paintings have come down to us to enable us to judge of him better than we can of Dubreuil, the happy thought of an intelligent copyist has preserved the design of a large decorative work that he directed at Fontainebleau, the most important in the whole palace after the Ulysses Gallery; I mean the Diana room which a few years later was added to the queen's apartments.

* *Op. cit.*, vol. i. p. 358.

† Laborde: *La Renaissance des arts à la cour de France*, p. 680.

‡ Cassiano del Pozzo, *op. cit.*

Before describing it in detail, it is well to ask how far these two painters acquired the manner of Primaticcio from copying his works, which no doubt they did. They adopted his whole style of composition, which deliberately places half-length figures in the foreground, while the rest, which is seen from above, stretches away into strangely empty space. But Dubois is not free from a certain heaviness, which, it is true, does not occur in his paintings; Dubreuil is lightness itself. His agile, delicate and pleasing penwork is equal to that of Niccolo himself. We feel that he was born to be a master of ornament, and to reign over that happy kingdom in which this order of work borders on figure-painting, a mixed and fertile soil in which the three arts of architecture, sculpture and painting are mingled and drawn up in order under the control of the painters, if any there be who are capable of directing them. Primaticcio was of the number in his time; possibly Dubreuil might have been, had he lived longer, and there is no proof that he failed to show promise of something of the kind during his lifetime.

It is certain that Henri IV., whose resemblance to François I. was maintained even in this particular, was anxious to restore the industry of tapestry-weaving; and finally, in 1597, with the determination to instal it in the house of the Jesuits who had been driven out of the Faubourg St. Antoine, he sent Dubreuil himself to lodge in the house with the tapestry-weaver Girard Laurent, and the sculptor Barthélemy Tremblay, who was Dubreuil's brother-in-law.* This was a favourite project

* Sauval, quoted by Lacordaire : *Notice sur les manufactures de tapisserie des Gobelins*, p. 6.

of the king's; and although the mediocrity with which
it was carried out in after days tends to bring it into
discredit, it is none the less true that any attempt at
direction of that kind implies a controlling influence on
all the provinces of art. Dubreuil was the first to exert
it, and it is to this excursion of his into manufacture
that we must refer a tapestry of Diana which was woven
after his designs.*

He died, as I have said, in 1602,† two years after
the king's marriage, when the painters, who till then
had been busy with Gabrielle, had already begun to
combine in their work the king's cypher with the new
cypher of Marie de Medici.

Roger de Rogery and Caron had gone a little before
him, the former in 1597 ‡ and the latter in 1599§; both
were very old, though their length of life had not succeeded in making either of them famous, or assigning
either more than a secondary rank in the French school.

Meanwhile any number of schemes were being carried
out at Fontainebleau. The Bathing-hall was being restored, the Emperors' Closet was being made, and the
Clorinda Chamber and the room which the guides now
call the Salon of Louis XIII. were being painted.

In the old King's Chamber, in the Pavilion des Poèles,
above the chimney-piece and on the very spot where

---

* Guiffrey : *Inventaire du mobilier de la couronne sous Louis XIV.*,
vol. i. p. 296.

† On the evidence of Lestoille : "Journal," quoted by Jal : *Dictionnaire critique de biographie et d'histoire*, p. 280.

‡ Félibien : *op. cit.*, vol. i. p. 712.

§ On the evidence of a portrait mentioned on p. 222, note *, which was
engraved in 1599, and bears this inscription : *Antonius Caron Bellovacus
pictor vixit eximius a. 78.*

Niccolo had placed a picture, now, no doubt, too far gone to be of any service, Ambroise Dubois painted a "Mars and Venus." * In the Clorinda Chamber, which formed part of the queen's apartments, he painted eight pictures, representing the story of that heroine as told by Tasso in his poem of "Gerusalemme Liberata." Bailly gives the details as follows † : "Argante and Clorinda before a besieged tower," "Clorinda presenting herself to Soliman," "Tancred leading the Assault on Jerusalem," "Tancred in Camp," "Tancred contemplating Clorinda," "Fight between Tancred and Clorinda," "The Birth of Clorinda," "The Baptism of Clorinda." On the ceiling, besides a "Louis XIII. as Jupiter," which, no doubt, was added later, there was also to be seen a painting by Dubois of the "Four Elements" in the cyphers and mottoes of Henri IV. This decoration has perished, and nothing of it has been preserved except scattered scenes, one of which, "The Baptism of Clorinda," is in the Louvre. ‡ "Clorinda before Soliman" and "The Birth of Clorinda" are in St. Louis' Chamber at Fontainebleau. In the Salon of Louis XIII., on the other hand, which was formerly known as the King's Great Closet, a decoration of the same kind has been preserved to the present day. It was once composed of fifteen scenes, taken from Heliodorus' celebrated romance of Theagenes and Chariclea. New household arrangements and the enlargement of the

* Dan : *op. cit.*, p. 128.

† *Op. cit.*, p. 334. Dan's description, *op. cit.*, p. 145, is inextricably confused. A slight mistake in editing the inventory quoted above has headed the list of these pictures with the words *Cabinet du roi*, which refer to previous works.

‡ Catalogue, No. 272.

doors afterwards compelled the removal of four of them,
one of which may be seen in the Louvre,* and the rest at
Fontainebleau itself. The list of them is as follows:
" Chariclea in a Chariot going to the Sacrifice," "Theagenes
in Love with Chariclea," " Calasiris undertaking to learn
Chariclea's sentiments," " Apollo and Diana appearing
to the Great Priest," " Calasiris deciding to flee with
Theagenes and Chariclea," "Theagenes rejoining Chariclea," " The Two Lovers joining Calasiris in flight, in
sight of the Isle of Crete," " The Corsair Trachinus seizing
Chariclea," " Chariclea imploring Calasiris to save her from
marrying the Corsair," " Pirates seizing Chariclea as she
tends the wounds of Theagenes," "Theagenes declaring
his Love," " Theagenes and Cremon wandering on the
shore at the sight of a fire," "Theagenes and Cremon
believing that they recognise the Corpse of Chariclea,"
" Chariclea recognised as his Daughter by King Hydaspes,
who wishes to sacrifice her " (this is the painting to be seen
in the Louvre), "Theagenes married to Chariclea." It
was stated that in this last scene the painter introduced
his own portrait, together with that of Sully, the minister
of Henri IV., and the famous financier Zamet. On the
ceiling also, vilely repainted, may still be seen several
other subjects by the same painter.†

One thing we must not omit from the description of
these rooms; that is the addition of several landscapes,
painted on the panelling, which old descriptions attribute
to Paulus Bril. The attribution is extremely doubtful,
since we find no mention anywhere of this painter's staying in France at this period. He had appeared there on

---

* Catalogue, No. 271.

† Dan : *op. cit.*, p. 143.   Bailly : *op. cit.*, p. 331.

CHARICLEA RECOGNISED BY KING HYDASPES

AMBROISE DUBOIS, PAINTING FROM THE ROOM OF THEAGENES AT FONTAINEBLEAU,
NOW IN THE LOUVRE

his way to Italy, according to Van Mander,* about 1576 ; but there is nothing to prove that even on that occasion he left any work of his in France. Moreover, his fame as a landscape-painter was so great in the time of Louis XIII. that they were quite capable of assigning anything to him without further proof. The important point to be re-membered is the mere fact of the use of landscape at all, which is in accordance with a fashion totally unconnected with anything this history has touched upon, and the herald of a time outside the limits of my subject. It is clear that the epoch of Henri IV. was acquainted with this decoration at its apogee.

I even believe it to have owned a specialist in the art, who was entrusted with the painting of this kind of orna-ment, which consists of decorative landscapes relieved with architectural ruins and monuments in perspective. His name was Etienne Dupérac, and he combined his powers of painting with celebrated ability as an architect. Father Dan, in a passage which has been copied by Félibien and all the dictionaries, gives him as the painter of the my-thological subjects that decorated the Bathing-hall at Fontainebleau. These are the paintings which absolutely incontestable evidence has compelled me to restore to Primaticcio.† There is no reason, however, for supposing that Dupérac has been mentioned gratuitously in con-nection with this room. We know that the decoration of it was completed by oval medallions, placed lower down ‡ ; and in the adjoining room similar adventitious pictures represented ruins in landscapes. What more natural than to believe that these last subjects were by Dupérac, and

* _Op. cit._, vol. ii. p. 241.          † See p. 106, note †.
‡ C. del Pozzo, _op. cit._

that he had also painted something of the same kind
in the medallions in question? That is the explanation
of the confusion I have spoken of. It affords a very
plausible reason for providing Dupérac with a definite set
of works, which he had lacked till then, in the style which
he was known to have cultivated.

Thus Dupérac comes back into my subject. He had
studied long in Rome, since 1565 at least, in which year
he is shown to have been there by some prints he engraved, up till 1572.* We are not concerned now with
the series of antiquities which he engraved or drew there.
We find him in France again in 1578,† and he died in
1604,‡ only two years after Dubreuil.

The Bathing-hall, of which we have just spoken, was
the occasion about this time of the issue of an important
commission to a number of painters who were working at
Fontainebleau. I have said that King François I. placed
his collection of pictures there. Henri IV. had them taken
away, to stop the damage they were suffering from the
dampness of the place,§ and replaced by copies. Later
documents have preserved the names of the painters who
made these copies. Ambroise Dubois was entrusted with
Lionardo da Vinci's "Gioconda" and Titian's "Magdalen."
Another painter, called Michelin, whose name has only
survived in this solitary instance, but with some credit
therefrom, painted Raphael's "Madonna," Lionardo's
"Virgin of the Rocks," and Andrea del Sarto's "Charity"
and "St. Elizabeth." Others, whose names are not known,

---

* *Nouvelles Archives de l'art français*, 1897, p. 143.
† *Société des Beaux-Arts des Départements*, 1897, p. 129.
‡ Herluison: *Actes d'état civil d'artistes français*, p. 127.
§ *Le Primatice*, p. 281.

CHARICLEA IN A CHARIOT GOING TO THE SACRIFICE

AMBROISE DUBOIS. DESIGN FOR A PAINTING AT FONTAINEBLEAU. COLLECTION OF M. MASSON AT AMIENS

copied other pictures; but there are still two of which the copyist's name is given: Piombo's "Visitation" and Raphael's "St. Margaret," which were entrusted to Josse de Voltigeant.

This painter was a native of Flanders like Dubois; the original form of his name was Voltighen. We find him mentioned in 1593 and the following years, always at Fontainebleau,* but without being able to attribute to him with certainty anything but the copies we have mentioned.

I have ventured to include him in the number of the Flemings who must have worked under Dubreuil, with Jan Dhoey, who demands a large place in this history.

He derived his origin from a famous painter of the Low Countries, being the grandson of Lucas van Leyden by a descent which M. Herbet† has perfectly elucidated. He appeared at Fontainebleau in 1595 ‡ and continued to live near Dubois, with whom, after the death of Dubreuil, he appears to have shared a leading *rôle* at Fontainebleau. To judge by the ages of their children, Jan Dhoey must have been much the older. His eldest son, Claude, was close on twenty-five at the death of Henri IV., from which we may fancy that the ability which he afterwards displayed as a painter had had time during that reign to develop in the neighbourhood of his father and no doubt under his direction. It is true that there is no painting of the reign of Henri IV. which can be attributed with certainty to this painter from Leyden, and we can do no more than imagine the part he may have taken in such works of that period as have had no artists assigned to

* Laborde: *Renaissance*, p. 877.

† *Extraits d'actes et de notes concernant les artistes de Fontainebleau*, p. 31.

‡ Laborde: *Renaissance*, p. 680.

S

them; in the decoration, for instance, of the Emperors'
Closet, or, especially, in that of the celebrated Conference
Hall, which the special attention of Henri IV. had made
the most magnificent part of the Bathing-hall.   Dan has
left the description of it.*  If from the list he gives we
subtract the copies of old pictures I mentioned above,
there remain eleven compositions, taken from Ovid's "Metamorphoses," which certainly were not the least important
ornaments of the resuscitated Fontainebleau.

No one can tell exactly when the Diana Gallery was
painted; but I can no longer delay the description of this
great work, the famous masterpiece of Ambroise Dubois.
It formed a pendant to the Small Gallery of the Louvre,
and the two combined form the illustrious and long
admired testament of the school of French painting of
the sixteenth century on the threshold of the seventeenth,
which was to see it replaced by another.

Father Dan has left us a complete description of the
paintings with which it was decorated.†  They were
painted in oils on the plaster of the walls, and consisted
of twenty-eight pictures.  Two above the chimney-pieces
represented Mars with the features of Henri IV. and
Marie de Medici as Diana.  Ten others showed the battles
the king had fought and the cities he had taken; and the
rest were mythological, as follows:—

"The loves of Diana and Hippolytus," in two parts;
"The realm of Œneus, King of Ætolia, ravaged by a boar
sent by Diana to punish him"; "The story of Callisto,"
in three parts; "The judgment of Midas"; "The education of Achilles"; "The story of Apollo and the nymph
Coronis," in two parts; "The flaying of Marsyas";

* *Op. cit.*, p. 97.                    † *Op. cit.*, p. 147.

DETAIL OF THE CEILING OF THE GALLERY OF DIANA AT
FONTAINEBLEAU

AMBROISE DUBOIS, AFTER A COPY BY PERCIER, LIBRARY OF THE INSTITUTE
OF FRANCE

" Clymene showing the god of the sun his son Phaeton ";
" Apollo pursuing Daphne "; " The peasants of Lycia
changed into frogs by Latona." Single figures formed a
subsidiary series to these paintings : " Hercules," " Saturn," "Neptune," " Bacchus," "Ceres," "Venus," " Mars,"
" Jupiter," " Juno," " Mercury," " Diana," " Vulcan," &c.,
all painted in camaieu and life-sized. There was also a
" France Triumphant " in the guise of a woman trampling
her vanquished enemies under her feet.

The vaulted ceiling was no less richly ornamented.
It had a quantity of arabesque in the style of the Ulysses
Gallery, of perfect taste and execution, intermingled with
landscapes, views of towns, seaports and various per-
spectives, which all lent a novelty that bears out what I
said of this style above. These ornaments supported the
following twenty large subjects, painted in oils on plaster,
like the rest of the ceiling : " Phaeton praying the son his
father to let him drive his chariot"; "Phaeton driving the
chariot "; "Apollo playing the flute and Pan mocking
him "; " The fall of Phaeton "; " Flora borne on the
clouds "; " Juno and Venus enjoying a concert given by
the Graces and Cupids "; " Mercury flying towards
Olympus "; "Jupiter seated on an eagle "; " Henri IV.
ascending to heaven in a chariot drawn by lions "; " Neptune on a dolphin "; a " Dance of young girls " round the
cypher of Henri IV. which was supported by Cupids ;
" Flora accompanied by the Graces "; " France " per-
sonified, holding a sceptre and crowned by Cupids ;
" Hercules received into the number of the gods"; an
allegory of " Commerce flourishing through the concord
of princes," represented by Mercury with two nymphs,
one of whom was holding two hearts together ; " Diana

in a chariot drawn by horses"; "Latona, Apollo, and Diana"; "Syrinx changed into a reed." Besides these large pictures there were a number of smaller ones, which served as an accompaniment. They come in the following order: "The Danube"; "The Rhine"; "Neptune and Ceres"; a "Concert of Nymphs"; "Naiads with a Satyr"; "Venus bathing"; "Wisdom teaching Infancy"; "Orpheus in Hades"; "The rape of Proserpine"; "Leucothoe and Apollo in the guise of her nurse"; "Semele burned with the fires of Jupiter"; "Apollo and Diana slaying the children of Niobe"; "Mars surprised with Venus"; an allegory of "The plenty enjoyed by the kingdom under Henri IV."; an allegory of the same king's "Good fortune"; "Diana reposing"; "Diana and Endymion"; "The Rhone"; "The Po."

This enumeration will give some idea of the fertility and decorative genius of Ambroise Dubois, and, at the same time, of the new splendour that Fontainebleau put on under Henri IV. This gallery, like the Ulysses Gallery, has perished, and we are less fortunate here than in the case of Primaticcio in being unable to compare it with the original designs. It is true that some portions of this ceiling were removed, and so escaped destruction; they may be seen on the ceiling of the little gallery which King Louis Philippe composed under the name of the gallery des Assiettes; but they have been so thoroughly restored and remade that it is impossible to look to them for any features of the original work. And yet, deprived as we are of examples from which we might judge of the execution, we are fortunate in possessing a document of inestimable value for the information it gives on the arrangement and general merits of the gallery. The

DETAIL OF THE CEILING OF THE GALLERY OF DIANA AT
FONTAINEBLEAU

AMBROISE DUBOIS, AFTER A COPY BY PERCIER, LIBRARY OF THE INSTITUTE
OF FRANCE

document is a water-colour copy made by the architect
Percier shortly before its demolition. This excellent
work, very poorly engraved by Baltard, may be seen in
the library of the Institut de France.*

Judged by this copy, the work shows a great talent
for distributing ornament and breaking up the surface
to be painted, and at the same time a thorough knowledge of how to balance the various compositions. It
presents the most general qualities, at least, of historical
and decorative painting under Henri IV.; they are by
no means to be despised, not only in the apportionment
of the ceiling, but in the actual composition of the particular parts. There is every reason to suppose that
Dubreuil, who excelled Dubois in the latter point, was
his superior also in the general arrangement of parts;
and it must be confessed that the men of the succeeding
age were right to attach the value they did to the small
gallery of the Louvre, and that the two works together
composed a highly honourable testimony to the ability
of the age, sufficient, at any rate, to silence all the con-
temptuous criticism it has received and the efforts that
have been made to deny its very existence.

We need not hesitate to go further, and say that,
regarded solely from the point of view of the art of
decoration, the Diana Gallery reveals an advance on what
we know of the Ulysses Gallery, and, in general, on all
the works of Primaticcio and Rosso. A more discreet
employment of figure subjects, greater variety in the
distribution of them, a much cleverer management of
the points of repose procured, in form by the faint
modelling and in colour by the use of camaieu, wider

* Album, No. 125 F *.

resource in ornament, and a much lighter and pleasanter
general disposition, all go to make up a superiority, which
cannot fail to be apparent on a comparison of Ambroise
Dubois' work with the ballroom, for instance, where the
crowding of the figures without end and without repose
has been censured in all ages by the best judges of the
subject. In the Henri IV. painter the architectural
episodes, which are frequently used among the historical
pieces, introduce order and variety. The pleasant effect
they produce is a happy forecast of what was to come
later under the reign of Louis XIV.; and while Primaticcio in this respect is still but little in advance of the
monotonous arrangement of Raphael and Giulio Romano,
Ambroise Dubois turns our thoughts rather to Vouet and
Lebrun with their magnificent disposition of space and
their exquisite and inexhaustible resources.

He completed the Ulysses Gallery with a profusion of
different devices on the panelling, and a composition that
was still wanting to the ceiling, in which he represented
the surrender of Amiens. The addition of two more
figures, a Diana and an Apollo, which he painted in the
famous aviary at Fontainebleau,* will give us the complete list of his work at that time.

Meanwhile, the gallery of the Louvre, which Dubreuil
left unfinished, was being continued by a painter whose
name only has survived—Jacques Bunel, a son of François Bunel, whom we have seen in the service of the King
of Navarre as a portrait-painter. Jacques occupied himself with history-painting, and painted the second half
of the gallery in question.† He was a native of

* Dan : *op. cit.*, p. 159. † Reiset : *op. cit.*, p. 294.

Blois,* where his father lived, and came to settle in Paris. He was forty-four years old, at least, at Dubreuil's death, and probably followed his designs in completing what remained to be done.

We know of two other works by him, a "Descent of the Holy Spirit" in the Church of the Grands Augustins, and an "Assumption" at the Feuillants in the Rue St. Honoré.† Both have perished, without leaving any known traces either in engravings or in the original drawings.

These pictures in the Paris churches began to be multiplied by the brushes of the painters of this school. Thus Jan Dhoey painted a "Last Judgment" for Notre Dame,‡ which has been missing since the Revolution. In 1612 again, two years after the death of Henri IV., he was commissioned for similar sacred pictures§ for the Chapelle Haute at Fontainebleau, concurrently with Dubois, who had painted "The Pentecost" and "The Resurrection." Dhoey painted "The Assumption" and "The Church Militant."‖ All these pictures are lost.

At the Louvre, moreover, and the other royal palaces, there were painters at work whose names are all that Félibien has preserved ¶—Pasquier Testelin and Jean Debrie. In addition to these there were two of whom we know a little more: Guillaume Dumée, whose name is now beginning to be rescued from obscurity, and Gabriel Honnet,

---

* Though Marolles makes him a native of Tours. See Bernier: *Histoire de Blois*, in Laborde's *Renaissance*, p. 322.

† Félibien: *op. cit.*, pp. 712, 713.

‡ *Revue universelle des Arts*, vol. xxi. p. 80.

§ Herbet: *op. cit.*, p. 54. Dan wrongly puts them in 1608, and makes a still greater mistake in combining them with two pictures by Jean Dubois, the son of Ambroise, who was then only four years old. His pictures were not added till 1631.

‖ Dan: *op. cit.*, p. 60.     ¶ *Op. cit.*, p. 712.

whom, so far as I can discover, no other writer has mentioned. Both took part with Bunel and Dubois in the decoration of a certain great closet of the queen in the Louvre. Félibien,* who gave the details, has not defined the date. It must certainly have been before 1614, the year of Ambroise Dubois' death; and everything points to this series of paintings as having been, with the Theagenes and the Clorinda rooms, one of the most famous examples of the style of the painters of Henri IV. The subjects were again chosen from the " Gerusalemme Liberata." Dubois painted " Olindo begging to be allowed to die in place of Sophronia," and " Sophronia maintaining that she committed the theft of the image for which Aladine was punishing her"; Bunel painted " The enchantments of the magician Ismeno," and " Aladine condemning the Christians to death"; Dumée, " Clorinda on horseback arriving at Jerusalem," " Clorinda demanding pardon for Olindo and Sophronia," and " The condemned pair delivered from their doom"; and Gabriel Honnet, " The magician Ismeno demanding the image of the Virgin from Aladine," " The carrying off of the image," and " Sophronia accusing herself before the Sultan of having taken it." In all there were ten compositions, which deserve a place of honour in our history.

In 1601 Guillaume Dumée became one of the painters of Fontainebleau.† He had also painted at St. Germain-en-Laye, and was appointed painter to the king in 1605.‡

The continued efforts of Henri IV. for the encouragement of tapestry form no part of my subject, but I cannot omit a brief mention of them, because the names of several of these painters occur in that connection.

* *Op. cit.*    † Laborde : *Renaissance,* p. 686.    ‡ *Ibid.,* p. 866.

THE LAST SUPPER

LERAMBERT. CABINET DES ESTAMPES, PARIS

It appears that, after the death of Dubreuil, the duty of superintending the work and of furnishing an occasional design was entrusted to Henri Lerambert, whom we mentioned in a preceding chapter. Twenty years before, in 1584,* he had furnished the designs for the famous hangings in the Church of St. Merry in Paris. Félibien states that in 1600 he supplied cartoons for the Artemisia tapestry,† a supplement to Caron's compositions, of which I have recently discovered six original drawings.‡ These drawings, with the series used for St. Merry,§ give a singularly feeble idea of this artist's talents. He seems, however, to have played some part in the art of the day until 1610, when he died.|| Four painters then applied simultaneously for the right of succeeding him in the studios of the royal tapestries, which, since the return of the Jesuits, had been set up in the Louvre. The four were these very men, Dumée, Honnet, and Dhoey, and one now mentioned for the first time, Laurent Guiot. Dumée and he came forward in partnership; and in the competition that was set, the subject being a series of cartoons on "The story of Pastor Fido," they presented their designs together; and both being accepted at the same time, they were appointed in conjunction to the supervision of the tapestry factory in the Louvre.¶ Their Pastor Fido was

---

* Guiffrey, Müntz and Pinchart: *Histoire générale de la tapisserie*, p. 91. Félibien wrongly gives the date as 1594.

† *Op. cit.*, vol. ii. p. 126.

‡ *Le tapisserie d'Artemise et le peintre Lerambert.—Chronique des Arts*, 1902, p. 327.

§ Cabinet of Prints, Paris. Ad 104.

|| Laborde : *op. cit.*, p. 868.

¶ *Ibid.* In the document Dhoey is written De Hery, an orthographical corruption of De Hoey, of which there are several examples. Hence Jal

woven, and the hanging is mentioned, with the names of
the two artists, in the inventories of Louis XIV.* The
cartoons by Honnet and Dhoey for the same subject were
considered unworthy of the appointment.

I have but a word to add of Laurent Guiot. Like
Lerambert, to whose place he succeeded, we only find him
mentioned in connection with tapestry. He designed
several hangings mentioned in Félibien and the inventories,
the most celebrated of which, immortalised by Molière in
" L'Avare," was that of Gombaut and Macée.† We know
it from the prints ‡ and a complete series in the museum
at St. Lo.

After these painters comes one more completely forgotten than they, the second of the Bollerys, Nicolas, son
of Jérôme. We find him married in 1584,§ which proves
that he was then old enough to be a painter. I cannot
help thinking that it is of him that. Van Mander, whose
work was printed twenty years later, wrote as follows':
" There is still a certain Bollery, who paints beautiful
night effects, masquerades, and other such entertainments,
as well as flocks in the manner of Bassan. He has the
air of a great lord, and rides on horseback followed by a
groom." This last detail, nevertheless, marks a painter
of some importance.

And that brings me to the end of my history. I have
only now to wind up the long list and crown it with the

has taken him to be Martin de Hery, the son of Claude de Hery, the
engraver of the French coinage.

* Guiffrey : *op. cit.*, vol. i. p. 333.
† Félibien : *op. cit.*, vol. ii. p. 126.
‡ Cabinet of Prints, Paris, Album Ed 5 g.
§ Jal : *op. cit.*, p. 243.

## THE FLAGELLATION
FREMINET.  FROM A PRINT

splendour of a great reputation by the mention of one whose career was then only at its outset, and whose most famous works were not painted till well on in the reign of Louis XIII.

It was only in 1608 * that the roof of the Chapel of the Trinity at Fontainebleau was put in hand under Martin Fréminet. The paintings, restored, are still there, and an enumeration of the principal subjects will be sufficient. They were as follows: "Noah building the Ark"; "The Fall of the Angels," "The Eternal Father," "Gabriel chosen for the Annunciation," "The Fathers of the Church" with the "Four Elements"; "The Prophets and figures from the Old Testament"; "The Virtues," and fourteen subjects representing the life of Jesus Christ. The author of these famous and important works had studied in Italy. We find him back in France and present at Fontainebleau about 1603,† and he died in 1619.‡ He had painted a St. Sebastian in the church of St. Josse in Paris § and eight fathers of the Church in the Castle of Richelieu, which are now in the Orleans Museum.‖ His style is completely Florentine in origin, and sensibly different from that of Dubreuil or Dubois. With him this history closes, and he is the last of the French painters of style who may be said to belong to the epoch of the Renaissance.

Dubois, as I have said, died in 1614 and Lerambert in 1610. Hieronymus Franck also died in 1610 ¶; Jan Dhoey in 1615,** and Josse de Voltigeant no doubt before

* Dan: *Trésor des Merveilles*, p. 64.
† Laborde: *op. cit.*, p. 689.    ‡ Félibien: *op. cit.*, vol. ii. p. 116.
§ *Ibid.*, p. 114.    ‖ Catalogue, Nos. 141 to 148.
¶ Herluison: *op. cit.*, p. 230.    The document calls him Lefranc.
** Herbet: *op. cit.*, p. 36.

1622.* They were all Flemings; and, strange to say,
they bore the old French art with them to the grave.
Henri IV. died in 1610. Others were destined to achieve
the task of joining the thread of his schemes to works of
another kind, and of reaching with a totally new school
the goal which the genius of this king had marked out for
the efforts of French art.

* Herbet : *op. cit.*, p. 163.

ST. SEBASTIAN

DUBREUIL. LOUVRE

# CHAPTER XIII

Portrait-painting under Henri IV.—The Dumoûtiers, Etienne, Côme, Daniel and Pierre—The exceptional ability of the last named—His travels—The Quesnels, François and Nicolas—The presumed works of the former—A criticism of them ; their importance—Benjamin Foulon ; his mediocrity — Other portrait-painters, Darlay, Rabel, Recouvrance, Ledigne—The master of the monogram I. D. C.—The new feature he introduced—Imitated by the last Dumoûtiers — Italianism in portrait-painting—Supposed works of Caron—Jacques Bunel—Louis Poisson—The small gallery of the Louvre—Incorrectness of the general idea of the portraits it contained—Bunel and his wife the painters of them—Frans Pourbus the younger—His place in French art—Final fate of the last Dumoûtiers.

WE must now pass to the art of portrait-painting under the reign of Henri IV., which marks the end of our course.

It is chiefly remarkable for the full expansion of a family which was thenceforward to be famous in that sphere; I mean the family of Dumoûtier. We have seen its first appearance already with Etienne, the most celebrated of the sons of old Geoffroy, who came upon the scene in the reign of Henri II. Owing to the absence of precise information about his life and his works, we were unable to do more than mention him in passing; but his name occurs regularly in the Accounts of the royal household from the end of the reign of Charles IX. to the date we have now reached. His epitaph * shows that the office of painter to the king, which he held under Henri II., continued to be his without interruption under François II., Charles IX., Henri III. and Catherine de Medici, and finally under Henri IV. By this time he had grown very old, and no doubt had left behind him an extremely large quantity of work, and many drawings in chalks, the remembrance of which descended as far as Félibien.* He reports that several were taken into Flanders by his son and purchased by the Archduchess Isabella, which would prove his talent to have been deservedly recognised and his fame to have been extended. As for particular mention of his works, it is true that we do find one, by a poet named Ledigne.† It refers to a portrait of the poet's mistress, entitled Marie B. with the surname suppressed. The poem dates from 1606, which proves that Etienne Dumoûtier continued in extreme old age to practise his art and enjoy the praise of the public.

He had a brother named Côme, generally taken to be a portrait-painter; but since we have no proof of this, and in general do not know in which branch of art he was distinguished, a few notes on his score will be sufficient. He was painter to Catherine de Medici and to the king, and we find his name in the Accounts from 1581.‡ The lateness of the date and the youth of his children proves him to have been younger than Etienne. Mariette,§ after a manuscript by Sauval, says that he received commissions from several courts; and his own celebrity, combined with that of Etienne, brought the

---

* *Entretiens sur la vie et les ouvrages des plus fameux peintres,* ed. 4to, vol. i. p. 706.

† *Nouvelles Archives de l'art français,* 1878, p. 272.

‡ Jal : *Dictionnaire critique de biographie et d'histoire,* p. 881.

§ In Reiset : *Notice des dessins du Louvre,* part ii. p. 299.

whole family into an eminence by which the successors of both must have profited.

It is about this time that they begin to appear. Pierre, a son of Etienne, is mentioned from 1581,* when he was apparently at a very tender age, for none of the earliest works of his that are known date from before the reign of Henri IV. Thomas de Leu engraved, after him, the portrait of Guillaume Legagneur in 1594, and that of Jean de Beaugrand in 1595. Daniel Dumoûtier, a son of Côme, was born in 1570,† and was about twenty when Henri IV. recovered his throne. These two cousins, though no doubt unequal in age, were both concurrently endowed with eminent abilities, and the footing at court which they owed to the fame of their fathers could not fail to draw its attention to them. And so we find them both from that time forward giving proofs of a period of production which was destined to last for not less than half a century. It is not surprising that this long career should have resulted in stamping the name of Dumoûtier on the public memory to such an extent that at last ancient France knew of no other artists in chalks; and, while indiscriminately ascribing every single French portrait in oils to Clouet, came finally to put the name of Dumoûtier to every single portrait in chalks.

We have seen that Thomas de Leu engraved portraits by Pierre. It is probable that Pierre was responsible for the small preparatory sketches in chalks reduced to the dimensions of the print and possibly taken from some other master. A chalk-drawing in the Cabinet in Paris,‡ dated 1601 and signed with his name, is an example of

---

* Jal: *ut sup.*  † Mariette: *Abécédario*, vol. ii. p. 131.
‡ Album Nᵉ 32.

one of these small copies of which we possess the original.*
Two portraits,† signed and dated 1618, show the talent
of this master on the larger scale, and enable us to com-
pile a list of his other chalks, some of which are dressed
in the fashions of Henri IV.  On the other hand, a
number of works by Daniel, of much later date, and,
like the others, signed and guaranteed in several ways,
enable us to discern his earliest manner and to ascribe to
him with perfect assurance several works of this period;
among others a portrait of Gabrielle d'Estrées ‡ painted
before 1600, the year in which this favourite died, and
another of Mme. Dubiez.§

Of the two manners which we find at this time in
the two Dumoûtiers, Pierre's is far the better.  Daniel's
work is clever but feeble; and the impression he gives
is that of a man in haste to acquire a specious and rapid
manner, rather than of an artist in love with his art and
anxious to keep it renovated by the study of nature.
His facility is great, and from the very beginning it limits
his ambition; his ability is singularly agile and completely confined to settling the rules of an honest routine.
Pierre, on the other hand, shows an exquisite taste, a
delicacy in his aims and ideals, and a constant ardour
for improvement which from the very first give a fore-
taste of the choice works he was afterwards to produce.
In him we meet with one of the kings of French chalk-
drawing, and the name of Dumoûtier rises to its apogee.

* Album Na 23 a ; old No. 127.
† One of Lavardin-Beaumanoir, framed ; the other of a woman, Album
Na 24 b, in the Cabinet in Paris.
‡ Cabinet of Prints, Paris, Case I., old No. 83.
§ Cabinet of Prints, Paris, Case III., old No. 45.

But it seems that he was of an adventurous spirit. The years that his cousin spent * in building up what was to be a considerable reputation, Pierre devoted partly to travelling. In 1603 we find him in Flanders † with the Archduchess Isabella to whom he sold his father's works. Did he go on to England? It is a fact that a portrait of King James I. in the Cabinet in Paris ‡ is unquestionably his, and that another drawing § has an inscription in his own hand, "the wife of James I."; that is, Anne of Denmark.

Etienne Dumoûtier had died shortly before, in the same year 1603, at the age of eighty-three. He was the last survivor of the generation which had seen the second of the Janets at his height, and he brought to the threshold of the new century the traditions founded in France by the masters of the ancient portrait-painting.

Others, like the two brothers Quesnel, added their labours to the work. These two were François and Nicolas, both sons of the old Pierre whom I have mentioned. François, and possibly his brother also, was born in Edinburgh at the time when their father was in the service of James V. François was not yet fifty at the accession of Henri IV., and this reign saw his chief period of production. There are no fewer than eight works known, which were engraved after him by Thomas de Leu. He also was painter to the king. Marolles ‖ adds that he

---

* To Daniel, known as Dumoûtier the Younger, we must ascribe, no doubt, a chalk-portrait of Louis XIII., drawn in 1604, which is mentioned by Héroard : *Journal de l'enfance et de la jeunesse de Louis XIII.;* edited by Soulié and Barthélemy, vol. i. p. 64.

† Félibien, *ut sup.*                    ‡ Album Ne 30.

§ Album Na 32 a ; old No. 34.

‖ In Reiset : *op. cit.*, p. 413.

T

was highly favoured by the Chancellor de Cheverny. In 1602 he painted Louis XIII. in infancy, full-length.* The Constable Henri de Montmorency commissioned him for five pictures at once: portraits of himself, his wife, and their three children, which were intended for the Princess of Orange.†

Unfortunately all this does not put us in possession of a single authentic work by this master. The famous amateur Fevret de Fontette had a portrait by him of Jacques Quesnel, a child of six,‡ which is now lost. In the absence of any works certainly his, M. Bouchot remembers that a portrait of Henrietta d'Entragues, engraved by Thomas de Leu, on which his name appears as the painter, has been discovered among the chalk-drawings in the Cabinet in Paris,§ and thereupon proposes to attribute to François Quesnel this drawing and all others of the same kind, which certainly form a numerous and characteristic family. The author of this observation does not speak of certainty, but there is good reason to believe that the hint is not to be despised. We may presume, therefore, pending further knowledge, to complete this information on the life of the elder Quesnel by some consideration of the manner of the works thus presumed to be his.

They have brilliance in plenty, but little solidity. The knowledge is limited and the display excessive. There is much softness and finish; the hair shines, the eyeballs gleam, a peculiar tint of rose heightens the cheeks

---

* Héroard : *op. cit.*, vol. i. p. 21.
† *Nouvelles Archives de l'art français*, 1877, p. 150.
‡ Lelong : *Bibliothèque historique de la France*, vol. iv. p. 254.
§ Na 21 a, fol. 77.

Catharine Henriette de Balsac d'Entragues, marquise de Verneuil, maitresse de Henry 4. morte en 1633.

HENRIETTE D'ENTRAGUES
ATTRIBUTED TO FRANÇOIS QUESNEL.   CABINET DES ESTAMPES, PARIS

and sweetens the complexion. With these qualities we find a dashing air and a discreet enthusiasm which, coming on the top of this sweetness, must have been highly prized. And, indeed, we find that drawings of this kind were produced in great numbers. Two large volumes in the Cabinet in Paris, which came from the Gaignières collection,* are principally made up of them. M. Bouchot declares that there could be no better illustrations to the letters of Henri IV. In the eyes of the hasty amateur, the whole art of the reign is summed up in this style; and the men of that age are imagined in the light of the means and the manner of the presumed Quesnel.

The extant work of Nicolas Quesnel, which is proved to be his by authentic evidence, is far from being equal to his brother's. A portrait of his father, drawn in 1574 and bearing his signature,† may serve as a measure of his ability, which was of a very low order. What success it had is not known.

There was another painter of famous origin, of whom I have given nothing so far but the name, but who nevertheless found patrons, though he never rose to any height; I mean Benjamin Foulon, Janet's nephew. Several of his chalk-drawings are to be found among the anonymous works which make up the Lecurieux album. After 1577 we find him on the king's household.‡ On the death of Henri III., he passed into the service of Henri IV. before his restoration. He was then in retirement at Tours. In 1592 we find him summoned to the king's camp and staying there for two whole months, at work on

---

\* Na 21 and Na 21 a.

† Cabinet of Prints, Paris, Na 31.

‡ Jal : *op. cit.*, p. 292.

several pictures,* the subjects of which are not known, but in view of this special commission must almost certainly have been battle-pieces. Later he was living in Paris, as a number of family documents testify. He had obtained, somehow, the post of controller-general of the coinage in the place of Germain Pilon. Philippe Damfrie, who occupied the same post and claimed to be declared the sole possessor of it, obtained a decree against Foulon in 1592.† Of the previous history of the case we know nothing. The story, combined with his numerous drawings and the illustrious people who stood god-parents to some of his children,‡ seems to prove that he was prosperous.§ He was painter to the king for the rest of his life, which lasted beyond the reign of Henri IV.

One of his drawings in the Lecurieux album bears, as I have said, his authentic signature.|| This being taken as a model of his manner, the large number of works of the same kind which have been found to resemble it, have made Benjamin Foulon one of the best known of the artists in chalks of the sixteenth century. He has no cause for congratulation in that, for his talent is of the most beggarly description. The most rudimentary elements of drawing are all he can lay claim to, and he lacks the art to make the most of them, or even to show the feeble work he has to offer to its best advantage. I need only mention the Fair Gabrielle and the Duc de Mercoeur in the Cabinet of Prints in Paris,¶ and the

* *Revue de l'art français*, 1890, p. 137.
† *Ibid.*, 1892, p. 299.
‡ Grandmaison : *Documents inédits sur les arts en Touraine*, p. 90.
§ On the question of his salary, see p. 240, note ¶.
|| Bouchot : *Les Portraits au crayon de la Bibliothèque nationale*, p. 31.
¶ Case I., old No. 53, and VI., 46.

Mme. de Sardini, the wife of a famous banker, who became his patroness, in the Louvre.* The César de Vendôme, which bears his signature and was engraved on a reduced scale by Thomas de Leu, is a more wretched performance than any of the others, owing to the greater difficulty he always found in painting children.

To this long list of painters sprung from celebrated families, I need only add Charles Decourt, the son of Jean. We have already seen him appointed, like his father, painter to the king; but none of his works survive. We know, at least, that he made four chalk-drawings of Louis XIII. between 1602 and 1607, when the young prince was six years old.† The first of all was intended for the Grand Duke of Tuscany, his ancestor, the father of Queen Marie de Medici.

Side by side with these more or less eminent artists there lived and worked on the same lines a number of others still very little known, who, nevertheless, helped to fill up a very imposing tale of artists of the period, and to prove the persistence of a taste which is all but perennial in the public mind. Among these were Darlay, Rabel, Antoine de Recouvrance, and another, whom no one ever mentions, Nicolas Ledigne, a native of Champagne.

Darlay is principally known by a portrait of Catherine, sister of Henri II., which was engraved after his drawing by Thomas de Leu. Other works also prove that he was in fact painter to this princess. ‡ Possibly, too, it is he that a modern writer § mentions under the name of Darly,

---

* No. 33,474. It was by means of this portrait that M. Bouchot identified Foulon's handwriting. See above, p. 212, note *.

† Héroard : *op. cit.*, vol. i. pp. 18, 30, 79, 262.

‡ *Œuvres du poète Laroque de Clermont*, 1609, p. 336.

§ Chalmel : *Histoire de la Touraine*, vol. iv. p. 129.

adding that he was said to be of Touraine, and enjoyed as a portrait-painter the patronage of the greatest nobles of the time.

Rabel, whose Christian name was Jean, was, like Caron, a native of Beauvais, and a publisher of his own engravings as well as a painter. Thomas de Leu engraved three portraits after his drawings, and these are all the works of his that we possess. One is of Drake at the age of forty-three, and drawn, therefore, in 1583; one of Don John of Austria and Alexander Farnese together, and the third of the French poet Garnier. The portrait of Queen Louise, which is added to the plates in a book of "The Sibyls," which he published for the poet Dorat, may also be his work; the plates certainly are. He also painted flowers, and was a friend of the famous Malherbe. It is not known that he held any official title. He died in 1603,* in the same year as Etienne Dumoûtier.

Antoine de Recouvrance was painter to the king from 1588. Henri IV. continued him in the office. Indeed, it is probable that at that time he enjoyed, like the Huguenot painters, the special favour of the intimate members of the court of Navarre. It is certain that he painted for Duplessis-Mornay, the celebrated minister of Henri IV., whose gallery of portraits I have mentioned. In 1609 he was commissioned by this noble for four portraits, the names of which have survived.† They represented Mornay himself and Mme. de Mornay, M. de Boves, and Mme. de la Vairie.

---

* According to Lestoille, quoted in Mariette's *Abécédario*, vol. iv. p. 232.

† B. Fillon: *La galerie de portraits de Duplessis-Mornay à Saumur.—Gazette des Beaux-Arts*, 1879.

The text of the evidence itself informs us that these pictures were only copies taken from originals by an artist whose name is not given; and thence we must conclude that Recouvrance's work was destined for the Saumur Gallery, and lacked the interest which would be taken in portraits intended for a different purpose. The works themselves are missing; and here, again, we should know nothing of the artist, except from his lost productions, if it were not that the little town of Chaumont-en-Bassigny possesses a work of his, signed and dated with unquestionable authenticity, as follows: *Anth. de Recouvrance me fecit et delineavit* 1604. It is now in the possession of the merchant, M. Scordel. It represents a scene, which has not yet been explained, displayed in a church in the midst of several allegories. The very numerous portraits in it form the whole interest of the work.

Of Nicolas Ledigne, mentioned above, who was a friend of Etienne Dumoûtier, we have evidence that he himself drew portraits in chalks. He was a poet, and the author of an album called " Les Fleurettes," which appeared in 1601; and with this talent, like Denisot, he combined the gifts of an artist. Three poems in his book * are proof of this. He styled himself Sieur de Condé and Prior of L'Enfourchure, and his poems continue up till 1610.

His name is the last on the list we have succeeded in compiling of portrait-painters under Henri IV. But in this period, as in the rest, there are the unknown artists to be reckoned with; and, since the number of works produced went on increasing incessantly, the task

* See above, p. 286, note †.

becomes harder here than before.   It belongs, however, more properly to museography than to history; and in the scanty light that the former science is able to supply at present, there is no hope of our being able to draw on it for anything essential to the task before us.   There is only one list of works that deserves to be made an exception in the present instance: one which reveals a singular ability that sets the unknown artist in the highest rank of the long procession of drawers in chalk of the sixteenth century.   With the two Janets, Pierre Dumoûtier, and the presumably Flemish unknown artist of the reign of Henri IV., he forms the fifth of the exquisite chosen few, and deserves to be described at length.

M. Bouchot was the first to discover this admirable master, and to make a classified list of his works.   One of them* has on the corner of the sheet the letters I. D. C. In the absence of other information, this monogram ought to help in his identification.   M. Bouchot refrains from deciding on its meaning, but suggests several interpretations.   He examines Jean de Courmont, or Gourmont, who was an engraver and publisher about this time; then Jean Decourt, or de Court, whom we mentioned above. Neither of the two satisfies him, for various reasons, the most remarkable among them being that we are not even sure that the monogram is that of the artist at all.   The portrait on which it occurs represents a woman of the middle classes, as the head-dress shows, perhaps even the wife of an artisan.   These artists in chalks never on any account painted middle-class people, with the exception of those of their own families, for no doubt they could not have paid for their portraits; it is possible, therefore, that

* Cabinet of Prints, Paris ; Na 23 a ; old No. 5.

GABRIELLE D'ESTRÉES

THE MASTER WITH THE MONOGRAM I.D.C.  CABINET DES ESTAMPES, PARIS

this woman was the artist's own wife, and, if the monogram is hers, it still might some day become a means of
verifying her husband's name. However it may be, the
following is a list of the works that may be attributed to
this master, I. D. C.: two chalk-drawings of La Belle
Gabrielle d'Estrées, Mme. de Carnavalet, Claude du
Bellay, abbot of Savigny, Mdlle. d'Urfé, and five portraits of men unknown; * these, with the portrait mentioned above, make a total of eleven works, which their
strong individuality of style declare to belong to this
master.

They are recognisable, not only by their perfect science
and infinite charm, but by a turn for the ornamental, a
pride of execution, even a suspicion of mannerism, which
are unique in the whole of this history. All the chalk-
drawings we have mentioned, for all the obvious differences they show between one master and another and
one-period and another, agree at least in one thing—a
closeness of execution that is completely devoid of style.
Gravity in execution and simplicity in method are the
common features of the whole school. The master with
the monogram I. D. C., on the other hand, has a dash, a
softness, a filminess, which reveal the charms of more
refined schools; a fugitive delicacy in the features and
a sinuosity in the outlines which add new fascination to
the distinctive merits of the school. It is at least remarkable that with all his refinement, he has nevertheless conformed to the traditional simplicity in composition.

* Cabinet of Prints in Paris, Case I., old Nos. 12 and 120; II., 59 (not
observed by M. Bouchot); III., 79 (also passed over by M. Bouchot);
VII., unnumbered; Album Na 23, old No. 115, unnumbered. Louvre,
Nos. 33,497, 33,535, 33,536.

We find in him no inversions, no foreshortening, and no contrasts except one that must be mentioned, in the relation between the direction of the eye and the position of the head. He is fond of turning the eyeballs a different way from the face, of putting his model three-quarter face, and then making him look at the spectator. This is no slight or negligible detail. In that small beginning, in that feeble effort after elegance, lies the germ of the whole difference between the archaic school of portraiture and the modern school as the state painters have formed it; to make my meaning clear by examples, the whole difference between Holbein and Vandyck.

On comparing the younger Janet, the presumably Flemish anonymous artist, and the master I. D. C. together, I find in the second a consummate perfection, a vivacity, and a charm which are lacking in the extremely simple and only slightly abstract art of the first. But there is nothing in his charm that goes beyond nature; it only results in giving all the fascination of nature, which was partly neglected by Janet; in the master I. D. C. art comes to the front, and the pleasing superiority of the painter in the management of his material and the interpretation of his model. With him we have ceased to be rooted to the soil of old Flanders, of which the elder Pourbus remains the symbol. We have taken the first step towards a freer, more brilliant art, with more of those charms of the mind and the imagination of which Italy stands for the perfection. These works go beyond character to aim at something of style.

And this is all the more noteworthy because the two Dumoûtiers, Pierre and Daniel, did not fail to enrich

their own manner with this new quality. I need say
nothing in detail about Daniel, for in him this new
artistic resource was merely combined with several others,
and so steeped in the common stew of his facile and
tedious works; but Pierre proved himself hardly below
his model in this direction. His brilliant and bold
handling was admirably suited to these contrasts of
direction between the eye and the face, and the Lavardin-Beaumanoir in the Cabinet of Prints in Paris * must
be acknowledged to be in this respect a masterpiece of
French art.

The foregoing considerations lead naturally on to the
subject of the Italianism which began to make its way
among some of the portrait-painters of the end of the
century. Not that the term is applicable either to the
master I. D. C. or to those who followed him. It only
concerns the art of portraiture as men like Antoine Caron
were able to conceive it, as silhouettes of princes on
caracoling steeds, or royal robes sweepingly enveloping
kings and princesses in heroic guise.

In the Castle of Chantilly there are two drawings in
this style, said to represent Charles IX. and the Duc
d'Alençon, both on horseback. They are ascribed to
Caron, and are perhaps the work of one of the heirs
of Niccolo. In the time of Henri IV. we see this type
taking form ; the prints designed by Isaïe Fournier are
the most striking examples. They mark a style very
different from that which reigned throughout the whole
of the sixteenth century, but since the change was chiefly
due to the influence of Fontainebleau, we cannot omit all
mention of it here. Jacques Bunel and Louis Poisson

* See above, p. 288, note †.

appear to have painted in this style. The second I have not mentioned before, and will take this opportunity of giving his history at once.

He was painter to the king from 1596,\* and at work, on what branch of art we do not know, at St. Germain and at Fontainebleau. The inventory of the pictures of Louis XIV. by Bailly † gives the title of the only picture of his of which any mention has survived, a portrait of Henri IV. armed and striking down the Lernæan hydra. Now this composition, which could not have been common, is found exactly reproduced in an engraving in the work of Léonard Gautier; and this fact has induced me to believe it to be the work, now lost, by Poisson.

If we now compare this work with a state portrait of Henri IV. by Bunel, the drawing of which is in the Louvre,‡ we may form an idea of this new style of portrait, a style that is insipid enough, it must be admitted, but interesting as a contrast. Moreover, it is certain that this was the style in which the celebrated portraits in the small gallery of the Louvre were executed.

We described the ceiling of this gallery in the preceding chapter, and it is now time to pass on to the work of a different sort which decorated the walls.

And, first of all, the current idea of the tendencies of art at this period, an idea which we find at the root of much criticism, is absolutely void of foundation. It is commonly supposed that this gallery contained a regular series of kings and queens of France, alternating with ornament, from the earliest days of the monarchy

* Laborde : *La Renaissance des arts à la cour de France*, p. 875.

† Edited by Engerand, p. 577.

‡ Catalogue, No. 33,594. Fréminet also painted him in 1606. Héroard : *Journal*, vol. i. p. 235.

down to the time of Henri IV. The name of "The Gallery of Kings and Queens," which every one has followed Sauval in giving it, and that writer's story of the whole of France being scoured in the search, among painted windows and tombs, for the authentic features of each monarch, in order to compose these historical pictures, combined to give this opinion a force which only an incontrovertible document could suffice to overthrow. Still, in spite of its having been printed for some time, that document has not yet succeeded in obtaining due consideration, or in prevailing against the beaten track of the oldest descriptions. Nevertheless, it is nothing else than the inventory of the portraits that formed the decoration of that gallery, drawn up by order of the king in 1603.* I shall not transcribe it here, because the lengthy particularisation of so uniform a list of pictures would carry little instruction with it. But the summary of it which follows will give a good idea of it.

It consisted of 130 pictures, among which the kings and queens of France, so far from occupying the whole space, were not even of secondary importance. There were only four of them in the gallery: Henri IV. and Marie de Medici, whose presence was a matter of course, Henri III. and his mother Catherine. The last named, again, was doubtless there only in honour of the queen, the wife of Henri IV. and a Medici like herself; for it is quite certain that the sole object of the gallery was the glorification of that family. With the exception of these four, indeed, every large portrait in the place represented a Medici. There were eighteen of them,

* *Archives de l'art français:* Documents, vol. iii. p. 55.

including Cosmo, the father of his country, Lorenzo the Magnificent, Francisco II., Grand Duke of Tuscany, and his wife Christine, all of them relatives of the queen. Then came John, Julian, and Alexander, all three popes and all three members of the family, Leo X., Clement VII., and Leo XI. Those are enough to prove the intention I have just stated. The gallery was the result of a gallant design of the king's, and was ordained for the glorification of the relatives of the new queen; of the twenty-two large pictures it contained, only two represented kings of France, and two others, though indeed they represented queens of France, were still Medicis. It is certain that these large pictures were painted quite as much, and even more, with a view to decoration than to historical information. Bunel worked at them, with the aid of his wife, Marguerite Bahuche.* The date is indicated by what I said above. The king was not married till 1600, and the inventory is of 1603. The work, then, must be placed between these two dates.

When we pass to the rest of the 130 portraits, all works of smaller dimensions, and intended to be a subsidiary series to the large ones, we are struck by the absence of all system in the choice of the persons represented. Charles the Bold, Duke of Burgundy, appeared there side by side with Basil, Prince of Muscovy; Ferdinando Cortez by Odet de Foix-Lautrec; Tamerlane by Marsilius Ficinus; Artaxerxes by Charlemagne; Sir Thomas More by Michael Angelo; St. Bernard Tolomei by Andrea Doria; and the Cardinal de la Bourdaizière by Porsenna. And that gives rise to the question whether so complete a chaos can possibly be

* Jal : *op. cit.*, p. 295.

considered to be the effect of systematic choice, or whether rather, in haste to make up the gallery in the style then fashionable, and having only three years in which to work on it, the people responsible did not simply seize hurriedly on any historical portraits they could find, and make copies of them.

The answer would be uncertain, without the aid of some useful comparisons supplied by the catalogue of Paolo Giovio's museum, which has been elaborated by M. Müntz.*

The titles of more than fifty pictures in the Small Gallery correspond with those of the same number in the museum; and since there is nothing to show that the remainder were not to be found among Paolo Giovio's pictures, all traces of which have since been lost,† we have evidence enough to conclude that Henri IV., following the example of several contemporary monarchs, took copies of Paolo Giovio's pictures for the Louvre. Among others, the Archduke Ferdinand of the Tyrol had done the same, and before him Cosmo I. de Medici, who had at Florence a replica of the *Jovianum*.‡ This last fact puts us on the scent of a still stricter proof of the certainty of my suggestion. It is this. A copy which Duke Cosmo had made of a Nicolas Orsini from the *Jovianum*, has the false inscription *Virginium Ursinus*.

---

* *Mémoires de l'Académie des Inscriptions et Belles-Lettres*, 1900.

† The inventory of the Small Gallery of the Louvre is exactly fitted to be of assistance in all future attempts to complete the list of portraits in Paolo Giovio's museum. For instance, we know, on the evidence of Giovio himself, that the list must have included some popes, while M. Müntz has not discovered a single one. The Small Gallery contained seventeen, and perhaps these might fill the gap.

‡ Müntz, *op. cit.*

Now that same inscription may be found in the inventory
we have quoted,* taken from a picture in the Small Gallery
of the Louvre. That proves that the pictures in this
gallery not only reproduced the portraits in Paolo
Giovio's museum, but that they were copied in Florence
from the first copies, which, no doubt, were put at the
disposal of Henri IV. by his father-in-law, the Grand
Duke of Tuscany.

Who went to copy them? The question cannot be
answered yet; but it would be an interesting point to
solve, and would prove, no doubt, that Marguerite
Bahuche, who was at work on the eighteen large portraits, had nothing to do with the others, as is commonly
believed at present. No more can we continue to credit
her with the work of historical reconstitution which has
been attributed to her on the evidence of Sauval. Most
of the pictures were brought over completely finished, and
with them, no doubt, the chalk-drawings necessary for
painting in full-length the fourteen Medicis to whom the
four kings and queens of France were subsidiary.

That is as fair a picture as can be drawn, here set
down for the first time, of the famous Small Gallery of
the Louvre, which exhibited, as it were, the consummation
of a taste, the outset and origin of which I have given
above. Historically, it comes between the Gallery of St.
Ange, which was created before 1600, again by Henri IV.,
for Gabrielle d'Estrée, to whom the castle belonged, and
that of Beauregard, still to be visited, which dates from
later than 1614. The fashion was suggested by Paolo
Giovio's collection, and we find it ostensibly returning
after fifty years to its original, while other contem-

* No. 71.

poraneous works, like the gallery of the Mornays at Saumur, represented rather a collection of family portraits, or at any rate a selection from the national subjects, than a universal iconography.

The gallery of the Louvre, as I have said, was burnt down. The accident happened in 1661. But it is usually forgotten that only the paintings on the ceiling were destroyed, and that the portraits were saved. Loret's " Muse," in fact,* informs us that a few days before the ceremony which caused the fire, they were put in a place of safety, so that, were it not for the negligence which, no doubt, followed these stringent precautions,† the disaster would never have prevented our forming an idea, from the pictures themselves, of the combined abilities of Bunel and his wife in the domain of the state-portrait.

It is highly probable that the above-mentioned drawing of Henri IV. had been placed in this gallery. Other portraits by Jacques Bunel also, no doubt painted in the same style, are mentioned elsewhere. The physician Héroard ‡ bears witness to two : one of Mme. de Mornay, ordered in 1602,§ and one of Louis XIII. in infancy, painted in 1610.

We must pass now to the last of these names, and close this long story with the mention of the Fleming Pourbus, the latest in date of a dynasty of painters, of whom the two first have already found a place in previous chapters.

* Jal: *op. cit.*, p. 294.

† M. Müntz, *op. cit.*, mentions a portrait of Giovanni Pontano in the possession of M. le Président Girard at Rouen, which is copied from Paolo Giovio's museum, and may well be one of these lost pictures.

‡ *Op. cit.*, vol. i. p. 429.          § B. Fillon, *op. cit.*

Pourbus appears in history as the leading portrait-painter of the reign of Henri IV. No reputation was ever better won; but it must be admitted that his style of painting recalls none of the men we have hitherto met with. On the contrary, he resembles a painter who was to work in France under the reign of Louis XIII. and even later. His name, therefore, is included here rather as the consummation of the preceding remarks than as closing an epoch in which he had no share. Henri IV. took him into his service soon after 1600, but certainly before 1603, for, according to Sauval, it was he who painted the portrait of the queen which hung in the Small Gallery, and is now preserved in the Louvre.* He lived till 1622,† and carried far forward in the reign of Louis XIII. the precepts and examples, which, after the death of Henri IV., were seconded by newcomers and favoured by the change of taste, until they put an end for ever in France to the school inaugurated by the Clouets, just as in another domain the school formed by Primaticcio was disappearing.

Benjamin Foulon must have died shortly after the year 1612‡; Ledigne did not live beyond 1614§; Charles Decourt died that same year,‖ and so did Jacques Bunel.¶ Nicolas Quesnel and Pierre and Daniel Dumoûtier alone survived. Quesnel, it is true, who died in 1632,** could do no more than carry on in obscurity, drowned, as it

---

* Catalogue, No. 2072.
† Herluison : *Actes d'état civil d'artistes français*, p. 359.
‡ The last mention of him occurs in that year. Jal : *op. cit.*, p. 592.
§ Goujet : *Bibliothèque française*, vol. xiv. p. 140.
‖ Herluison : *op. cit.*, p. 90.　　　　　¶ Jal : *op. cit.*, p. 294.
** Jal : *op. cit.*, p. 1025.

were, in the flood of a new art, the feeble achievements
that were all he was capable of. Not so with the two
Dumoûtiers. Pierre, however, was always travelling;
since 1625 he had deserted France to settle in Italy,*
and, in spite of his great abilities, his countrymen must
soon have forgotten him. Daniel, on the other hand,
lived till 1646,† winning renown and popularity to the
last, till he seems to gather round his own name the
whole fame of the school. In him the art of the deceased
masters of chalk-drawing continued to live and to bear
fruit, but fruit that, in spite of its appearance, was ever
more and more tasteless. Dimensions grew, colours were
heightened, a style more mechanical than ever was exhibited in innumerable examples, of which no one was
a more active producer than he, and which everybody
prizes as curiosities. His work was a belated caricature,
in the new world of those days, of the once glorious
career of an art, the very remembrance of which was to
perish with him.

After Daniel Dumoûtier's death, a kind of ghost of
the past was seen to reappear in France: his cousin Pierre,
whom all the world had forgotten, and whose family connection there was scarcely a soul alive to remember. He
was nearly ninety years of age. Six years later, having
seen his native land once more, he expired in the Rue des
Tournelles in Paris, in 1656‡; and with him was extinguished the last spark of the art which has formed
the subject of this history.

* Mariette : *Abécédario*, vol. ii. p. 131.
† Reiset : *op. cit.*, p. 307.
‡ Herluison: *op. cit.*, p. 127.

# CHAPTER XIV

Later destinies of French painting—Dearth of painters after the death of Henri IV.—How the school was revived by Vouet—Causes to be noted of this decadence succeeded by such a revival—The endurance of schools dependent on their transformation—Why the changes in French painting were preceded by an interregnum—Effect of this interregnum on individual artists—Fontainebleau thenceforth only a provincial school—The art of portraiture—The new school founded by Pourbus and other Flemings, and made famous by Philippe de Champaigne—No Frenchmen included in it—Nanteuil and the engravers, the sole descendants of the art founded by the Clouets —Conclusion.

At the end of so long a course, it is inevitable that we should cast a comprehensive glance at the road we have travelled, and at the same time obtain, by a kind of comparison, a view of what the school of French painting was destined to be on the morrow of our period.  In fact, it is only by an examination of the kind that we can determine the real bearings of our history, and draw some of the general conclusions which make it possible to understand a complete epoch and retain its principal features.

Our first impression is one of a certain resemblance between the epoch we have reached and that from which we set out,—the beginning of the reign of François I.

The first years of François I. and the first years of the reign of Louis XIII. are separated by a whole century, and by all the various fruits of the double effort made at once by the Valois kings and by certain excellent painters

in their service to endow France with a school and a
tradition alike of historical painting and of portrait.
Both veins were now worked out; those hundred years
mark a perfect circle, a complete revolution of history.
From Janet the Elder to Pierre Dumoûtier and from
Rosso to Ambroise Dubois, the two schools had passed
all the stages that they seemed able to furnish. Insti-
tuted by foreigners, they were brought to the full by
the hands of several Frenchmen, whose names deserve
not only to fill the otherwise empty pages of a feeble
history, but to figure honourably in the triumphal procession of the national art. Both schools offer a similar
spectacle to the inquirer. After a period of apprenticeship, during which the national painters are merely the
assistants and the anonymous imitators of the examples
given by foreigners, there comes a second stage, in which
France herself is found producing work which, though
feeble, is already abundant. The third age realises the
promise of the second, in the full activity of a school
sufficiently powerful to satisfy the demands of a court
greedy for the productions of the arts, and possessed of
merits worthy of the admiration of posterity. It looks
as if the destinies so begun should be able to continue
their course under the succeeding reigns. On the contrary, we find the thread broken; or rather the current
is lost and dried up by a natural exhaustion. Twenty
years after the death of Henri IV. it appears that France
no longer owned a single historical painter capable of
carrying out the plans of a court which increasing prosperity and long habituation to artistic splendour kept
incessantly prepared to engage in new undertakings. I
have shown elsewhere the isolation in which the last

artist who drew portraits in chalks dragged on the barren extension of his career in spite of the support he received from a popularity inspired by curiosity.

In 1620, when Marie de Medici desired to have the history of her deceased husband's life and of her own painted in a gallery of her palace of the Luxembourg, there was no one but a foreigner she could apply to. Rubens, as we know, was entrusted with the work. The Antwerp master was commissioned, as Andrea del Sarto and Rosso had been before by François I. On the side of portraits, Pourbus had appeared before the death of Henri IV. in the *rôle* of the elder Janet. A century later we seem to perceive that the history of art is beginning again in France in symmetrical and similar limits. The masters of Fontainebleau are dead: the country seems as empty of celebrated artists after 1615 as it was in 1515.

And in fact, when Fréminet was gone, it would be hard to name a single painter of any importance in the eyes of posterity, a single painter whose name would not seem to have been disinterred from an oblivion as profound as it was deserved. That is the first of the points we mentioned, and it shows a close resemblance to the past.

The second shows a remarkable difference; which is, that the appearance of Vouet ten years later, in 1627, was sufficient to revive the school of French painting which was apparently dead, and in one moment to repair its complete decadence. Blanchard, Laurent de Lahyre, Perrier, and Bourdon all appeared at the same time as Vouet. There was a second outburst of great works; the galleries were covered anew with paintings which were the work of French artists. This wonderful revival of

art was accompanied by the rare magic of the name of
Poussin, of Claude and Lesueur. The decorative splendour of the reign of Louis XIV. was ushered in. The
French school took new life for two centuries, in the
course of which its sway, the heritage of the masters of
Fontainebleau, was to be imposed over the whole of
Europe. I am definitely speaking now of historical
painting and decoration only. Without any question
of a comparison of Vouet and his companions with
Rubens, one thing must be admitted: there can be no
doubt that when, only ten years later, Marie de Medici
formed the project of the gallery of the Luxembourg, she
dispensed with the services of Rubens, and was content
with what France could thenceforth produce.

There is one other comment that we cannot escape
from passing. It is, in a manner, a contradiction of what
we have just said, and is all the more urgently in need of
explanation, because the reflections it sets on foot make
up the whole philosophy of this volume.

We must realise at the outset that a school of painting cannot endure without incessant renovation. The
most auspicious beginnings, and the firmest foundation
of principle, cannot achieve durability without the help
of a series of masters, posted, as it were, at intervals
along the road of time to refresh the strength of the
school, and to come to its aid, so to speak, like relays
of history. The collective genius of a people peters out
in monotony; that is the inevitable result, when the
lessons of the master of a school are repeated, no matter
how cleverly, by men of meaner temper and a lower flight.
To reinvigorate it, and to fill it with new courage, there
is need for new lessons and the spur of hitherto unseen

examples. And so the most firmly rooted of schools cannot prosper or endure without incessant transformation, not by the effect of any interior law conditioning originality, but in a manner that contradicts the assertion of a certain kind of criticism, by the absorption of new elements which are foreign to its original tradition. This is not the place to furnish instances drawn from other periods of the French school. The lessons of the Roman school, which Poussin handed on to Lebrun, caused the renovation of the French school in the hands of the latter. Later, the suggestions which Jouvenet took from Rubens, Lemoyne from Correggio, and Largillière and Watteau from Vandyck, were the causes of the new lease of life taken on by the old tradition, thus rejuvenated at each new epoch. Without such assistance the strictest adherence of pupils to the lessons of the preceding age could not have achieved the durability of the school. There is no cause for surprise, therefore, in the fact that the traditions of Fontainebleau could not avail, unaided, to perpetuate the French school. The intervention of Vouet need not set us searching for any particular cause of feebleness in the school he was to replace; for it is given to no school in the world to escape the danger of a corresponding exhaustion.

The only remarkable features of the present case are the extent of the void and the interval that preceded the renovation.

The cause arose from matters of detail rather than any profound necessity. In so common a circumstance, the like of which occurs in the history of every great school of painting, the man who was to revive the French school was never connected, from his earliest days, with

the masters of the preceding epoch.   Vouet was twenty
years old at the death of Henri IV., and there was nothing
to prevent his having worked, at any rate, under Fréminet
on the Chapel of St. Saturnin, and possibly under Dubois
on the Diana Gallery; but, as a matter of fact, he received no instruction from either.   He was neither their
pupil nor their assistant.   He was out of France when
they died, and he came back from Italy entirely detached
from the past, with nothing of all that these masters
might have been able to teach him, or of the lessons
of a school which, even when instructed in its practice,
he did not allow to transform him.

Thus the most exterior links in the continuity of
things were no less broken than the essentials.   And this
epoch in the French school was marked by an interregnum.
That, however, does not mean that the overplus of a past,
on which the historian could not fail to lay stress, if these
exterior bonds, at least, had remained unbroken, should
be considered as of no account.

However great the initiative of the Louis XIII.
painter may have been at the outset of the revived tradition, it is only in externals that his work has anything
in common with that of a founder.   There was no longer
any question of launching the French school on the world,
as there had been in the days of François I.   All that the
nation had acquired during its century of apprenticeship
was at hand to reply in the nick of time to Vouet's efforts.
All the material previously acquired, and the effects of
general culture, spread far and wide, and brought to
visible expression in a few chosen spirits by the reign
of Henri IV., were there to fructify the impulse exerted
by the new painter into the rapid results I have pointed

out, which without such aid could have been nothing
but miraculous.

At the same time, the interval that had elapsed
joined with the fact that Vouet's education had been
entirely gained abroad, to bring about a divorce between
the men no less than between the styles.  The youngest
artists, who were connected with Fontainebleau not only
by the ties of the school, but, it is worth noting, by
family ties also, were destined to play no part at all
in the history of painting in the seventeenth century.
Their failure was partly due to their indifferent ability;
none the less, it is one of the most interesting features of
the period.

Claude Dhoey, the son of Jean ; Jean Dubois, the son
of Ambroise ; Henri de Voltigeant, the son of Josse ;
Toussaint Dumée, the son of Guillaume ; Pierre Poisson,
the son of Louis ; and Picou, the nephew of Bunel,—we
find them all in this new period, cast ashore, as it were,
out of the common stream of history.  The men of Fontainebleau continued to produce even feebler and feebler
works in the palace that had fallen from its high estate,
and was thenceforth to drift into provincial rank ; they
intermarried, they handed down their posts of doorkeeper,
or gardener, or keeper of the king's pictures, and they
and their children continued to appear throughout the
whole century, and to carry on in obscurity the nursing
of the last embers of a fire which had illuminated France.
It is a strange example of persistence, and worthy of a
place in our concluding chapter.  The school of Fontainebleau, in that advanced stage of history, is like some
town, once famous and the capital of a flourishing empire ;
now some village marks its site, as if, let the wheel of

history turn as it will, so much glory could not utterly perish.

It must not be judged, therefore, from these appearances that the hundred years of painting, the history of which we have read, had been lost to France. I have mentioned the obscurities which prevent our noting in detail the effects and the evidence of the very wide services they rendered. I have no intention of pointing out here that Nicolas Bollery taught Blanchard or that Gilles Testelin, the son of Pasquier, was himself the father of one of the able men who appeared in the studio of Lebrun; for these exceptions to what we have just said are still deprived of any conclusion drawn from a comparison of their works. But in default of the valuable information on this head which the future may have in store, it is necessary here to recall the important fact of the resemblance that exists between the school of Vouet and that of the time of Henri IV., in the general management of decoration; the abundance of architectural episodes, the refinement in the divisions, the use of landscape, and the just employment of camaieu, which to this day declare the relationship of one epoch with the other.

In the case of the art of portrait-painting, these reflections must be slightly modified.

We find none of the masters of portrait in the succeeding age who can trace their descent from the Dumoûtiers and Quesnels; and yet it is certain that those masters are directly connected with several of the artists who worked under Henri IV. And, in the second place, we must observe that, long after the end of his reign, the school was recruited from none but foreign masters. That is an important point in this history, and I am not aware that it has ever been noticed before.

I have said that Pourbus owed nothing to any of the portrait-painters of the preceding age, or even to his contemporaries. To take only his most external feature, he is outside the school of all our makers of chalk-drawings. We do not find that he ever worked in that branch of the art; and that would only be worth noting as an exception due to his foreign origin, if Pourbus did not occur exactly at the moment when the vogue of chalk-drawings was ceasing to be general in France, and if the works of the masters who set themselves to supply its place did not very clearly reveal a relationship between their manner and his.

At the end of the reign of Henri IV. two new portrait-painters from the Low Countries came to settle in France: Ferdinand Elle of Mechlin, who was known under the name of Ferdinand, and one Vrains, a Hollander, who is mentioned by Félibien. The mere fact of their arrival is not the only thing to be observed here. It agrees in date with the beginning of one of the most noteworthy practices in old French painting, that of painting the assemblies of aldermen, which we find to have first been ordered about this time. Now the first artists to paint these assemblies were precisely these three Flemings: Pourbus, Vrains, and Ferdinand.

Two French painters soon followed their example, Louis Beaubrun of Amboise and Georges Lallemand of Nancy. The first group of aldermen by Lallemand was painted in 1611, Ferdinand's first in 1609. From at least as early as 1616 Beaubrun bore the title of painter to the *messieurs de la ville*. But the names of the three

Flemish painters are not the only thing I have to point out. The reader will already have noticed the number of portraits of Dutch corporations, governors of hospitals and aldermen which this branch of the art included, and will have perceived therein its double mark of origin. When we meet in Félibien with the constantly repeated references to works of this sort, we become aware of the large part they played in the origins of the school of which this author became the historian. The style was properly Flemish, and was practised by Flemings, whose manner agreed, as an extant picture by Ferdinand may prove, with what we know as the manner of Pourbus; and the success it enjoyed deserves to be considered the most famous feature of the new Flemish education which France was then receiving in the art of portraiture. That education may be recognised by innumerable signs in the painters of the reign of Louis XIII. The school even had a leader in the indubitably Flemish person of the admirable Philippe de Champaigne, himself the painter of several of the portraits of aldermen and magistrates.

Now this is the comment I wish to make, one which is directly opposed to that commonly passed.

While the education received in the sixteenth century had prepared the French school to profit instantly by the teaching of Vouet and to prosper under his direction, in the realm of portrait-painting, when once the stream that sprang from the Clouets had run dry, there was nothing to take its place that was deserving of any rational commendation. With the exception of the Lenains, all the French portrait-painters that flourished in the time of Louis XIII. were of very little value. It will be enough to mention the Beaubruns or the elder Nocret to show the obscurity of these painters. Bourdon's works in this domain are execrable. We must go on to the minority of Louis XIV. to find in Claude Lefebvre an artist worth mentioning. But, as if it had been decreed that French portraits in this style were only to appear for an instant with any credit, in order to emphasise the general dearth of them, there is no master so difficult to discover as Lefebvre; and any one in search of examples in this branch of art is obliged to go to Rigaud and Largillière, painters of an extremely different order. As to portraits with the gravity of composition, the symmetry and simplicity of attitude and the closeness of execution of the old style, which are said to be the special features of the French school, the only example to be found after forty years is the one I have just mentioned, with no link with the past and no influence over the future.

Throughout the reign of Louis XIII., therefore, the Flemings, and after that reign some works of a different kind, are all that we have to show; and there is no escaping the admission that so far from preparing the French school to receive instruction from the painters who were to arise, the art of the drawers in chalks left it incapable of turning out portrait-painters, and that, too, in spite of the wisest teaching it could hope for, the teaching of Pourbus and of Philippe de Champaigne.

This conclusion is so true, that if we are asked who was the great portrait-painter of the seventeenth century in France, we can only reply with the name of an engraver, Nanteuil.

In striking the balance, therefore, as is sometimes done, between the tradition of the small portraits of the sixteenth century and the lessons of Fontainebleau, there

must be no more depreciation of the latter for the benefit
of the former; there must be no more vaunting, so far at
any rate as painting is concerned, of the vigour and
fecundity of the lessons which sprang from the Clouets.
Fecundity there was for French painting in the influences
of Fontainebleau, which paved the way a hundred years
before for the great development of the art of decoration,
which forms the principal feature of that painting, and
the definitive reason for its success in the world.  The art
of small portraits, on the other hand, originally entrusted
to talents which only valued the chalk-drawing as a means
to the painting, and soon submerged in the fashion which
looked at the drawing for its own sake, left the new school
nothing but the material and substance of mere drawers
in chalks.

As Lebrun sprang from the seed of Primaticcio, so
from the seed of the Clouets there came Nanteuil and his
long posterity of engravers, who, side by side with the
portrait of style and of state, which itself issued from the
influence of decoration and historical painting, maintain
the tradition of a very different order.

Let us think ill of neither; let us try only to settle
their respective places, and, in considering the origins of
a great modern school, to classify the influences, to measure
the merits, and, passing equitable judgment on their difficult beginnings, to recognise the good and the excellent,
which are the sources of the success that came after.

That success France owes above all to the constancy
with which, through four changes of reign, the Valois
monarchy maintained the practice of its patronage.  I
have pointed out the extreme sterility of the earliest days
of her art.  We have just seen the disposition into which,

after a century of this patronage, the least touch of
brilliant direction, the slightest spurring of rejuvenation,
were able to bring her with ease. In France these results
were the fruit of the patience and the will of man. What
England was to see later as the marvellous result of the
determination of an artist, the creation of a national
school achieved by the efforts of Reynolds, was due in
France to the patronage of the kings.

This is not the place to compare the two developments
or weigh the merits of the two schools. But if we wished,
in the case of France as in that of England, to refer the
whole merit to a single man, to write at the end of this
work a single name, it must be admitted that the last
Valois and Henri IV. did no more than carry on a wonderful continuation; that the whole scheme of an able,
universal, and far-sighted patronage had been laid before
their time; that the preparations made by its inventor
far surpassed the ability of his auxiliaries; that France, in
fact, owes all that her painting became, the renown it
won for her throughout the world, and the advance
towards perfection which she herself achieved by it, before
all others and beyond all comparison, to the genius of
King François the First.

# INDEX

# 324 INDEX

THE END